ROGER

P9-DFA-220

Women in the Kibbutz

Women
in the Kibbutz

LIONEL TIGER

and JOSEPH SHEPHER

HARCOURT BRACE JOVANOVICH

 NEW YORK AND LONDON

A Harvest Book

Copyright © 1975 by Lionel Tiger and Joseph Shepher

All rights reserved. No part of this publication may be reproduced or transmitted in any form or by any means, electronic or mechanical, including photocopy, recording, or any information storage and retrieval system, without permission in writing from the publisher.

Printed in the United States of America

Library of Congress Cataloging in Publication Data
Tiger, Lionel, date
Women in the kibbutz.

(A Harvest book)
Bibliography: p.
Includes index.
1. Women—Israel. 2. Collective settlements—Israel. 3. Sex role.
I. Shepher, Joseph, joint author. II. Title.
HQ1781.P2T54 1976   301.41'2'095694   76-13603
ISBN *0-15-698300-1*

First Harvest edition 1976

A B C D E F G H I J

Contents

Acknowledgments

A long and demanding research project such as the one documented here cannot possibly be the exclusive product of one or two people; a considerable number of talented people have contributed in varying degrees to *Women in the Kibbutz,* and here we wish to express our gratitude to some of them. Our research assistants, Gila Adar, Ety Ben Ziv, Zivit Gilad, Vered Muller, and especially Kathi Fishov accomplished the trying work of interviewing, coding, and calculating, and prepared the statistical tables. Kathi Fishov also discharged the secretarial duties in Israel, which included the typing of several drafts of the manuscript (on this she was joined by Genevieve Breitstein, Jill Bloomberg, and Doris Bergmann). In New York, Elizabeth McCreary and then Beatrice Indursky administered the official aspects of the project, and Beatrice Indursky ably and agreeably supervised the preparation of the Bibliography for publication. Joseph Koenigsberger smoothly managed the accounting and budgeting procedures.

We are very grateful to Steven M. L. Aronson of Harcourt Brace Jovanovich for his constructive overview of the book's history and for his long-standing commitment to books that make scholarly research at once dignified and accessible.

We owe a particular debt to Arno Karlen, who served as editorial consultant and who contributed a great deal to the final draft.

We are grateful to Dr. Menahem Rosner, Dr. Miriam Dornstein, Dr. Michael Saltman, and Dr. Marilyn Sefer who read parts of the manuscript and whose remarks were important antidotes to our mistakes.

Hundreds of members of various kibbutzim, especially those of Ofer, patiently tolerated our questioning and our scrutiny. Shepher wishes to express special gratitude to his friend Yacob Gluck, whose great fund of humanistic wisdom helped to crystallize thoughts and ideas. Tiger wishes to thank Virginia Tiger and Sebastian Tiger for their helpful understanding of the long absences of their close relative. He is grateful to Zelma and Norbert Rubenstein of Herzliyah Pituach for their congenial hospitality.

Mrs. Agi Meinhard of the University of Haifa generously offered her solutions to some complex problems of research design. Dr. Benyamin Kedem (Kimmelfeld) of the University of Haifa and Professor Roy D'Andrade of the University of California at San Diego assisted us in approaching complicated questions of statistical measurement. Professor Robin Fox has been both a consistently useful stimulus and helpful critic.

The Committee of Research of the University of Haifa made important financial contributions to this project; the Department of Sociology and Anthropology contributed generous forbearance and understanding over three years.

Tiger wishes to thank Dr. Henry Torrey of The Graduate School of Rutgers University and the Officers of Rutgers University for their hospitality to the overall project of which this study is a part.

The major financial support for this research came from the Harry Frank Guggenheim Foundation. We are grateful to its chairman, Peter Lawson-Johnston, its president, Dr. Mason W. Gross, its executive director, George Fountaine, the Fellowship Committee, and the Board of Directors. Their interest in our work has been abiding and constructive in much more than a financial sense.

We wish to emphasize that we alone, and no other organization or person, are responsible for what this book reports, assesses, asserts, and how it does so.

J.S.
Haifa

L.T.
New York City

Perhaps because so many of us suspect that our lives are insufficiently joyful, the zest for utopia has been a recurrent and powerful ingredient of countless theories of ways of life. Whatever the source of the restlessness that drives people to change their lives, their ideas, and the trajectory of their destiny—to try to form a better life in common with others—that source rarely runs dry. As in the past, people now and in the future shed their skins and move to, or make, an exquisite new tribe. Utopias sprout in the desert, in the cities, by the sea—as well as in books.

Of the successful communes that are not cemented by loyalty to a ruling God, the Israeli kibbutz is perhaps the most influential and long-lived. The encounter of Palestine with Zionism, and that of radical socialism with the very matter of survival, have yielded a sturdy and complex social reality of abiding interest to all who understand the lure of the communal way, and yet whose own lives are committed to goals relatively selfish and ideologies plainly flawed. The heat of the achievement of the Israeli communards affects not only Israelis and Jews (there are more communes in Japan than there are in Israel); the kibbutz has assumed a place in public and private legend as a symbol of the life of socialist assertion and structured compassion for one's fellows.

Because it is people who are the stuff of legends, it is important to scrutinize their lives. What follows is such a scrutiny, with a special and strategic focus on the role played by gender in the scenario of this particular legend. We have divided people into the simple, widely evident classification of boys and girls and men and women, to see what we can see.

Women in the Kibbutz

Chapter 1

Notes on the Origins of Gender

What happens to women who entrust their children's care to communal nurseries from the age of two to six weeks on? What happens to women who are supported not by their husbands but by the collective to which they belong? To women whose communities are ideologically devoted to equality and for decades have stressed the ideal of sexual equality? To women who are drafted into military service, wear uniforms, and carry rifles? To women whose food is cooked in communal kitchens and whose clothing is cleaned in collective laundries? What happens to girls who are taken away from their mothers? To sons? In other words, what happens to women of the kibbutz, and to their husbands and children?

As a social and political innovation, the kibbutz movement of Israel has always aroused attention and controversy, tantalized and repelled. At the center of life in a turbulent, complex country rich in symbolism, it implies a great deal about Israel and about Jews. The kibbutz has been influential in Israel far beyond the numbers of its members and their contribution to the economy. It has also had a moral and political impact around the world—far beyond what one would expect from several hundred rural settlements involving only 100,000 people over three generations. Certainly part of the impact stems from the kibbutzim's dramatic transformation of desert land into a fertile and livable home for people who were victims of extreme prejudice and unparalleled disaster in war. The kibbutzim are also inviting and intriguing in their zest for equality and their commitment to the always lustrous ideals of political brotherhood. In a direct, practical way, the people of the kibbutz have created and sustained socialist communities; the object of many people's dreams and of decades of rhetoric and planning is reality in the Israeli countryside.

It is a provocative reality. The change from capitalistic, religious ghettos with a close, extended-family life to rural communism, with dormitories for children and no serious connection with God, was enormous. In shifting from the busy web of urban European life to a primitive existence in remote and isolated communities, the Jews who settled Palestine and became Israelis were aiming high ideologically, and they made an uncompromising—even virtuous—effort to meet the challenges of the demanding land and their harsh situation.

The kibbutz is not only a practical attempt to create a way of life but an extraordinarily elaborate, long-term experiment. The founders of the kibbutzim wanted to develop a new kind of human being, motivated by communal commitment and uncontaminated by private greed. This determination to share all benefits and responsibilities extended beyond property to children, who were reared by the collective—they were a gift and a concern to the entire group. The kibbutzniks (their own semiaffectionate term for themselves) would not re-create the intensely loyal but convoluted family many of them had fled in Europe. They would not restrict women to being only mothers, children to being the exclusive property of harassed parents. Nor would the sex roles of ghetto Europe be re-created in village Palestine, especially the historical antifemaleness of many ghetto traditions—ritual baths to wash away the alleged impurity of menstruation, the devaluation of women's religiosity, elaborate assertions about male superiority. They would take care that none of this was thoughtlessly repeated in the new way of life. Men and women would do the same work, have the same privileges and obligations. They would equally be politicians and cooks, equally have the freedom to make love with whomever they wished, unbound by the old association of sex, marriage, and procreation. Indeed, they would be free not to marry at all; they could live together, and could separate as easily as they had united. No man would be any woman's master, no woman would have to shiver with fear at any man's edict. And no one would use sex to achieve social ends. In short, gender would not mean coercion. This was to be a revolution not only in living but in spirit.

This book is a report on the three generations of women who chose to live in this new way—on their work, play, schooling, political activity, their attitudes toward other women and toward men, their relationship with children, their military experience. We hope we have succeeded here in capturing both the sweep and some of the intimacy of their lives.

This is also a report on a massive experiment that no social scientist could have ever devised. The results are relevant to what men and women throughout the world think about their own lives and about utopia; to science; to statements about people's freedom to change their ways; to the relationship between sexual ideologies and people's lives; to the consequences of radical social measures concerning child care and money.

This book appears at a time of great interest in, and turbulence about, sex roles. A revolution of half the world's people—women—is going on, a prospect where not a reality. Some aspects of the revolution may not take practical form for a while, or ever; but in communities where it has been even rumored or partially felt, at least a great deal of public discussion and action have taken place. The conventional ways of being men and women are under challenge in home after home, workshop after workshop. The information and attitudes offered to children are being challenged and reviewed. Boys and girls have become members of a cooperation, and sometimes of a contest, about how to become men and women.

And what kind of men and women? The question has launched a veritable industry of speculation, assertion, research, synthesis, consciousness-raising, debate, friendly and unfriendly discussion, inner monologue, and, not least, legal action. In the chapters that follow, we attempt to deal with the details of a representative sample of this material.

One urgent major theme enters much that is written and thought on the subject: if certain primary circumstances in women's lives are changed, the broad difference in what men and women do will also change. If women do not participate as much as men in politics, managing industries, the conduct of war, it is because there are powerful, traditionally sanctioned barriers standing in their way, whether they know it or not—and, of course, not knowing about them would increase the barriers' efficacy. Remove these impediments and the unalterable fact of gender will no longer so severely control the division of power and of labor.

The women of the kibbutz live in circumstances very different from those of their sisters in England, Pakistan, the United States, Russia, Spain, Peru. It is important that we know the effect of communal life and child rearing on women's political and economic status, and how effective social changes are in creating new conditions of gender-related experience. Ours is the first extensive study of kibbutz women; we deal not with a small sample of the contemporary kibbutz population but with about two-thirds of it. We have used information about three generations of kibbutz women to find historical consistencies and to examine the directions of social change. Because of the quality of census data, to which we have had complete access, and because these data are accessible to computer analysis, we are confident that within the limits we define, this study is comprehensive and reliable in depicting the broad conditions of kibbutz women's lives.

The results startled us. We had had some general notions about the relative intractability of sex roles despite basic social change; we were nonetheless surprised at how the major innovations in kibbutz women's lives have failed to stimulate the expected new social patterns. Having learned perhaps too well the principal lesson of sociology—that social circumstances affect other social circumstances—we were unprepared to find, for example, how little three generations of communal child rearing had affected the way kibbutz women respond to their children and how they conduct their work lives. The statistical profiles we produced with the help of the computer unexpectedly revealed that men and women seemed to live as if in two separate communities and met mostly in their dwelling places. It is almost as if we had been studying two distinct villages. We were equally unprepared to discover, as several previous researchers had in specific kibbutzim, a strong, general, and cumulative tendency of women and men to become less, rather than more, similar in what they do and evidently want to do.

The kibbutzim have successfully realized their ideals of making property and child care communal, remaining agricultural, contributing leaders to Israeli society, and reducing the importance of religion. But they have failed to create the sociosexual conditions they had hoped for. Does this mean that sexual patterns are more conservative than other patterns? That the kibbutzim have misconceived the problem of sexual equality and its solution? That it will be difficult for women elsewhere to achieve sexual equality even under kibbutz circumstances? That the women's liberation movement is based on hopeless goals? What does it say about the needs, passions, pride, and fears of kibbutz women and their responses to their men, children, and communities? Finally, what does this experiment mean to all the rest of us?

Our main theoretical concern as academics has been to scrutinize the methods and findings of such social sciences as sociology, political science, and anthropology in the light of many recent discoveries and theories about human and animal biology, and to learn more about how the human genetic heritage is related to habits, conventions, and economic systems in cultures around the world.

Shepher, a Hungarian by birth, has been an Israeli since the inception of the state of Israel. He has lived within the kibbutz movement for twenty-eight years, most recently as a research sociologist. He was the first director of the Central Research Institute of his kibbutz federation. One of his research concerns was the widely noted but inadequately understood pattern of incest-avoidance in the kibbutz. As a student and research associate of Yonina Talmon at the Hebrew University in Jerusalem, he became interested in how young kibbutzniks decide whom to marry and whom not to marry. Kibbutz boys and girls who are reared together in the same children's house never marry each other, in violation of the sociological "law of propinquity," which holds that people marry people who are geographically near and with whom they share a set of life experiences. Using the census data presented in this volume, Shepher demonstrated that there was a tendency against such "incestuous marriages"; in fact, out of some 3,000 kibbutz marriages over three generations, there was not one between men and women who had been together during the ages of three and six. We cannot be sure what mechanism underlies this extraordinary finding, but the firm correlation with a maturation stage in the life cycle suggested to Shepher that it may be comparable to the "imprinting" which some biologists (most prominently Konrad Lorenz) have conceived to explain certain regularities in some animals' social behavior. Whether such a process occurs in humans—even in the reverse, or negative, way which Shepher maintains—remains an open question; still, his research strongly implies that some infrasocial process in individual growth inhibits men and women from engaging in sex and marriage if they have spent a particular, long period together as boys and girls.

Shepher also investigated families in the kibbutz. As a by-product of research he conducted for his federation comparing different housing systems for children (children who sleep in their parents' apartments compared to those who sleep in dormitories in the children's houses), he found basic incompatibility between collective social systems and a powerful nuclear family. This directed his attention to the sexual division of labor within the nuclear family and the general work scheme of the kibbutz.

Tiger's first research was on a scientific research institute in Canada, where creative scientists were housed in a business-oriented organization administered uneasily by scientists turned executives. Later he studied the Ghanaian higher civil service during its transition from a colonial ruling group to a professional organization subservient to the emerging power structure of Kwame Nkrumah. A period of teaching politics at the University of British Columbia stimulated some general questions about sex differences, which led to his dissatisfaction with conventional notions of the origin of the marked differences in male and female political behavior. Tiger then conducted a survey of material about human and other primate cultures and reviewed theories about the evolutionary history of *Homo sapiens*. The results led him to an hypothesis about the bonding associations of human males, which he described as being antifemale. His work also tried to assess what the biological fact of belonging to one of the sexes may imply for the sociological fact of gender role. He continued this general line of investigation—the relationship between biological givens and social options—in an extensive study, with Robin Fox, of the infracultural components of a variety of social patterns, seen in the context of comparative primatology.

This book continues that research trajectory, which originated in both the natural and the social sciences. While we are convinced that the biological and sociological themes are intrinsically related, we realize that many social scientists will disagree with this approach. We have therefore prepared the material so that anyone committed to classical sociological methods, data, and explanations can approach it and use it easily. Those who doubt that evidence about human evolution and physiology and about other animals is closely related to how and why humans act can discard the argument and focus on our findings. There is not such a wealth of useful empirical work on female social behavior that anyone can dismiss contributions on the grounds that they have been contaminated by biology. We are confident that the sociological and anthropological data stand on their own.

But this does not absolve social scientists from the responsibility of offering stronger explanations than those we propose. We have hypotheses about some provocative data, and the burden of proof is upon those who prefer exclusively sociological explanations to render biological ones unnecessary. The matter cannot be settled by a priori decisions or on principle, only by weighing and testing both approaches. We are aware that for many reasons this study may even provoke some fervent antipathy. Fair enough: but the colloquy will be fruitful only if we are held responsible for what we actually say. We are not accountable morally or scientifically for what people on the kibbutz do and for the situations of women there, only for accuracy in our report and for the cogency of our analysis. Some readers are bound to regard us as bearers of ill tidings, but as we see it, there is neither ethical nor practical advantage in denying reality.

To those concerned with the implications of modern biological thought, we wish to say that we hope such studies as ours will be useful to biologists as they occupy themselves increasingly with the complex social behaviors of complex animals, including man. When data are available, and the context that gives rise to them is known, hypotheses about human biology can be tested with the same care and significance as animal biology. Indeed, one facet of our program here has been to use well-tested sociological and anthropological techniques as part of a human ethology. The availability of computerized data and the computer itself enabled us to process numbers reflecting countless human actions, emotions, and attitudes, and so to discern patterns in a social group.

The extent to which we can generalize from one group of people to any or all others is questionable; we recognize that at best it is limited. However, unless we are so foolish as to assume that human behavioral nature is formless to the point of randomness, we must admit that comments about one human group—particularly one that boasts unusual and intriguing social experiments—may help us form some general conceptions of human nature. This has, of course, been the traditional justification of all ethnographic and sociological study of human variation.

Our evidence comes from a variety of research techniques. We will describe them in detail in later pages, but we sketch them here to show the nature of the enterprise. First, we subjected the 1968-69 census figures of two of the three agnostic kibbutz federations to elaborate scrutiny by computer programs, seeking relationships between factors we will describe. Since we were interested in the effect of ideology on social behavior and sex roles, we took the most conservative and liberal federations, assuming that the remaining moderate group would fall between. Because ideology is central to kibbutz life, and is a major source of social energy and cohesion, we expected that the sharpest ideological contrast would yield the strongest contrast in behavior. For cognate reasons, we excluded all data about religious kibbutzim. Second, to provide illustrative and revealing personal statements, we conducted standardized interview studies of adult members of four kibbutzim—one old, one new, one conservative, one liberal. Then we interviewed, individually and in groups, members of the founding generation of kibbutzniks, people who could give us a sense of the early kibbutz world from which present social patterns developed. We also consulted diaries, public speeches and statements, books, correspondence, and other materials in the archives of the kibbutz federations. To gather information in depth about the sensitive matter of extramarital relations, we used anthropological techniques in an intensive, long-term study of one kibbutz. Whenever we report data, we will report from which of these sources they came, unless it is markedly obvious.

Of course, our study has a broad context in scientific theory. We must briefly step back from the kibbutz to ask a fundamental question: Do the physical and physiological differences between the sexes inevitably produce social differences in how men and women live and in how communities organize themselves? Or, as it is sometimes put in extreme terms, are the genitals the only serious sex distinction, and is their influence restricted to specifically sexual acts?

Even those who dispute the Freudian canon accept the tremendous impact of sexuality on social life. The psychoanalytic school and its offshoots take for granted the central relationship between genitals and individual social development. They also assume important endocrinological and other physical influences on human behavior. While they have proposed a bewildering variety of approaches to what they variously describe as happiness, even the relatively novel therapies (Esalen, encounter sessions, Rolfing) use tactile techniques to express a healing physicality. And the ascetic religions of the world testify to the power of sexuality in human experience by their very effort to restrict it.

Yet many recent approaches to sex differences have neglected the facts that sex has to do with reproduction, and that for complex mammals reproduction is never simple. In the 1970's, interest burgeoned in sex roles and their bases. Much of this has plainly been stimulated by the outrage of both men and women at inequities and rigidities in women's lives. This has yielded a considerable crop of publications, ranging from the polemical (e.g., Millett 1970; Greer 1971; Davis 1971; Figes 1971) to the more academic (e.g., Epstein 1971; Sullerot 1971; Holter 1970; O'Faolain and Martines 1973; Bernard 1972). The consensus of these contributions is that the situation of women is unfortunate, should be changed, and can be changed; that the major levers of change are altered economic and social conditions; and that when these changes are great enough, the causes of female deprivation will have been permanently removed, and new relationships will emerge that produce a satisfying sexual equity.

As we have already suggested, in some communities, this has already happened to some extent in a surprisingly short time. Perhaps most dramatically in the United States, government statutes, judicial decisions, and responses to public pressure have begun to remove at least formal barriers to the participation of women in many groups that had been mainly or exclusively male. Informally, in organizations beyond the control of governments, there has also been heightened attention to the concerns of women, their installation in positions of authority, their artistic and literary output, and their general situation as they engage in the traditional roles of wife and mother while entering new roles in the labor force and in arenas of self-expression. In education, more attention than ever is being paid to the persistence of stereotypic images of gender that are believed to narrow freedom of choice for men and women, especially for women. An outpouring of enthusiasm for teaching and learning subjects of special interest to women has accompanied efforts to reduce the formal and informal channeling of people into sexually segregated careers and avocations. Newspapers, legal offices, and businesses have taken more or less effective steps to increase the number of female employees.

In medicine and associated professions, greater sensitivity to the needs and priorities of women has led to liberalized abortion and contraception practices, and to an adjustment of medical routines to accommodate the domestic situations of married women professionals. Furthermore, groups of women have formed to dispense information to one another by various formal and informal means, thereby reducing the dependence of women on the medical profession. They urge physicians to revise what they consider a male-oriented view of health care. They have made frequent and angry attacks on psychiatry, alleging antifemale bias among its founding thinkers, Freud in particular, and a strong tendency for male and even female psychiatrists to influence women to succumb to social roles that serve the interests of men.

Male and female homosexuals have also entered the issue, lobbying for acceptance of their sexual and social activities as legitimate and unthreatening to the moral integrity of society. A small but attention-getting group argues that homoerotic relations are desirable for women, since these avoid the inevitably pernicious consequences of association with men and assert the importance and solidarity of women (Johnston 1973; Hedblom 1973).

In sum, there has been rapid enhancement of female consciousness of the meaning and effect of sociosexual roles, and some enlargement of male understanding. At the very least, there has been considerable change in the expressed ideal value system of a number of countries—a change in values about women and the practices that separate them from men in seeking equity and self-expression. It would be both foolish and inaccurate to become sanguine about what has been achieved in this relatively short time, or to overrate the effect of pronouncements and rhetoric; nevertheless, there has been a significant shift in attitudes and a reduction of personal and public rigidities about the rights and needs of women—a necessary if partial basis for real social change.

We say necessary but partial because we do not know which social realities relate to the biology of gender, or whether changing

attitudes and even laws will induce people to act in ways that con-
travene, contradict, or distort what may be natural mammalian patterns. That is the heart of the problem dealt with in this book. We will
report data which we think convincingly demonstrate that changing
social variables designed to provide formal structural opportunities
for men and women to act similarly in public life have failed in their
purpose in an important and adventurous case. Our information proves
that the segregation of women need not be a function of the size or
kind (capitalist or other) of community in which they live, of dependence or independence of a husband's support, or of whether they
raise their own children.

One even wonders whether current standards for assessing female equity are male-oriented. If they are, is it likely or even inevitable that women will continue to suffer comparisons with men?
Of course, again, it is impossible to settle so large a question on the
basis of one case, but the kibbutz movement is as good a source of
information as any other about the situation of women in communal
settlements of ethnic, economic, and geographical diversity. In any
case, our evidence is certainly relevant to assessing the role of such
social variables as communism of property and children in stimulating particular social patterns.

We have voiced our hope that this study will be part of an
attempt to review a difficult scientific and human problem—how much
human biology shapes human society, or—putting the question in
more sophisticated terms—how much, if at all, the form of human
society reflects the behavioral biology of our species. This is an old
question; since Darwin's *Origin of Species,* the relationship between
freedom and genetics has preoccupied many scientists. Our first principle, following Hegel and then Marx, is that "freedom is the recognition of necessity." This book is, in part, an exploration of what that
necessity may be. Our second principle is that no unifactoral explanation of major social phenomena is likely to be correct, since human
behavior is so varied and complex, and scientists cannot agree on
which dimensions of behavior can be consistently perceived and described. Our third principle is that what people do usually reveals
more about their commitments and enthusiasm than what they say;
as we shall see later, there is a negative correlation between what
people say about sexual equality and what they do about it. This

implicitly criticizes survey-research sociology as a faithful direct reflection of behavior.

Our final principle may seem paradoxical beside the others: given information about social and economic forces, and given the will, people can define ideal patterns of life and make them a reality. Of this the kibbutz movement is ample proof. The early kibbutzim emerged from urban, mercantile, theocratic, capitalist communities, yet have remained rural, agricultural, communist, and agnostic. This striking change casts in sharp relief the relative failure of the kibbutzim to transform men and women into people able to live the roles of their founders' dreams. But social dreams are real, and because they are real we must examine why this one, with its sexual theme, has found such limited manifestation.

These questions fundamentally concern a mammal that is potentially sexual all its adult life—perhaps one reason discussions of sex behavior and sex roles are invested with great emotion. Especially since the emergence of a well-articulated feminist critique, many people writing and thinking on these matters have taken or felt pushed into partisan stances on whether human sex roles are biologically or culturally determined. Here we will quickly review some of the findings, contentions, and agreements; such as excursus must be lightly sketched, for a survey even approaching comprehensiveness would demand a book in itself.

Immediately we come face to face with a contradiction. On one hand, an extensive and persuasive body of work argues for the cultural determination of existing sex roles. It denies both traditional and new claims that these roles are in any sense natural. On the other hand, a rapidly growing body of sophisticated and detailed studies is elaborating the biology, physiology, and psychology of human male-female differences.

In publications of varying scope and competence, women commentators in particular have been portraying what they define as a failure of sexist social and medical science to identify pervasive sexual inequality. For example, Kate Millett on literature (1970), Juliet Mitchell on psychoanalysis (1974), Michelle Rosaldo and Louise Lamphere on anthropology (1974), Jane Lancaster on primatology (1973), and Jessie Bernard on sociology (1972) all have claimed there is a male bias in the social sciences, and have stressed its negative implications for social policies affecting females. Generally such statements contain a commitment to social change and imply distrust of scientific positions without activist and/or feminist points of departure. Indeed, commitment in print has often been accompanied by participation in consciousness-raising groups and other means of exchanging both personal experience and social support for what may be strenuous personal experiments.

The mélange of personal activism and scientific critique may blind some observers, perhaps even some participants, to the genuinely radical and innovative implications of what is being attempted. The male bias in the social sciences has unquestionably been pervasive; it is amazing that in the past, sexual differentiation and sex roles received so little crisp and forthright attention. When social scientists spoke of people, societies, politicians, or values, they were speaking principally of men (see also Smith 1973). Tiger's *Men in Groups* (1969), though it was (incorrectly, we submit) held by some to support the scientific and political sexual status quo, attacked this serious deficiency. It argued that by assuming that men and women behave similarly, and that understanding the biology of gender is not usually necessary for understanding social behavior, social scientists were losing a major tool for explaining our social life. While the book explored the possible evolutionary background for some human sex differences, it strongly affirmed the need to describe the old, widespread discontinuities between men's and women's experiences and opportunities for experience.

We are committed to some aspects of the feminist perspective for more than historical reasons. Insisting on exploring gender will provide a basis for more accurate social science and permit more realistic, sensitive study of what women do and why. Whatever the extent of our agreement with many feminists, we share their search for the ethnographic female and their commitment to understanding why what is "male" has been transformed into "human," and what is "female" has remained just that—female.

The core of the argument of the major feminist proponents is sociological. As Ralf Dahrendorf (1973:v) has put it, the sociological effort assumes that human behavior "follows certain rules which, while they are like everything human, historical, and thus subject to change, acquire a life of their own. Human behaviour in a given context is predictable to the extent of making the individual actors interchangeable." From this argument it follows that social conditions result from other social conditions: this is the main operating assumption of modern sociology, certainly since the time of Durkheim. In its most radical formulation (for example, in Erving Goffman's work), this principle denies that any serious realities arise from gender except those caused by the social categorizing of the sexes, and from what these attitudinal definitions imply.

So according to Dahrendorf's classic argument, *not only are different men interchangeable in given situations, but men and women would be interchangeable were it not for coercive customs and prejudices that have arbitrarily marked them as different.* Changing prejudices and customs, and thus preventing the growth of otherwise groundless distinctions, would align the roles of men and women; ideology, the antidote to lethargy, would permit the emergence of unpolarized society. Juliet Mitchell (1974:414) says: "Women have to organize themselves as a group to effect a change in the basic ideology of human society. To be effective, this can be no righteous challenge to the simple domination of men (though this plays a tactical part), but a struggle based on a theory of the social non-necessity at this stage of development of the laws instituted by patriarchy."

As a partial explanation of why society is as it is, such a position is incontestable. Social circumstances do flow from social circumstances; there are probably no direct physiological causes for most social behavior. The strength and appeal of this argument lies in its attention to human variability and flexibility, and in not raising the unappealing specter of determined limits on human freedom. The feminist argument reflects the cultural relativism that has long characterized those social sciences which rejected locating human behavior in biological processes. This view can be traced to John Locke's theory of the *tabula rasa,* which attributes human variation to virtually complete flexibility in the human infant, permitting it to be molded by communal wishes. The child brings little or nothing to the interaction. Girls and boys are the same in what they bring to the world; any differences in what they do depend wholly on the models and demands of the world around them. This is also, in a certain sense, incontestable; unless children are raised in solitary confinement, they will inevitably respond directly to their social milieus.

The difficulty with this as an exclusive explanation is evident when our entire species' behavior is held to be primarily a fixed or arbitrary imposition operating over the whole world. Thus, when Kate Millett seeks to explain why it is men who dominate and manage social systems everywhere, she concludes that the symptom is also the disease—pronouncing, with stunning disregard for the possibility that she is dealing with a characteristic of the human species, that "Patriarchy's greatest weapon is its universality and longevity." In the cultural-relativist canon, when cultures are the same in one or more respects, this does not invite biological theory; rather, it underlines how pervasively an interest group or culture area can inscribe itself on the human *tabula rasa.* In this view, the structure of the world depends on manipulation and more or less rigorous persuasion rather than on the biosocial natures of human beings.

Some of the tenacity with which extreme cultural relativists cling to their position may come from a misunderstanding of biological method and prediction. The assumption that biology determines behavior, especially in complex species, is wrong. At its strongest, biology *predisposes* animals to act in certain ways; at its weakest, it is but one influence among many. Biology is not destiny, it is statistical probability. Genetic codes determine some phenomena firmly, others loosely; all people die, but when and of what varies enormously, and depends in part on the individual's interaction with his environment. Appreciating the reciprocity between what the individual brings to his social situation and how the situation affects him avoids the sterile, obsolete contest between nature and nurture. It then becomes possible to scientifically inquire into both the conditions and preconditions of social life: one can seek to determine what behavior is predictable if one knows the species, and when the surrounding conditions must be known as well.

Such interaction is certainly necessary in therapeutic situations. In a recent review of therapies for sexual dysfunctions, Helen Kaplan (1974) stresses the need for understanding the basic biology of sexual activity before exploring the causes of an individual's difficulties. One must know the endocrine system, reproductive physiology, neurophysiology, etc., to determine whether a person is in fact behaviorally aberrant, and if so, which mechanisms must be examined. This information, of course, is useless without elaborate data reflecting the patient's socioeconomic and psychological circumstances. Again, biology does not determine; rather, it is the instrument upon which the changes of individual experience are rung.

There is a growing literature representing such a synthetic approach. Questions have been carefully asked, and answers offered, about what men and women bring to their societies because of their gender, and how certain biological functions—reproductive rates, hormonal patterns, perceptual capacities, etc.—relate to social ones. In the words of John Money and Anke Ehrhardt (1973:1), who have both engendered and described much recent work on sex differences and sex roles:

"In the theory of psychosexual differentiation, it is now outmoded to juxtapose nature versus nurture, the genetic versus the environmental, the innate versus the acquired, the biological versus the psychological, or the instinctive versus the learned. Modern genetic theory avoids these antiquated dichotomies, and postulates a genetic norm of reaction which, for its proper expression, requires phyletically prescribed environmental boundaries. If these boundaries are either too constricted, or too diffuse, then the environment is lethal, and the genetic code cannot express itself, for the cells carrying it are nonviable. The basic proposition should not be a dichotomization of genetics and environment, but their interaction. Interactionism as applied to the differentiation of gender identity can be best expressed by using the concept of a program. There are phyletically written parts of the program. They exert their determining influence particularly before birth, and leave a permanent *imprimatur*. . . . Postnatally, the programming psychosexual differentiation is, by phyletic decree, a function of biographical history, especially social biography. . . . The social biography program is not written independently of the phyletic program, but in conjunction with it, though on occasions there may be dysjunction between the two."

When a male fetus is in its mother's uterus, at a certain "phyletically written" part of the pregnancy program, there are secretions of the hormone testosterone; the gonadal system is imprinted to read "male," and certain brain cells of the fetus are selectively primed for male behavior programs. If maternal or fetal hormones are not produced in the right amounts, the organism remains basically female. Unless synthetic hormones are accidentally or deliberately administered to the mother, this phenomenon is subject to little environmental influence. Before it became clear how immensely complex such mechanisms are, and how interdependent the factors are that influence life patterns, attention to such a process was called reductionist by most social scientists. Some still mutter that imprecation, accusing the biologist of seeking to reduce so complicated a thing as sex role to so "simple" a matter as hormones, and contentedly consider it neatly understood. If hormonal influences on behavior were indeed simple, their point would be just. But adding the wide range of complex information from biology to what already exists in the social sciences is no simplifying procedure. In fact, the reductionists in this field are those who limit the scope of information they gather and, on a priori grounds, define as unnecessary to their purposes data from sciences other than their own involving processes (chemical, neuroelectric, etc.) they may not understand and do not care to encounter.

Though we reject efforts to limit the scope of cross-disciplinary inquiry, we are aware of its difficulties. We also know that the use of biology in the social sciences has often had bitter political implications and inferences. Biology has been misused in the miserable effort to assign higher or lower ranks to human races; there is no need to reiterate here the neobiological justifications advanced for racist programs and their vast, grotesque consequences. This intellectual and political pathology originated in efforts to use Darwinian concepts to justify inequities that already existed—in colonial systems, between social classes—and to foment yet others, for political purposes (see Tiger 1973). This process has not ceased, though in more recent times the supposed signs of "racial quality" have had to become increasingly indirect and modest. Instead of grandiose talk of master races, we now see such limited, fragile concepts as intelligence used to imply inherent racial or cultural inequality. Thus, questions are posed under highly artificial circumstances by Euro-American scientists to people in other culture areas; the few percentage points in score that predictably separate the groups are then used by scientists and commentators to support splenetic affirmations. Perhaps the best indication of how questionable such testing of different cultures is comes from Israel itself. There is a 15 per cent difference in IQ scores between urban-dwelling "Oriental" Jews (those from Morocco, Algeria, Syria, etc.) and "European" Jews (from Europe or North America). But in kibbutzim, where education is highly specialized to fit individual needs, and social processes more inclusive and egalitarian than in the cities, Oriental and European children perform equally well on IQ tests. In fact, both European and Oriental kibbutz children score ten points higher than European children in the cities. The conclusion is inescapable that these differences are stimulated by the children's circumstances rather than by their racial origin (see also Nichols and Anderson 1973).

Racial differences, then, are very difficult to define, and biological arguments made in their name are not useful for the serious biological study of human behavior (see Fox 1973: Ch. 2). Are sex differences of the same order? As we have already noted, there has been systematic bias against sympathetically appreciating women's contributions to social systems. The very foundations of modern sociology, as Jill Conway has persuasively argued (1970) depended on an unwarranted and bizarre assumption that biological evolution had been arrested in women but continued in men. This was strongly marked in Spencer's and Comte's theories and in the work of the Scottish biologist Patrick Geddes. Similar concepts abound not only in folk thought but, more elaborately, in academic positions (for a critique see Sherry B. Ortner, in Lamphere and Rosaldo 1974; Charles Urbanowicz 1970). A cognate argument asserts the greater naturalness of women by claiming the existence of a primitive matriarchy from which our species unfortunately lapsed into contemporary patriarchy. This baseless position—enthusiastically taken by Gloria Steinem (1975), among others—is effectively rebuked on historical and ethnographical grounds by Joan Bamberger (in Lamphere and Rosaldo 1974).

However, the fact that prejudiced theory has thwarted efforts to produce an accurate human sexual biology should not preclude seeking one anew. Considering the quality and range of recent information, the social sciences may now more readily and usefully assimilate material from physiology and psychology. Whatever the political consequences, and however unfortunate earlier formulations, there is too large a body of carefully gathered information about sex differences for even biased investigators to dismiss or explain it away. For example, such general reviews of the data as Corinne Hutt's (1972 a, b) and Judith Bardwick's (1970) underline the consistency of findings about male-female differences in various areas such as verbal skills, spatial skills, aggressive behavior, and choosing to solve general rather than intimate problems. Christopher Ounsted and David C. Taylor (1972) have collected detailed studies of sexual differentiation and the implications for social life.

Work on newborn infants, both experimental and empirical, shows how early sex-linked differences appear which are presumably independent of social circumstances. For example, Garai and Scheinfeld (1968) have described differences that begin at the moment of conception and emerge later in life as radical and significant divergences. Furthermore, it has become clear that the basic course of reproduction in mammals, including *Homo sapiens,* is to create females; the additional Y (male) chromosome mobilizes and organizes male development. The derivative or augmented character of maleness may be reflected in men's greater vulnerability to stress, disease, and early death.

Some have argued that women are generally underprivileged as controllers and recipients of resources and opportunities; nevertheless, except in seven Asian and African nations with very high rates of maternal death in childbirth, women live longer than men—some six years longer, for example, in the United States. Many social factors influence death rate, but at least one study has suggested their unimportance compared to the simple fact of sex difference. The TIAA life insurance group for college and university teachers in North America investigated the hypothesis that men died earlier than women because they worked harder, and that women who worked as long and hard would show the same mortality. The TIAA compared academic women who had worked full-time throughout their adult lives with nonworking wives of academic men. Both groups enjoyed roughly comparable standards and styles of living. The mortality of the groups was the same. The insurers concluded that the difference between male and female mortality was not, at least on the face of things, caused by work (*The Participant,* TIAA-CREF, N.Y., July 1973).

Beatrix Hamburg has provided an extensive review of materials describing *The Biosocial Bases of Sex Difference* (1975). She makes a methodological note with which we concur:

"Throughout, terminology referring to masculinity and femininity is used. It is important to recognize that these are modal terms which refer to behaviors which are performed characteristically or more frequently by one sex rather than the other. The only behaviors performed exclusively by females are those which are linked very directly with childbearing. Ejaculatory behavior with discharge of seminal fluid is the only exclusively male behavior. It is important to emphasize this overlap in masculine and feminine attributes because there is a tendency to think in terms of polarized sex stereotypes."

Hamburg's review emphasizes the importance of maintaining an evolutionary focus on sex difference and of employing no single analytic perspective, but rather a range encompassing the various aspects of sexuality (see also June Reinisch 1974 and Irving Singer 1973). She relates individual psychological factors underlying large-scale social differentiation by sex to patterns deep in our species' evolutionary history. The volume on this broad subject edited by Bernard Campbell (1972) examines the social implications of gender in a variety of species, using the powerful tools of modern biology and genetics.

Our conception of biology is statistical rather than proscriptive, a notion that will become clearer in the context of individual psychological and social performance. The reviews of research cited above document differences in male and female responses under a variety of circumstances. Many of these circumstances are formal test situations whose artificiality may affect their wider meaning. Still, enough has been carefully observed about "free-ranging" human behavior to suggest that we are discussing a real phenomenon. Again, this is only relative; there will always be, with exception of childbirth and ejaculation, overlap between what men and women do. This is true of many physical characteristics as well as of behavior. Most men are taller and heavier than most women, and this is very probably genetic. However, many women are taller and heavier than many men. Most women appear to be more skilled at verbal activity than most men, but many men are more skilled than many women. We are describing differences between groups, not necessarily between individuals. Let us assume that most human characteristics fall along a normal bell-shaped curve of measurement. The curves for the two sexes will more or less overlap, depending on what we are examining. If we look at weight, the overlap may be about 75 per cent, men being approximately 25 per cent heavier on the average. If we are concerned with longevity, the overlap will be about 90 per cent, women living about 10 per cent longer. If we examined the capacity to write or appreciate poetry—if such a skill could be measured—we might find the overlap complete, the curves identical —meaning that as groups, men and women were equally apt at the poetic process. This would mean there is no biological reason why any men and women cannot equally do almost anything they wish with excellent prospects of success. We do not know why men and women should not do certain things, experience certain emotions, be stimulated by certain problems, or be exhilarated by certain activities. If biological sex differences do exist, they are not proscriptive; they are usually relative, and they plainly do not imply that particular men and women lack skills and enthusiasms that are statistically more common in the other sex. Many men are better caretakers of children than many women, and many women better mapmakers than many men, though it has been widely held that these skills exist disproportionately in one sex or the other.

This point cannot be stressed too heavily, since the confusion between "is" and "ought" has so effectively dissuaded exploration of gender and its implications. Indeed, it is plain that knowing what sex differences exist would make it easier to overcome or eliminate their effect—knowing any system's components and how it operates is a good basis for changing it, if one wants to. Even if the role of biological sex differences turns out to be limited, and the number of differences few, it is important to know what they are. If the feminist argument is correct that women are made to live lives greatly and unpleasantly different from men's, it is imperative for reshaping social policy that we discover even those relatively small differences that apparently help produce such significant major ones.

One interesting area for investigation, for instance, is certain hormonal differences between the sexes. These have been extensively described (e.g., Money and Ehrhardt 1973; B. Hamburg 1975) but we do not yet know much about their relationship to behavior in complex social situations. A study by Kreuz, Rose, and Jennings (1972) discovered that among Marine cadets, the levels of testosterone increased as personal status and confidence increased. In one of the few studies of female hormonal experience, Heather

Fowler (1973) found in three groups of five women an inverse relationship between social dominance and testosterone levels; other substances that may be related to dominance were not assayed, but this remains a provocative finding and deserves retesting and expansion. Kedenberg *et al.* (1974) found a positive correlation between recovery rates of male psychiatric patients and increasing rates of testosterone secretion; mental health related not only to cognitive and social circumstances but to endocrine ones. David Hamburg (1971, 1972) has described adolescent growth and its changes in hormonal secretions; from a lower base than men's, women double their testosterone secretions, whereas men increase at least twenty to thirty times. The implications of this difference in stimulating aggressive behavior may be considerable. On such hormonal factors, Steven Goldberg (1973) based a popularized argument about the inevitability of male dominance of social arrangements, which has been criticized by Eleanor Leacock (1974), Frank Livingstone (1974), and Eleanor Maccoby (1974). It is in this area—commenting on social patterns from what is known about individual experience—that the controversy is greatest, especially among scholars in different disciplines, using different kinds of data (see also Gilder 1973, 1974).

We have already acknowledged the various writings that survey sex differences from nonbiological viewpoints and actively reject biological factors (e.g., Epstein 1970; Rosaldo and Lamphere 1974; Sanday 1973; Janeway 1971; Brown 1970; Holter 1970; Sullerot 1971). Again, these arguments imply that generally social conditions are consequences of other social conditions. Rosaldo and Lamphere, for instance, make the important but unwarranted assumption (1974) that "although we are certain that biological studies will illuminate our understanding of the sexes, we feel that the issues are too complex for definitive treatment in this volume, and furthermore, that they do not *determine* the relations and evaluations of the sexes in contemporary forms of social life."

We cannot share their trepidation about the complexity of this matter. We are less convinced than they about the undetermined nature of sex; we think it more prudent to consider the amount of determination, if any, open to assessment. To ascertain precisely what any member of a system contributes to the system, one must have detailed knowledge of both the individual and the system.

Harlow and Lauersdorf (1974) urge understanding of the importance of sex differences as bases of social behavior. Seligman and Hager (1973) suggest that individual organisms are limited by their genetic inheritance in the range of what they can learn from their environments. Or as Tinbergen (1972) has put it, "What is relevant . . . is the fact, now becoming increasingly clear, that learning is not random, but is often a highly selective type of interaction with the environment." He turns to the questions of human limits in the light of the present dilemmas of our species, to ask whether there are "signs that this new situation imposes demands on 'human nature' that exceed the limits of its phenotypic adjustability? Are there intolerable pressures, and are there, conversely, gaps, pockets of missing outlets for behavior patterns that are strong, perhaps compulsive internal determinants?"

This major question requires major elaboration and data before we can form even the beginnings of a reply. We propose that the kibbutz can help us make such a beginning. That this must be a controversial matter is clear, but we hope that we have at least sketched the scientific landscape around this study, and that both its limitation and possible significance will be estimated in that context.

Chapter 2

Sex Roles
in the Kibbutz Movement

In most cities with large Jewish populations, Zionist groups have been formed to train young people to emigrate to Israel and join a kibbutz. In these groups, Hebrew terms are used and the forms of collective life are introduced as an earnest of life in the kibbutz. The endeavors of these Zionist groups are felt to be significant not only for the survival of Israel and the Jewish people, but also for the lesson about human perfectibility which the kibbutz teaches. Simultaneously one can reach back to the deep past of the Jewish tie to Israel and forward to a future in which communal sympathy, equity, and absolute human dignity exist everywhere through the kibbutz example. The question stands posed: If kibbutzniks can make a dream come true, why can't everybody else?

It is difficult for a casual visitor to appreciate how far-reaching and intensive the kibbutz innovation is. As we have seen, it represents a thorough, carefully considered effort to destroy some central social formulae of the Western tradition, and to manifest through novel social organization the ideals of pure equality, non-exploitiveness, and close identification of social practice and moral goals. All the major social patterns of capitalist Europe, from which most of the kibbutzim's founders came, are denied or at least challenged by the kibbutz way of life. The close ghetto family with its overprotected children, quest for money and property, devotion to religion, sharp legal and practical distinctions between the status of men and women —all have been replaced by new forms appropriate to the scale and situation of the kibbutz and to Zionism, socialism, and nation-building.

What has been achieved is a measure of the ardor and labor of the founders, the support of the wider Israeli and Jewish communities, and the special historical and geographical situation of Israel. We have already noted the importance of the idea of social determinism in the feminist position on women's social situation. Two of sociology's central concerns have always been the relationship between ideas and societies and the relationship between ideology and action. While ideological positions may not actually determine social patterns, they are often decisively influential, and theoretically this should be no less the case with sex roles than with attitudes toward property, free expression, and religion. Since many revolutionary movements have included a program for achieving sexual equality, this important aspect of radical action must be evaluated in the context of any political program.

In this regard, the kibbutz movement has shown perhaps more consistently than any other movement a rigorously egalitarian position. Other radical communities make extensive theoretical assertions about the equality of women, but the realities of their lives are scarcely affected and are sometimes even made more onerous. For example, in the U.S.S.R., the revolution lifted elaborate legal and procedural barriers against women, but now their day-to-day lives consist of full demands as members of the labor force and conventional domestic responsibilities as well. Because of time-consuming shopping arrangements and the relative scarcity of labor-saving domestic appliances, Russian women have not only signally failed to earn equal participation in the political economy but have also had inroads made in their time and leisure (Dodge 1966; see also Sidel 1973a, b).

Even in China, where the emancipation of women is as great as their historical oppression was overwhelming, the same dual demands on women exist, with commensurate female nonentry in major decision-making bodies and political cadres (Langton 1973). Efforts to provide communal dining facilities and the existence of a resourceful extended family (for child care, domestic management, etc.) somewhat mitigate these problems. But women's rights remains an area in which less progress has been made than other areas of Chinese society (see Sidel 1973b for an account of changes that have taken place).

There is always a gap between ideology and achievement. Even in the most venturesome of radical societies, several structural factors in social life seem to militate against complete equality of the sexes. A woman remains economically dependent on her husband, especially where birth rates are high, crèche facilities poorly developed, and employment opportunities oriented to men and nonmothers. A woman generally derives her social status from her husband's, particularly if the family is physically very mobile. Furthermore, governmental, military, and educational functions aside, economic consumption revolves mainly around the family; for example, in the United States, women spend most of the family's money on the goods and services women are responsible for supervising. And of course the raising of children is principally the work of families. Families are also responsible for the guidance of children until they are at least sixteen, and have legal responsibility for several years thereafter. The family system is the most intimately pervasive moral and attitudinal force in many communities. These factors place a heavier burden on women than on men and create the problems of "women's two roles."

There are some exceptional cases, such as hypogamic marriages and an increasing but still small number of families that establish different patterns for themselves. However, the most common pattern of family life, especially in industrial societies, is that in which the adult male of the household provides its main income and determines its status in the community. Even if the female is gainfully employed, she is presumed to care for or supervise the household and to be the most active, responsible figure in the lives of the children. Whether or not the actual exercise of authority is the father's, his intervention is often considered more important than the mother's because it is less routine—even if the mother orchestrates these interventions in a way that allows the father few options except those she wishes him to have (Barbara Anderson 1973 describes this as it occurs in France).

It has long been asserted in the literature of feminism that the patriarchal family must be dismantled. Engels believed this, and many others have come to accept it as a prerequisite for equalitarian change. Eleanor Burke Leacock (1972:44) writes that "it is crucial to the organization of women for their liberation to understand that it is the monogamous family as an economic unit, at the heart of class society, that is basic to the subjugation." Eva Figes (1971:181) writes that "Until marriage is either abolished completely or has become a hollow sham, I am afraid women are going to make far too little effort to improve their own positions."

However drastic the remedies proposed, the nuclear family has clearly acquired uniquely extensive reponsibilities in industrial society (Goode 1963), at the very time when its moral, legal, and economic structure is under attack. Especially in suburban communities, the isolation of each family from wider networks and its economic individualism are extreme. Indeed, some families possess equipment that could service a village under other circumstances— full laundry facilities, power mower and tractor, power saw, elaborate television antennae, tool shop, snow blower, etc. While this may reflect poorly developed communal services or "public squalor" (Galbraith 1958), the fact remains that the nuclear family is the focus of social and economic life. Restaurants, especially "fast food" outlets, and prepared foods do represent a degree of communalization, but supermarkets are nonetheless geared to women, who are their chief customers. Most exchange of prepared food still takes place within the home of the nuclear family, and most of the preparation is done by women, for men and children.

The kibbutz system has met most major criteria for radically restructuring such family life. Indeed, it may meet Engels's demands more completely than any social system about which we have good, long-range information. Here is why:

1. All the major household services are collectivized. Meals are served in communal dining halls and prepared and served by all kibbutz members on a rotation basis. Therefore women in principle are required no more than men to cook, serve, wash dishes, and carry out demanding esthetic performances in presenting food—something that may expose women's egos two or three times daily to the test of their families' approval. There is no individual shopping for food.

2. A collective laundry cares for all washing. A collective store does all ironing and mending, and a great deal of tailoring as well.

3. A doctor and nurses are responsible for health care, and no family is subjected to the expense and trauma of extensive home nursing.

4. Children of 90 per cent of the kibbutzim who are younger than fourteen live in dormitories, starting at the age of two to six weeks. They are cared for by trained nurses and teachers. Even in the 10 percent of kibbutzim where children sleep in their parents' apartments, they are cared for by trained persons during the day.

5. Men and women are economically independent of each other. Each adult member of a kibbutz works within a general labor-assignment scheme; and rarely, if ever, do families or couples work in the same branch. No one receives direct payment for labor; all receive the same, communally determined economic rewards. These rewards are independent of both the prestige accorded various tasks and the quality of job performance. The capitalist ethic of close relationship between individual effort and reward does not apply in the kibbutz.

6. Social status does not depend on marital, legal, and economic status. In fact, in terms of expenses for personal maintenance, marriage may be a minor disadvantage. No woman, whether pregnant, old, a new mother, a mother of five, unmarried, or divorced, need depend on her husband, father, or any other man. Economic support and legal status are hers by virtue of her membership in the collective, which is granted by the General Assembly of the kibbutz.

7. It has been cogently argued that in large urban communities and in modern society in general, most people lack opportunities for direct and serious contact with the political processes that govern their lives. In the kibbutz system, power is highly diffused; up to 40 and 50 per cent of the membership serve on governing bodies. There are no impediments to male or female participation in politics. One does not find in the kibbutz movement the political alienation that makes people regard their own efficacy with immense skepticism.

Obviously these important characteristics make the kibbutz very different from most societies. Because of the way in which it organizes domestic and legal life, it approaches absolute equality in the taking of jobs and in conducting personal lives. Neither men nor women are bound to each other or to their children by economic responsibilities. Women who have children outside marriage are not made to suffer any economic or moral handicap; neither will their children suffer economic disadvantage. The kibbutz system, unlike the nuclear-family system of Europe and North America, does not penalize one-parent children.

The kibbutz system, then, does not have a capitalistic or familistic pattern, except insofar as most people marry rather than remain single, or at least establish permanent liaisons. Of course, men and women are not completely interchangeable, if only because women are occasionally pregnant and normally breast-feed their babies, even though they are not their primary caretakers. Still, within these limits, and given some difference in aptitude for the most physically demanding tasks (which decrease in importance with mechanization), there are equal options for men and women, especially in administrative, managerial, political, and clerical jobs. It is interesting to see what happens when both men and women are workers, cooperative owners of their resources, and share an ideology of sexual equality that is reflected in their formal social arrangements.

We do not wish to gainsay the imperfection of this experiment. It exists within wider Israeli, Judaic, Middle Eastern, and Euro-American contexts, none of which shares its social practices and sociosexual attitudes. The mass media, visitors, and relatives of kibbutzniks, the cultural milieus that impinge on the kibbutz, all inevitably tend to erode its ideologically determined patterns. One cannot accurately weigh the effect of these factors in diluting social forms of the kibbutzim; when examining our results, one must bear in mind the necessary consequences of the kibbutz movement's involvement in the wider world.

Despite these involvements, the movement has sustained its ideals and practices in many important arenas, demonstrating that ideals do have effects, and that utopian communities can develop. The link between ideology and practice has proved sound in many respects; where it has not, and why it has not, may be especially interesting and significant, both theoretically and practically. The kibbutz movement is a long and intensely lived experiment in human rearrangement—one impossible to duplicate in controlled circumstances. A great deal can be learned from this colorful, thriving laboratory.

One could argue that the exceptional characteristics we list for the kibbutz also exist in socialist countries such as Russia and China and in communes elsewhere. We accept this; a comparative study of all these radical experiments would be revealing. Nevertheless, we argue that the kibbutz is the best subject for investigation if one is interested in what men and women will do *voluntarily* when both ideology and social structure promote the possibility of complete equality of the sexes, and have done so for a relatively long period of time.

Let us first glance at Russia and China, the largest Communist nations. Both present a basic problem; we can never be certain of the spontaneity of people's actions under an authoritarian political system. For instance, in Russia there are many more women than men, yet the centrally determined average income is so low that a family can survive only if both the husband and wife work. One cannot speak of spontaneity under such circumstances. Furthermore, most studies of the Soviet Union are macrosociological (such as Dodge 1966), so they do not enable us to thoroughly study Soviet women's everyday life. From China we still have only journalistic impressions (such as Sidel 1973a, b). Long years of détente will have to pass before we can obtain a well-documented study of the experience of Chinese women.

Moreover, in Russia collectivization is much less developed than in the kibbutz. City dwellers live in an individualistic system; every family forms an economic unit and has primary responsibility for the basic socialization of its offspring. The system helps working women by providing day-care centers, but the families must pay for them (Dodge 1966). The rural *kolkhoz* is a collective form, but far from the comprehensive collectivism of the kibbutz. Economic remuneration is proportional to the workdays delivered by the family, and hence consumption and basic socialization are still very much within the family framework.

The Chinese commune remains something of a mystery. The only well-established fact about it is that it includes tens of thousands of members, and from this we can assume that it is centrally directed.

Most voluntary communes probably resemble the kibbutz more than the state systems of Communist nations do. However, most seem to be quite small and short-lived, and the turnover in population is apparently very high. It is difficult to know what will happen to them in sexual and other spheres of life. The ethnographies available on these experiments are very elliptical, usually containing ideological principles but few data about how much they are implemented. We must wait to see whether the same tendencies and development we observe on the kibbutz appear in the communes that do endure.

Our strategy of investigating kibbutz communities depended on their having a large population (approximately 100,000), from fourth-generation veterans in their eighties to newborn babies. This account of their story is neither advocacy nor social criticism; rather, it is an effort to describe the experiment to, and discuss its meaning with, people who want to know to what extent the system works and why.

Chapter 3

The Way of Life in the Kibbutz

A recent bibliography of studies of the kibbutz (Shur 1972) registers 1,288 books and articles in English, French, German, Dutch, Norwegian, Danish, Swedish, Polish, Japanese, and other languages. Despite all this interest outside Israel, there still exists no exhaustive, up-to-date descriptive study of the kibbutz as a social structure.[1]

Some of the books devoted to the kibbutz draw their material from the early fifties (Darin-Drabkin 1967; Douard 1961; Spiro 1956). Others deal with only one aspect of kibbutz life (Bettelheim 1969; Jarus *et al.* 1970; Kanovsky 1966; Liegle 1971a, 1971b; Meier-Cronemeyer 1969; Neubauer 1965; Orbach 1968; Rabin 1965; Shapira 1971; Spiro 1958). Others limit themselves to one kibbutz or one federation; still others discuss the kibbutz movement as a whole but draw their evidence from the very general demographic data of the Statistical Abstracts of Israel. Our aims are also limited, but since women are part of every aspect of kibbutz life, we must explain the basic social structure of the kibbutz and how it functions.

Kibbutzim are collective rural communities in Israel.[2] Infield (1947) calls them "comprehensive" collectives, meaning that collectivism embraces every sphere of social life. Today almost 100,000 people live in some 240 kibbutzim.[3] These communities differ in size, economic structure, geographic locality, political ideology and affiliation, religiosity, members' cultural backgrounds, and members' seniority in the kibbutz and in the nation. However, they are all more or less alike in a number of important ways:

1. There is far-reaching collectivization of production. Most members work together in collective work branches, with less than 10 per cent of the working population employed outside the collec-

tive framework. In one of the three kibbutz federations, the Ichud, only 4.5 per cent of all workdays was expended outside the kibbutz; these accounted for 5.6 per cent of gross income and for 1 per cent of the costs, which include all expenses of the outside workers such as food, transportation, lodging (Sikumei Haavoda 1973; Sikumim Mishkiim 1973). Even those who work outside are registered in the general work-assignment list, and like all other members, work in the dining hall, kitchen, and on the night watch, according to a *corvée* system.

2. There is far-reaching collectivization of consumption. All members receive goods and services from the kibbutz, usually through collective institutions such as a communal dining hall serving three meals a day, a communal laundry, a communal clothing store that mends, irons, purchases, and—for part of the population (mainly women and children)—produces new clothing. There are communal cultural institutions, such as clubhouses and cultural centers and theaters, and communal health-care and educational services. House maintenance, landscaping, personal transport, and annual vacations are also organized collectively.

3. The socioeconomic role and level of performance of the individual kibbutz member bear no relationship to the goods and services he receives. The secretary and general manager, the highest administrative officers of the kibbutz, receive no more than anyone else, nor does a worker whose output is higher than his comember's. Most economic rewards are provided in kind, such as food, shelter, and most clothing; only about 4 per cent of the money value of all goods and services is given in cash. And only episodic conditions such as illness and pregnancy are held to justify any deviations from this system.

4. Education is collective in the sense that the kibbutz, not individual parents, is responsible for it. Both the aims and the means of education are established by the kibbutz, and all children receive twelve years of education. Each child's talents (musical, artistic, etc.) are identified and cultivated in accordance with the decisions of the educational authorities and economic resources of the kibbutz.

5. Membership is individual and voluntary, and it usually follows a one-year candidacy. It is granted by a two-thirds majority of the General Assembly. If the candidate is not granted membership, he

is usually advised to leave, which most rejected candidates do; however, on rare occasions a new candidacy is allowed. Membership can be ended by the member or by a two-thirds majority of the General Assembly, but this is rare.[4] Those who decide to leave the kibbutz receive a cash allowance fixed by the statutes of the kibbutz and its federation; this allowance grows with the number of years of membership and is usually enough for the person to start a new career.

6. The political system is direct democracy. A General Assembly consisting of all members (and in some kibbutzim candidates as well) is the highest political instrument. Every member has the same active and passive political rights, and one vote in the General Assembly, which must approve the annual plans of economic production and consumption. The Assembly also elects all important officials and committees and admits people to candidacy and membership. There is no party system. The criteria for election to office are fitness, talent, and experience of the individual. Every member may submit proposals for election either to the nominating committee or to the General Assembly itself. The right to make motions to the agenda and to question principal officeholders ensure each member direct access to the highest political institution. There are no judicial institutions; the kibbutz enjoys considerable autonomy in judging its members, and does so through the General Assembly and certain committees. Behavior considered deviant by the kibbutz is dealt with internally; only the rare incidents of such major misconduct as fraud, larceny, and murder are handed over to the state police. Only one murder is known to have been committed within a kibbutz (by a candidate who had spent three months in the community), and only one act of embezzlement.

7. Each kibbutz and its members are incorporated in concentric institutions—the kibbutz federation, the General Organization of Labor (Histadrut), the Zionist movement, and the state of Israel. These affiliations reflect the basic value of service to the society as a whole. So do the few requirements for membership: the candidates must belong to the Histadrut, accept Zionism, and be an Israeli citizen.[5] Each kibbutz is affiliated with one of the kibbutz federations, and federation offices are staffed by kibbutz members. Some decisions of the democratically elected bodies of the federation (congress, councils, and central committees) are binding on all kibbutzim,

while others are considered merely advisory. Each kibbutz is part of the Workers' Economy (Chevrat Ovdim) of the Histadrut and collectively affiliated with it and with the World Zionist Organization through the Colonization Department of the Jewish Agency. Each kibbutz is incorporated in the state as an independent municipal unit.

Within the general framework exists a great variety of patterns. While we cannot account for all the variations, we will try to explain the major aspects of kibbutz society that are indispensable to an understanding of the analysis of our data—the family, economy, stratification, politics, socialization (education), and value system. We will briefly cover each sphere's historical development and finally focus on the integration of the kibbutz in the wider social systems of Israeli and international life.

THE FAMILY

The changes the family has undergone in the kibbutz have been described and analyzed (Talmon 1972; Shepher 1969b), but a brief reiteration is necessary here in the context of the sexual division of labor.

The first kibbutzim (and to some extent new kibbutzim today) consisted of youngsters of both sexes organized in tight solidary groups; these required devotion to group values, and allowed relative neglect of economics and organization. Such a group has trouble absorbing the family system, which, especially in its modern form, is based on ties that may compete with group solidarity. Therefore tension frequently existed between the family and the early revolutionary kibbutz. Secluding one's spouse from the group was frowned on. Couples were tolerated but remained inconspicuous. Establishing a new family was wholly informal, without ceremony. Spouses did not act as a unit in any aspect of kibbutz life; they worked in separate branches and participated individually in the General Assembly.

In most kibbutzim, families were established slowly during the communities' first two decades. Childbearing was discouraged because of the severe economic and security problems. In the 1930's and even more in the 1940's, most members married and had children. Gradually the family gained full legitimacy. Meanwhile the small solidary groups could not cope with the demands of their share of the state's economic expansion; they absorbed new immigrants who helped the family to emerge as a unit. But strong solidarity was not the only characteristic of the early kibbutz. Its social structure was very similar to what Schmalenbach called a Bund (1961). Economic expansion required compromises between the original values of solidarity and service to society on one hand, and the emerging economic group interest on the other. After the establishment of the state, consumption became increasingly important. And this opened the way to giving the family certain functions formerly restricted to the collective, such as providing afternoon tea and spending the clothing budget.

In time the family became not only an important reference group for individuals but a basic social unit. Establishing a family became a formal act, not only because the new Israeli law required it, but because people wanted social acknowledgment of marriage. People spent more leisure time within the family (Meri 1973), made informal visits, and even carried out formal social activities together, such as night-watch service, annual vacations, and participation in the General Assembly.

Prosperity naturally stimulated a rise in living standards. Gone were the original tents, the barracks, the one-room apartments without toilets. Apartments were larger now, consisting of one and a half to two and a half rooms, with private bathroom, kitchenette, and small refrigerator. There was more and better furniture, private libraries, and sophisticated electrical equipment for comfort and convenience—all of which also generated more household work. These changes brought into relief the division of labor within the family, a question that had almost never come up when couples lived in a tent or single room.

In the beginning, families had hardly any authority over their children's education. The education committee and the *metapelot* (educational nurses) and teachers set standards with which parents had to comply. A few of the oldest kibbutzim lodged children with their parents, but by the early twenties the collective housing system was generally accepted, with youngsters of all ages lodged in special houses. Later, when families became powerful, and increasing numbers of children were entering the schools, parents demanded a greater voice in education. In the early fifties, the children's housing system came into question. The Federation Ichud Hakvutzot Vehakibbutzim was able to impose a delay, but after several years a half-dozen kibbutzim introduced familistic housing (Shepher 1967, 1969a, 1973). Today about twenty-five of the Ichud kibbutzim (and some of the religious kibbutzim as well) use the familistic system. (The two other federations have so far resisted the pressure to change, but the familistic system will probably soon break through, at least in the Kibbutz Meuchad Federation.) Families rose from a subordinate position to a salient one. Young mothers' participation in preschool socialization was also extended considerably. And the family now had a say in its children's higher education outside the kibbutz.

This emergence of the family as a strong, central unit was accompanied by an important change in women's image and in the relation between the sexes (Rosner 1973). The original kibbutz image of woman emphasized equality with man, hard physical work, austerity, and modesty. With the rise of the family, the romantic aspect of relations between the sexes received more consideration. More emphasis was paid by both sexes to women's appearance, and the styling of dresses was introduced for sexual appeal, along with sophisticated coiffures and cosmetics—even pedicures in some cases; these were frequently subsumed within the dour rubric of "health care." The absence of a parallel development for men suggests the basic asymmetry of sex roles on kibbutzim today.

In the early years of the kibbutz, there were almost no unmarried women. With the new importance given to the family, the social status of single people, especially of women, became precarious. An unmarried woman of twenty-five now presented a problem to be solved, not only by herself and her family but by the kibbutz and even the federation. The kibbutz sees to it that she receives a work assignment that makes it possible for her to meet potential mates or is granted permission to spend a year's leave in the city.[6] The kibbutz federations have coordinated their efforts to develop a uniform system with organized weekends, trips, and annual vacations. Thus a match is encouraged within the kibbutz system, so that neither partner will have a problem adjusting to kibbutz life.

In the kibbutzim established in the twenties, a rather balanced sex ratio and age pattern has recently developed, in marked contrast to the very distorted early ones. By 1948 the second generation in these kibbutzim had established their own families, creating larger units that might be called quasi-extended families. Two or more generations of the same family lived in the same village, but not under the same roof. They cooperated economically, but not exclusively within the family—a system quite different from the normative neolocality of modern urban and rural societies.

These large families commanded a new form and degree of solidarity and constituted a potential threat to the political system. A family group of fifteen to twenty-five adults, all with votes in the General Assembly, could easily become a power group defending the family's own interests instead of the collective's. An earlier study revealed that this potential threat was acknowledged by approximately a third of the population investigated (Shepher 1969a). These large family units are usually called *hamula,* a term used by Arab villagers for the traditional Arab patrilocal agnatic clan (Rosenfeld 1968). Although kibbutzniks proudly see these large families as proof of the continuity of generations in the kibbutz, *hamula* also connotes selfish factionalism, political maneuvering, and aspirations to dominate the village.

To summarize the present state of the kibbutz family:

—The kibbutz family has most characteristics of the "modern" family—free choice of a mate based on romantic love, comparatively narrow functions compared to most other rural societies, and an egalitarian attitude toward the sexes. There are also some tendencies to virilocal concentration of several generations within a village (Shepher 1971).

—The family legitimizes sexual intercourse and reproduction. Although premarital sexual relationships are not forbidden and are readily accepted, most long-term relationships result in marriage (Shepher 1971). Childbirth outside marriage is almost nonexistent.

—The family has become very strong and acquired several functions in consumption, education, and policy-making not officially sanctioned by kibbutz values. Families aspire to still more functions, especially in education. Acceptance of such family activity varies in the three federations. The Ichud Federation is more liberal, the Kibbutz Artzi Federation more restrictive, while the Kibbutz Meuchad Federation is in between. (Further differences among federations are discussed later in this chapter.) In all federations, though, people are well aware of the uneasy balance between the family and the collective.

—Spiro's discussion (1960) of the family's importance in the kibbutz has been supplemented by more recent analyses. Even though most kibbutzim do not allow children to live with their parents, the family's strength and its importance to its members and to the social structure is powerful and growing. In the kibbutz, marriage rates, already the highest among all kinds of locality and residence in Israel, are increasing; birth rates are higher than in the general population and increasing; divorce rates are lower and decreasing. Interestingly, all three statistics are higher in the second- and third-generation kibbutzniks than in the first, and higher in younger kibbutzim than in older ones—a point to which we shall return.

THE ECONOMY

The original economy of the kibbutz was limited to agriculture and was monocultural. From the twenties on, the kibbutz economy became mixed, including dry farming (cereals and hay), irrigated crops such as green fodder, vegetables, sorghum, corn, melons, and recently peanuts, sugar beets, cotton, European and citrus fruits, along with dairy, poultry, and sheep-raising. Industrialization began in the forties but did not become substantial till the sixties.

The economy of the kibbutz, based on collective ownership of the means of production, is operated by the general manager *(merakez hameshek),* assisted by the work assigner *(rakaz ha'avoda),* the treasurer *(gizbar),* and an economic committee. The general manager prepares an annual plan for production, consumption, budget, and investments, which is discussed by the economic committee and then submitted to the General Assembly for approval.

The work teams, usually called work branches, are headed by branch managers *(merakezei anaf)* appointed by the economic committee. In a few kibbutzim, the manager is elected by branch workers; in some service branches, such as kitchens and storerooms, the branch manager is elected by the Annual General Assembly. (By and large, "service" branches, unlike "production" branches, do not produce for external sale.) Branches are staffed by the work assigner, who is assisted by a work committee. Permanent workers are usually appointed by the committee, temporary workers (such as volunteers) assigned daily by the work assigner. The inclinations of the workers are respected, and no one is compelled to work in a branch against his will, whatever his reasons. Moreover, one can keep changing work branches until one finds a satisfying place.

The branch manager prepares his branch's production plan and is responsible for carrying it out. He is helped by members of the branch, though the participation of workers in management varies widely according to the kind of production, the size of the branch, and the personality of the manager.

In most kibbutzim, the workday is eight to nine hours for men and seven to eight hours for women, six days a week. The annual vacation of ten to fourteen workdays is graduated by age. Work usually starts at 6:00 A.M. (in some branches much earlier) and ends at 4:00 P.M. There is a one-hour break for lunch, and a shorter one for breakfast in some branches.

The educational system is rather complicated. The work teams of a single children's house or education unit are very small—usually a nurse with one aide who works a half day. The biggest unit is the kindergarten, where the team may be as large as three or four. These teams are not usually considered branches, even though in some kibbutzim one of the nurses is in charge of all the groups under school age. The result is that a responsible nurse can work with a high degree of independence. Elementary and high-school teachers are considered a separate branch; all high-school teachers are organized on an interkibbutzim basis, and elementary-school teachers are organized in many collective schools. So the production branches and service branches are organized differently; as we shall see, this is reflected in the sexual division of labor.

Work is considered the most important single activity in a kibbutz member's life. It is a major determinant of role and status. The attitude toward work is the classical communist one—from each according to his abilities. Differential material benefits, usually considered a major work motivation outside the kibbutz, are ruled out by ideology and are in fact nonexistent in practice.

The main work motivation is the esteem of one's comembers. Shirking is viewed with such disapproval, or even contempt, that disapproval is one of the chief forces in maintaining work discipline. This creates high sensitivity to satisfaction in work. (For perhaps the best socioeconomic description of the kibbutz system, see Barkai 1972.)

The economic system of the kibbutz seems to be very effective. According to a recent study (Shashua and Goldschmidt 1972), there has been overall economic growth of 32 per cent from 1957 to 1968, an annual growth of 2.5 per cent. The value of property per economic unit grew 220 per cent in these years, an annual growth of 11.2 per cent; the unit is defined as a family, but because of singles the number of units is usually half the adult working population. Even if we allow for inflation, the increase remains 86 per cent in production property and 54 per cent in consumption property. Investment grew 140 per cent, and the value of production rose 12.8 per cent annually. The contribution of industry and external work to overall production rose from 20.5 per cent to 27 per cent.[7] Work input declined 22 per cent, an indication of the economy becoming more sophisticated; but the contribution of capital rose 17 per cent, and of material 9 per cent. The effectiveness of production rose 7 per cent annually, and net annual income rose 3.8 per cent. The standard of living increased 2.9 per cent a year, creating a 0.9 per cent saving each year.

The success of the kibbutz economy is most conspicuous in industry. Although kibbutz industry owns only 4.8 per cent of all plants and employs only 5.1 per cent of the industrial manpower, the coefficient for the proportion of output per invested capital was 3.6 in kibbutz industry, and 2.6 in private industry. The proportion of output to labor was 12.3 per cent in the kibbutz and 10.3 per cent outside it (Rosner 1971).

The distribution of goods and services is based on the other half of the communist principle—to everyone according to his needs. Despite egalitarian distribution and a scarcity of some goods and services, special consideration is given in exceptional cases. Health care is provided according to need, from an open budget. All kibbutz members are insured through the Histadrut's Sick Fund (Kupat-Cholim), which covers almost all medical needs, including medicines, but not dental care. When special circumstances require health care outside Israel, this is financed by the kibbutz.

Education as well is almost free. Every child receives twelve years of general education, and special instruction according to need and talent. Psychological care is provided for every child who is disturbed or retarded in any way. Those who cannot cope with the requirements of high school are educated in special remedial schools run by the kibbutz federation. A quota of 5-6 per cent of the entire adult kibbutz population receives higher education each year.

Food used to be rationed, but recently restrictions have been relaxed. Dining-hall meals are now elaborate and diversified; materials for baking individually (such as eggs, flour, sugar) are usually free. Luxuries such as sweets and liquor are rationed under a separate budget. An overwhelming majority of the adults take their meals in the dining room; a minority may take food from the communal kitchen to eat in their apartments. Afternoon tea or coffee is usually enjoyed in the apartment; food for this is taken from the kitchen or from the "supermarket," as the kibbutz's small store is mockingly called. (This store also provides members with coffee, tea, sweets, liquor, soap, toothpaste, electric bulbs, cigarettes, cleaning materials, etc.) Children have their meals in the children's houses except for dinner, which they usually take with their parents in the dining hall.

Clothing, shoes, furniture, and such minor goods as postage stamps, stationery, and perfume, are distributed by various systems of rationing. Originally, clothing was collectively owned and randomly distributed among members after it was washed. Then individualized consumption of clothing appeared, and every garment was replaced when worn out. Still later, "quantity norms" were introduced; everyone received an equal number of items, whatever the extent of his wardrobe. This is still done in the majority of the kibbutzim, especially in the Kibbutz Artzi Federation. The early fifties saw another innovation in the distribution of clothes and shoes; an annual budget, called the "personal budget" *(taktsiv ishi),* was allotted to every kibbutz member, who was free to decide which items to order.

This change provoked a famous joke that reflects attitudes toward marriage and the sexes. The joke changes *taktsiv ishi* to *taktsiv ishti; ishi* means "individual," but *ishti* means "my wife." This pointed to the fact that as soon as a married person became free of the collective's control of consumption, he entered another, smaller collective—the married couple, in which discretion about choice of items was frequently given to the wife. In fact, the budget for married members quickly became a family budget in most cases.

After long and heated discussions, the Ichud Federation accepted this system, which today is also used in part of the Kibbutz Meuchad Federation and informally in part of the Kibbutz Artzi Federation. Members of many kibbutzim may not only buy clothing through the communal store but purchase it at considerable discount in city stores connected with the kibbutzim's purchasing cooperatives.

Originally, the personal budgets were divided—one for garments other than work clothes, one for shoes, another for small personal items *(haspaka ktana)*. At the end of the sixties, most kibbutzim in the Ichud Federation united these into a "comprehensive budget" *(taktsiv kolel),* which also included pocket money and an allowance for such items as theater and concert tickets outside the kibbutz and repairing and replacing furniture. This system is accepted only in the Ichud Federation; the other federations consider it a serious deviation from kibbutz ideology, though some of their own kibbutzim practice it. Supporters of the comprehensive budget claim that it is closer to the original kibbutz principle—to everyone according to his needs. Since each person can understand his own needs better than anyone else, he and no one else should decide how to apportion his budget. Opponents see a danger of opening the door to inequalities arising from more skillful individuals' better use of goods, and from the existence of external sources of income. "External sources" include presents and gifts from relatives and friends, and German reparation payments, of which a kibbutz member may keep part according to the specific decision of his kibbutz. People who are emissaries of their federation abroad may bring back certain goods. To a lesser extent, people who go on long leaves may bring back goods when they return. These external sources are very difficult to regulate and cause many problems. Generally, big items such as furniture and electric equipment coming from external sources are deducted from what the kibbutz usually supplies; small items such as garments and shoes are overlooked in most kibbutzim.

Because consumption is not connected to individual or family production, a kibbutznik's economic life takes on a special character. He must strive in his work without expecting direct results in personal consumption; conversely, he will enjoy a certain level of consumption without having to make special efforts. As we have seen, the complex system of informal social controls quite successfully prevents shirking and malingering. It is less successful in preventing waste—the parallel result of individual unconnectedness from the production-consumption link. Unnecessary waste is almost ubiquitous in kibbutzim, but it is counterbalanced by the advantages of collective wholesale purchasing and collectively organized consumption. The average income of a kibbutz economic unit (married couple and two children) in 1968 was I£ 649.50, slightly more than the national average of I£ 595 (Shashua and Goldschmidt 1972; Statistical Abstracts 1973). This is equivalent to the wage of a skilled worker in industry or the salary of a low-level white-collar employee. For the same income, the kibbutz can purchase more goods and render more services, so the average kibbutz standard of living is nearer to that of the upper middle class. Below is the personal budget for two working adults recommended by the Ichud Federation in 1973 and followed by most of its kibbutzim. This was during a year when a United States dollar was worth I£ 4.20, an Israeli pound worth $0.238.

This makes the gross family income for two adults and two children I£ 12,080, or I£ 1,007 per month. If one deducts annually I£ 600 a year toward pension, I£ 240 for kibbutz movement taxes, and I£ 600 for taxes, etc., the result is a net monthly income of I£ 887 for two working adults, or I£ 443.5 per person.

STRATIFICATION

Because of its complete socialization of the means of production, lack of differential economic rewards, and equality of access to political power, the kibbutz does not contain discernible stratified groups. Furthermore, the kibbutz has a highly selected population. The qualities and performance required for membership, and the process through which a person not socialized in a collective system reaches candidacy (usually a youth movement), assure this selectivity. It is expressed by many indicators—for instance, the much higher educational level in the kibbutz population than in Israel's general population. There are, however, differences in individual status. Differences in personality traits, talents, and skills acquired

Table 1
Recommended Budget for Two Working Adults, Ichud Federation
(in Israeli Pounds)

	I£	Notes
Food	987	2.70 per person per day
Kitchen Utensils	73	0.20 per person per day
Clothing	200	With home tailoring for women
Shoes	90	
Miscellaneous	155	Includes hygiene needs, sweets, liquor, postage, watch repair, cosmetics
Tobacco	50	
Personal Expenses	350	For personal use and for the "organic budget," from which the social affairs committee may grant cash for unforeseen, exceptional personal expenses, such as visiting a girlfriend or boyfriend in a faraway place
Short courses	40	Less than three months
Vacation	115	
Cultural expenses	138	Including clubhouse and theater outside the kibbutz
Newspaper	87	
Furniture	120	
Subtotal for Individual Comprehensive Budget	2,405	
Public Activity	5	Usually for those who work for the federation and require more "presentable" clothing for urban jobs
Laundry	20	
Young Generation	5	Additional cultural activity for the young
House Maintenance	210	
Gardening and Water	30	
Taxes, Insurance, and Contributions	300	
Subtotal for Collectively Rendered Expenses	760	
Total	3,165	

Another way to render the budget is

Budget per person	3,165
Additional collective expenses	625
Education 0.9 child per adult	2,250
	6,040

before joining the kibbutz all affect individual status. But the most important fact determining a kibbutz member's position is work.

In the original kibbutz ideology, work was an end in itself, which had to be "conquered" (see Chapter 5).[8] A person's labor was evaluated only according to his effort. "From each according to his ability" was interpreted to mean everyone doing his best in terms of his own talents and skills. A member who devoted himself completely to his work could be certain of commanding his comembers' esteem. The product was less important than the producer's devotion and commitment. This suited both the simple economic structure and the ephemeral, Bund-like structure.

But once the economic system became more differentiated, a new basis for evaluation appeared: specialized professional expertise. When everyone did similar and simple work, differences in performance were not always striking. As both agricultural and industrial production became more technologically sophisticated, the elaboration of work branches made specialization more pronounced, and differences in professional knowledge appeared among workers. Professional knowledge was not always equivalent to effort and devotion. Now a more intelligent person might achieve a higher professional level with less effort than relatively untalented comembers. In some cases, the new criterion replaced the old one.

Especially after the War of Liberation in 1948, the country's economic development was such that neither effort nor professional knowledge was sufficient for the survival of an agricultural branch; there had to be a profit. Despite widely introduced economic planning, unsalable surpluses gradually appeared in some crops and some sectors of agriculture, especially animal husbandry, and prices fell. Because of high capital investment in mechanization and a rise in prices of material, water, energy, etc., a net income was no longer certain. The kibbutz grew faster economically than it did in manpower; the branches that required high manpower but were not profitable were gradually abandoned. Vegetable gardens, sheepraising, and honey production were discontinued in most kibbutzim in the early sixties. Economic success became the criterion for evaluating work branches, and a branch's status partly determined the personal status of its workers. Prestige factors had now entered an esteem-based society.

The primary source of prestige in the kibbutz, that of membership, comes into play mainly when members meet nonmembers, such as candidates and temporary workers. Another kind of prestige, reflecting past achievement, is enjoyed by the old-timer (*vatik*); having mastered the hardship of the early, difficult years renders him more or less immune to criticism of his day-to-day activity. There is also prestige for "natives" of the kibbutz; socialized for eighteen years within the kibbutz before being admitted as members, they enjoy the automatic assumption by others that they are well suited to kibbutz life. Another source of prestige is having held a long series of offices. Someone who has been elected to central offices several times enters the informal but very real category of "important" members.

All these forms of prestige have weight in the broad set of social rewards, but however much they may soften the severe everyday controls, they do not neutralize them. What still counts first in the kibbutz is not who one is but what one does. Cynical disdain for the opinion of others is one of the most detested attitudes in a kibbutz member. That is why kibbutzim contain many stubbornly long-lived personal conflicts; people tend not to easily forgive any negative criticism of their performance.

In short, since economic rewards and very great payoffs through power and authority do not exist, informal social rewards are tremendously important. Personal status is based chiefly on the esteem in which one is held as a worker. Other factors in status are social relations, adherence to the norms of collective consumption, participation in the political system, behavior as spouse and parent (and sometimes as child or sibling), and performance in the cultural sphere. An ideal kibbutz member would be described as a good and devoted worker—energetic, enthusiastic, and successful—preferably in a prosperous work branch. He is kind and friendly, his house is always open to visitors. He is ready to help other members, quick to praise, slow to blame. He attends the General Assembly and volunteers for offices. He is a good family member, but not at the cost of stinting in his duties to the kibbutz. He is well-educated, well-read, and a producer of culture through active participation in the cultural life of the kibbutz.

It must be stressed, however, that differences in personal status do not constitute formal stratification. Only if persons with higher status are concentrated and organized in a distinguishable group, and transmit their status to their offspring, does stratification exist. There is no up-to-date or specific research on stratification in the kibbutz, but in the early fifties a group of American social scientists (most of them Jewish) studied this question.[9] Their results were divergent; Eva Rosenfeld's claim of a class structure in one kibbutz was completely refuted by Y. G. Talmon (1956) and Shepher (1952). Later research projects touching the issue supported Talmon's findings and interpretations (Leshem and Cohen 1968; Shepher 1974).

Talmon (1956) and Shepher (1974) explain the mechanisms that prevent the emergence of formal stratified groups in the kibbutz. First, the integration of subgroups based on age, seniority, and national origin is stronger than the integration of main officeholders.[10] Second, recruitment to the capital elite is by rotation, so that membership is temporary. Not only do important officeholders have no economic advantages, but the social disadvantages of exposure to constant criticism, and possible jeopardy of personal and family contacts because of work overload, discourage people from seeking elite positions. In fact, a person elected to such a position usually demands the right to stand down after two to three years. Elite positions are therefore constantly open to newcomers.

Third, political and organizational activity outside the kibbutz offers an outlet for people who have served within it. The influence of outside jobs on one's internal status is, in most cases, corrosive, as we shall show. This, too, prevents the crystallization of a closed and solidary elite group.

Two central ways of forming a stable class are by strategic placement of children and by endogamous marriage within the class group. Talmon (1972) has dealt with the first strategy, and Talmon (1964) and Shepher (1971) with the second. Status by placement is prevented largely by the egalitarian and collective system of education. Intermarriage between second-generation adults is relatively rare and limited to couples where there is an age difference of at least four years. The cohesion of age groups counteracts the formation of the extended family, which itself is under severe social control.

The egalitarian system of economic reward successfully prevents development of classes in the Weberian sense. (In the Marxist sense, this is prevented *a priori* by the complete socialization of production.) The relative absence of prestige differences also prevents the formation of (Weberian) status groups. The paradoxically mixed rewards of occupying elite political positions inhibit striving for such posts, and *eo ipso* the formation of groups aspiring to power (which would elsewhere become formal political parties). So there is no convergence of the various rewards which elsewhere greatly contribute to stratification. The rewards are independent (e.g., economic rewards) or even divergent (e.g., political-elite rewards).

THE POLITICAL SYSTEM

We have seen that social control is mainly informal. But a political system does exist. Initially, decisions on daily problems of economy and society were made through informal conversations among members in the communal dining hall. The General Assembly dealt only with important matters of principle. Later, as the economy and social structure became more complex, a ramified bureaucracy became indispensable to assure adequate division of labor, smooth coordination of the various branches of production and consumption, and a reliable level of performance.

At the head of the structure stands the General Assembly, with decision-making and judicial powers. There is no legislative activity in the parliamentary sense, but the decisions of the Assembly bind officeholders, committees, and members of the kibbutz. Some of the decisions are *ad hoc;* some cover a whole year (such as approval of the economic plan). Still others are statutory for long periods, creating norms of behavior and action.[11] Judicial actions are rare and limited to severe transgressions that call for the most severe (and almost the only) punishment for kibbutzniks—expulsion. The General Assembly has the exclusive right to award membership and to elect officials and committees who must report to it periodically. The General Assembly also serves as an administrative court, the last place for appeal of all decisions by officials and committees.

Each kibbutz member has the same political rights—to attend meetings and cast one vote in the General Assembly and to be elected to office. The General Assembly is presided over by the secretary (or, in a few kibbutzim, by a specially elected presidium, the members of which serve in turn as chairmen of the General Assembly). The agenda is prepared by the secretariat and published at least twenty-four hours before the Assembly begins, which is usually on Saturday evening.[12] Once a year the General Assembly elects officials and committees.[13] A special nominating committee is elected several months before the elections, to propose candidates. The list of candidates is published at least a week before elections, and members may add their own proposals. The rules of election vary from kibbutz to kibbutz; in some it is by secret ballot, in others by a show of hands. In some collectives, a specified majority, such as two-thirds of the Assembly, is needed to elect members to the most important offices.

The organizational structure has several levels, which are shown in Figure 1.

Three central officials are elected by the General Assembly—the secretary, general manager, and treasurer. The secretary is chairman of the secretariat and the General Assembly, and chief coordinator of the entire system. The general manager is chairman of the economic committee and thus head of the whole economic enterprise. The treasurer supervises the kibbutz's financial affairs and is its representative before financial institutions, the kibbutz federation, and the government of Israel. These three officers are relieved from all other work. They belong to the secretariat, and the general manager and treasurer belong to the economic committee as well. In most kibbutzim, other officials and committee members work in their leisure time. In big kibbutzim there are usually full-time jobs for a work coordinator and for two coordinators of education (for children under and over 6).

There are two main committees, the economic committee and the social affairs committee. These are in charge of the overall organization of the two main aspects of kibbutz life.

The economic committee organizes the production, marketing, financing, and manpower management of the work branches. All production branches and some branches of consumption may be subordinated to this committee. In some kibbutzim, a service committee may coordinate the branches of consumption and be responsible to the economic committee only in general budget matters. Even so, consumption branches are secondary to production branches. The economic committee is assisted by a work committee, which deals with the economic and social aspects of work. In some kibbutzim, other staff committees assist the economic committee (auditing committee, financial committee, agricultural committee, etc.).

Figure 1
Organization of a Middle–Sized Kibbutz

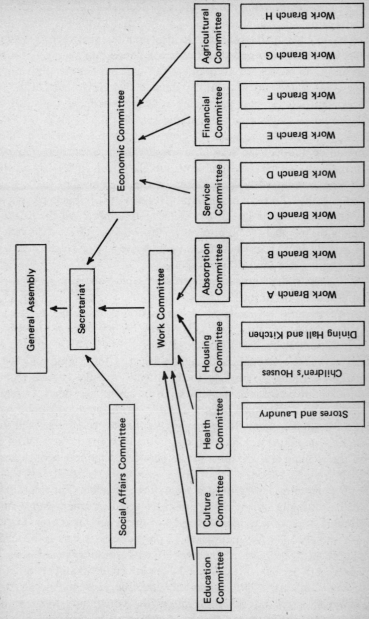

The social affairs committee [14] deals with health, education, culture, housing, interpersonal relations, and member's general well-being and personal problems. It also handles questions of membership, consumption, and distribution of goods and services. To some extent it supervises the committees for such services as absorption of newcomers and aid to relatives outside the kibbutz. It mediates in personal quarrels between members and sometimes even acts as a lower court. These various committees necessarily deal with social reality from different points of view; a synthesis is sought by the supreme committee, the secretariat. Every kibbutz member has access through the General Assembly to judiciary and legislative functions. On the average, 40–50 per cent of the membership takes part in running the affairs of a kibbutz (Barkai 1971). Such participation depends on the vitality of the General Assembly, which in turn depends on members' commitment to the value of direct democracy. It is usually harder to maintain a healthy General Assembly in a kibbutz with more than 400 members.

Despite the bureaucratic structure, everyone can share in decision-making at various levels.

Decisions are made at all levels of the executive structure. In the work branch, they are made by the branch manager, alone or in consultation with the workers (Rosner 1965, 1970, 1972). Most decisions are not publicized, since they are professional and specific; major decisions are brought to the attention of the general manager, with whom the branch managers are in constant contact. Committee decisions are published, unless they deal with purely personal matters (for instance, some decisions by the health committee and social affairs committee). Almost all committees except the secretariat meet in the evening and are open to the public, though few people exercise their right to attend.

Committees vary in size from three to nine. The central committees, usually larger, consist of the elected members and a smaller number of ex-officio members, such as the general manager. Decisions are usually made by consensus; if no consensus can be reached, a simple majority vote is decisive. Formal authority, used only as a last resort, is always exercised in an informal, unauthoritarian, and friendly manner. The values of equality and of human dignity (*shivyon 'erech haadam*) prevail in the community. And authority is specific rather than diffuse; a functionary is supposed to use his authority only within the strict limits of his job. Even a hint of exceeding the proper range would be rejected outright as illegitimate.

When attempts to exercise authority have not proved effective, the functionary's alternatives are to swallow the refusal and try an informal solution, or to take the matter before the appropriate committee or the secretariat. In the latter case, the adamant member is invited to explain his behavior to the committee. If the committee decides against him, and he still chooses not to yield, the matter may be brought to the General Assembly. Both the committee and the General Assembly may reprimand the recalcitrant member. The only further action the kibbutz can take if he remains obstinate is to terminate his membership. This ultimate sanction is reserved for the worst misconduct. Therefore the usual reaction to a final refusal to comply is a publicized formal reprimand—accompanied, of course, by informal pressure that may result in ostracism.

This enforcement system reveals the most characteristic trait of the political system: it is impossible to rule without the collaboration of the entire kibbutz. And the system works, for many reasons—wide participation in the political process and in daily decisions; direct access to the highest institutions; the tight network of personal relationships, which make the functionary a long-time comrade, friend, or at least coworker; deep commitment to the aims of the system and to its democratic management. In short, people usually obey orders because they believe that the orders serve a good cause and reflect a successful and proper way to get things done. There are, of course, apathetic individuals who do not participate politically or socially and are not committed to the group's aims and means. In most kibbutzim they form a periphery of alienation and anomie, although there is the danger that they will be more numerous in large kibbutzim. Such special problems of the political process that emerged with intensive industrialization in the sixties are now under investigation (Rosner 1969, 1972; Melman 1970–71).

SOCIALIZATION AND EDUCATION

The most elaborately studied aspect of kibbutz society is socialization. Psychologists, child psychiatrists, anthropologists, and sociologists have devoted years to describing and analyzing the kibbutzim's collective education. We will briefly summarize the available knowledge, emphasizing the facts most relevant to the emergence of sex roles and to differences in these between federations.

Collective education aims at socializing children to develop a personality suited to a happy life in the kibbutz. The responsibility for education rests not with the nuclear family but with the kibbutz. Basic socialization during the first years of life is carried out by trained nurses appointed by the education committee. Though children spend 9–19 per cent of their time with the nuclear family (the amount varies with age), the time is usually devoted more to purely social interaction than to goal-oriented activities associated with socialization and education. The situation is somewhat different in about twenty kibbutzim (about 8 per cent of all kibbutzim), where children sleep in their parents' apartments. But even there, most socializing activity is carried out by the nurse during the day, while both parents are at work. Every child is reared in a group of four to six until reaching kindergarten age, at about four. Then the child enters a new multiage group of ten to twenty children; therefore the child adjusts early to group life and develops a deep identification with his age group.

Early socialization de-emphasizes sex differences. Of course this is not completely possible. The Hebrew language distinguishes gender in nouns, adjectives, and verbs. Boys who use feminine forms of words are promptly corrected by their nurses. Children see each other naked, and realize genital differences very early (for the results of such socialization, see Shepher 1971). However, educational institutions try not to distinguish between the sexes in clothing, coiffure, and toys.

In the parents' house, the situation is very different. Even young children recognize the division of labor between the sexes. They visit their parents at work and learn that their fathers usually work in production branches and their mothers in service branches. Until the mid-sixties, children received all their clothing from the communal store, and it was not sex-typed until they reached kindergarten. But even at that stage, sex-typed clothing came only as presents from relatives and friends. In recent years there have been more and more deviant cases of purchasing "private clothing" for small children. Also, most toys parents are permitted to buy for their children are sex-typed. It is no wonder, therefore, that by kindergarten age, a sense of sex roles is fully developed.[15]

Of course these are not private processes; children interact with their group. By this time, identification with it has also been established. Kindergarten is a multiage group—from four to six or even seven; but the original peer groups usually stay together within the larger groups.

Early-childhood socialization differs little in the three kibbutz federations. In recent years, their departments of education have collaborated closely, and certain general principles have been accepted by all three. For instance, all kibbutzim are now inclined not to change children's nurses from birth till kindergarten (which is significant in itself), and to teach the first grade within the kindergarten. Differences among the federations are limited to parents' participation in socialization. The Ichud Federation is permissive compared to the stern Kibbutz Artzi; the Kibbutz Meuchad takes a position midway between them. The Ichud Federation has established familistic housing for preschool children in 25 per cent of its kibbutzim, but the Kibbutz Artzi has none; Kibbutz Meuchad has one such kibbutz, and is about to have discussions allowing more kibbutzim to make this change.

More differences among federations appear at five and six years of age. Because of a decline in the number of children, about half of the Ichud kibbutzim gave up the original comprehensive house (see Shepher 1973). These houses had provided all the needs for a class of children—living quarters, classroom, playrooms and playgrounds, and dining room. Instead, they sent their children to district schools organized by several kibbutzim. The Kibbutz Meuchad, which on the average has larger kibbutzim, uses only a few district schools. In the Kibbutz Artzi there are none; more age groups are combined in one class.

Another school-age difference is occasioned by the Kibbutz Artzi's attitude toward separation of the sexes in the bedrooms. The Ichud and Kibbutz Meuchad federations usually separate the sexes around ages nine to eleven; mixed-sex rooms persist in Kibbutz Artzi until age eighteen, though the custom of common showers described by Spiro (1958) has long been discontinued. The differences become even greater when children reach adolescence; then the Kibbutz

Artzi sends them to district boarding schools rather than the non-residential district schools used by the other federations. Sharing mixed-sex rooms with members of their own kibbutz is not embarrassing or complicated, since sexual attraction has not been found between cosocialized children. But at adolescence, the Kibbutz Artzi youngsters are suddenly forced to adjust to sharing mixed-sex bedrooms with students from kibbutzim other than their own. Perhaps because of this "priming" situation, the highest proportion of inter-kibbutz marriages within a federation exists in Kibbutz Artzi (Shepher 1971).

One sign of the success of kibbutz socialization would be the percentage of second-generation members who leave the kibbutz system. No complete comparative data on the subject have ever been collected from the federations; two surveys are known to us, but they are not comparable. The general impression is that the percentage of those who stay in the kibbutz is 70-80, which is very high compared to other collective experiments around the world. But even if these numbers were reliable, they would oversimplify the story. The percentage of second-generation people who left eighty Kibbutz Artzi kibbutzim during the forty-five years of the federations' existence may conceal such important facts as the existence of "good" and "bad" years and greater differences between kibbutzim and between periods of time than between federations.

If the success of collective education is measured by general adjustment to Israeli society, the picture seems even more favorable. People reared within the kibbutz are usually very successful in the army (Amir 1969) and in socioeconomic life outside the kibbutz. Of course, all these impressions still need validation by rigorous investigation, and at least one such attempt is now in progress.[16]

THE VALUE SYSTEM

Two basic values have always stood at the center of kibbutz ideology: service to the Jewish people and the state of Israel, and the creation of a new communist society. Historians are divided on the independence of the second value. Some say that communal life was the only solution to the extremely trying conditions of the first kibbutzim, and that the communist values, once applied, were incorporated in the value system and adhered to. When conditions became easier, communal values were gradually weakened. Other historians find earlier, independent communal values in the cultural background of the kibbutzim's founders. Many of the first kibbutzniks had been deeply influenced by populist social-revolutionary ideologies in their countries of origin, where some had lived communally for a considerable time.

The value of service ties the kibbutz to the Zionist movement. The kibbutz regards itself as the most radical means of implementing Zionist ideas and goals—the building of the country and the rebuilding of the people. At the beginning of this century, Palestine was severely underdeveloped and a new economy had to be created. A new economy requires an agricultural base, but farming was an uncommon occupation among the Jews of the Diaspora, if only because most European Jews were forbidden to own farmland. Several attempts at agricultural colonization in Palestine had failed, so the kibbutz assumed the task. Kibbutz groups were sent to where Zionist policy-makers decided to start settlements; sometimes the reason for choosing a site was not economic but political or even symbolic, so certain settlements were founded despite extremely harsh environmental and security problems.

Though all kibbutzim share socialist values, there are important differences in philosophical emphasis among them. The founders of the first kibbutzim, in the age of the Second Aliyah (for details see Meier-Cronemeyer 1969 and Bein 1952) stressed the idealistic, humanistic aspects of communal life and the central importance of group solidarity. Most of those who founded kibbutzim after World War I—the Third Aliyah—were Marxists,[17] who accepted Ber Borochov's analysis (Borochov 1920-28) of the situation of world Jewry. They argued that collective life is a socioeconomic historical necessity and the product of successful revolutionary class struggle. This difference in emphasis came to the foreground in the question of the best population size for a kibbutz. The first settlers argued that the *kvutza* (group) should be small and selective, no larger than twenty families, to ensure solidary relations. The economy would have to be correspondingly small.

The pioneers of the Third Aliyah criticized the small *kvutza* as a social form. They claimed it could not cope with the challenges of a steadily expanding economy of combined agriculture, artisanry, and industry, nor with the demands of public works such as paving roads and building ports and industrial centers. These needs, they felt, constituted a national emergency, a greater need than that for group solidarity. Selectivity in kibbutz membership must therefore be minimal. The kibbutz—this new name meant "gathering"—must be "a way of life for the masses," as the movement slogan put it.

In this dispute, paradoxically, the Marxists emphasized national values, the non-Marxists socialist ones. Two forms of settlements appeared gradually in Palestine—*kvutzot* (plural of *kvutza*), which deliberately remained small, and kibbutzim, which grew quickly and could send out work battalions to assist such public projects as the port of Haifa and the potash works on the Dead Sea.

Meanwhile, in the years after World War I, a new group appeared, a youth movement from Galicia, in Poland, called Hashomer Hatsair (The Young Guardian), whose members were influenced by the German *Wandervogel* and by such thinkers as Martin Buber and Gustave Wienecken. They stressed the submersion of the individual in the group, and his personal redemption through identification with it. The youth-movement immigrants founded their first kibbutzim in the early twenties, on the *kvutza* pattern.

After several efforts to unite the three groups of settlements in one federation had failed, three separate federations emerged in 1927:

—Hever Hakvutzot (Association of Kvutzot), consisting of the small settlements patterned after the first such group, founded in Degania, on the Sea of Galilee, in 1910.

—Hakibbutz Hameuchad (The United Kibbutz), consisting of the large kibbutzim.

—Hakibbutz Haartzi (The National Kibbutz), consisting of the small groups of the Hashomer Hatsair movement.

The initial ideological differences among the federations were greatly exacerbated by their political affiliations. Kibbutzniks, and kibbutzim as groups, have always shown unusually high political consciousness, and many of those who had no political commitment before immigration joined political parties in Palestine. Most members of the Hever Hakvutzot joined the right-wing, non-Marxist workers' party, Hapoel Hatsair (The Young Worker). Most members of the Kibbutz Meuchad became affiliated with the Marxist workers' party, Achdut Ha'avoda (The Unity of Labor). The Kibbutz Artzi originally had a non-Marxist outlook, but in the late 1920's, during the first part of its second decade of existence, it adopted an extreme left-wing position, accepted Leninist-Stalinist principles, and founded a separate political party called the Mifleget Hashomer Hatsair (Margalith 1971).

From their inception, the kibbutzim played an elite role in the country's political life. They contributed much energy and manpower to political activity, and their members were among the parties' leaders. In 1930 the two leading parties united to create the Mapai (Labor Party), without a union of the associated kibbutz federations taking place. This union lasted fifteen years. In 1944 the more radical Marxist element of Mapai left the party, disagreeing not only with its compromises in social policy but with its conciliatory attitude toward the Arabs and the British. The new party, which was later to reorganize under the old name Achdut Ha'avoda, included a majority of the members of the Kibbutz Meuchad Federation; a minority remained in Mapai. There was a gradual rapprochement between the left-wing parties Achdut Ha'avoda and Hashomer Hatsair, leading to their fusion in 1948 under the name Mapam (United Workers Party). This new party fiercely opposed the Labor Party, which was the core of the reigning coalition. An intolerable situation thus arose in the Meuchad Federation. On May 20, 1951, the Kibbutz Meuchad Federation split. Twenty-five kibbutzim left the federation after an extensive population exchange based on an extraordinarily potent ideological commitment. Even families broke in two. Mapai members who formed a minority in their own kibbutzim went to kibbutzim where Mapai members were a majority, and vice versa. The Mapai kibbutzim quickly united with the forty-seven *kvutzot* of Hever Hakvutzot. In October 1951, they formed the new federation called Ichud Hakvutzot Vehakibbutzim.

Developments in international politics quickly superseded antagonisms between the parties and federations. At first there had been party differences over foreign policy: Mapam was pro-Soviet, whereas Mapai had a Western orientation. But the gradual deterioration of relations between Israel and the Communist world through the fifties wiped out the conflict.[18] Mapam split once again, and the Kibbutz Meuchad returned to political independence by reestablishing the Achdut Ha'avoda Party. In 1955 this party entered the government coalition. The Six Day War of 1967 revealed the complete enmity of the Communist bloc toward Israel and hastened internal political fusion in Israel. Achdut Ha'avoda returned to the Labor Party (Arian 1972), and before the 1969 elections, Mapam entered a parliamentary alliance with the Labor Party. Now the three federations were united politically for the first time. But the old ideological differences are so deeply rooted that the federations maintain their separate organizations. Further splits and fusions are presented in Figures 2 and 3.

Figure 2
Development of Kibbutz Federations

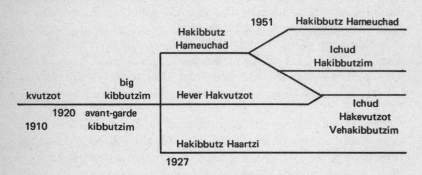

Of course, the differences are the greatest between the Ichud (politically right wing and socially liberal and compromising) and the Kibbutz Artzi (left wing and socially orthodox).

Let us return to the value system and to a discussion of issues arising directly from these differences. The most important one is hired labor. In the fifties, the kibbutz movement was plagued by an acute manpower shortage, just when there was an urgent need to expand agricultural production for Israel's rapidly growing population.[19] In World War II, much of East and Central European Jewry,

Figure 3
Items of the Ideological Tradition of the Three Federations

	Federation I Hakibbutz Haartzi	Federation II Ichud Hakvutzot Vehakibbutzim		Federation III Hakibbutz Hameuchad
Social Ideology	Avant-gardism; selectivity in membership; emphasis on solidarity; organic growth	Selectivity of membership; emphasis on solidarity, organic growth	Like Federation III	Open membership; mechanical criteria of growth; "the big kibbutz is home for the crowds"
Economic Ideology	Priority of agriculture, but industry is approved	Agriculture only	Like Federation III	Agriculture, artisanship and industry together with battalions for wage work outside the kibbutz
Political Ideology	Extreme left-wing, Marxist-Leninist, avant-garde of the Revolution, oriented toward the U.S.S.R.; binational state in Palestine; ideological collectivism*	Right-wing Social Democracy, non-Marxian, oriented toward the West; national state in Palestine; liberal approach to dissent		Moderate left-wing Social Democracy, Marxian, oriented toward U.S.S.R.; national state in Palestine; activism against the English and Arabs; liberal approach to dissent
Federation Ideology	Centralism in political matters; decentralism in economic ones	Decentralized federalism, almost complete freedom of the single kibbutz	Like Federation III	Centralism in economic settlement, youth education issues, freedom of political matters
Educational Ideology	Interkibbutz internship of high-school students, interkibbutz Children's Society, strong youth movement affiliation	Interkibbutz high school without internship, local Children's Society, loose youth movement affiliation		Local high school, local Children's Society, loose youth movement affiliation

*abandoned gradually after the 20th Congress of the CP of U.S.S.R.

the source of the majority of kibbutzniks, was exterminated: the great waves of new immigrants did not join the kibbutz. About half the immigrants of 1948-54 (352,000) came from Asia and Africa; to them, the idea of the kibbutz was utterly strange and unacceptable. The other half (343,000) came from Europe and the western hemisphere; most were survivors of the concentration camps who had become irreconcilably negative toward all collective ways of life.

If the kibbutz did not hire workers, it could not expand production and serve the state. If it did hire workers, it would violate one of the most important principles of socialist ideology by exploiting workers and pocketing "surplus value." Opposition to hiring help was universal in all three federations, yet all were finally compelled to hire outside laborers. The struggle to eliminate hired workers is still going on, more successfully in agriculture than in industry.[20]

Ideological conflict among the federations also appeared in political developments after the Yom Kippur War of 1973. From 1967 till 1973, the question of the "price of peace" has been pushed into the background by Arab intransigence. But after the 1973 war, it became obvious that a "price" had to be set, and this sharpened the conflict between "doves" and "hawks" within and without the kibbutz movement. In the matter of peace and occupied territories, most of the kibbutz doves are in the Kibbutz Artzi and most of the hawks are in the Ichud; many kibbutzniks remain undecided. It should be pointed out, though, that while the doves are an overwhelming majority in the Kibbutz Artzi, the hawks are a minority in the Ichud.

In summary, we can say that many of the original ideological differences among the federations have blurred, but that enough persist for us to distinguish easily between the Ichud and the Kibbutz Artzi. It is data about these groups which we use in this analysis.

SOCIAL DYNAMICS

A society's institutional framework includes norms for individual behavior. But within this framework, people crystallize into groups, communicate with one another, and are individually influenced by powerful personalities. Sometimes purposely, sometimes unwittingly, they deviate from institutional norms. Deviations that are not eliminated provoke social change, which in turn reshapes the institutional framework.

Although the kibbutz defines itself as a primary group, it has rarely been so except during its first years. The founders absorb new groups, families emerge, and children grow up and become members. Kibbutzniks belong to various work branches and devote their leisure time to various hobbies; they are elected to committees and are active in different political and cultural spheres. They interact with neighbors and with the parents they meet at the children's houses; such informal contacts may stimulate the formation of groups outside the institutional framework.

Most informal primary groups are of one-age and one-seniority categories. Neighborhood and children's-house connections usually do not cross lines of age and seniority. However, a common hobby or political or cultural activity may bring together people of different age and seniority. People with similar personal histories also appear to be close to one another socially. Thus a complex network of groups emerges, in which everyone has more than one place.

Aside from the correct and formally friendly relations among comembers of a kibbutz, warm, "real" friendships are reserved for a few individuals. As a kibbutznik would say, "You can't be friends with two hundred people." People spend much of their leisure time with this small friendship group, and it is there that they seek advice and unconditional help. Interestingly, such a group takes upon itself those tasks for which the kibbutz as a whole was originally responsible. Because the very size of the kibbutz today makes it impossible for it to provide what a small primary group can, the collective reluctantly accepts this shift. It does, however, object to primary-group relationships interfering with internal political considerations. For instance, political support in the General Assembly based on friendship would provoke criticism.

Almost every kibbutz publishes a weekly, biweekly, or monthly periodical for its members. But there is also a very intensive and alert informal communications system between members and groups. Physical proximity, overlapping membership in formal and informal groups, concern about what happens to other members, about what they do and how they do it, all encourage this multidirectional flow of information. People are quite conscious of this and may even speak of it sarcastically. "We live in a glass house—everyone sees everything, all the time." Or, "Everybody knows a woman is pregnant before she does." In fact, this intensive communication seems indispensable to the informal social control that maintains work discipline and general compliance despite the lack of an effective judiciary system.

Rumors are widespread, especially when formal communication fails to work properly. Because of the heavy emphasis on political values, no fact or deed remains unevaluated, and it sometimes seems that little goes unrepeated. Gossip is an absorbing kibbutz pastime—an excellent literary description of this is to be found in Amos Oz's novel *Elsewhere, Perhaps* (1973). Even the formal institutional system takes gossip into account. One often hears, "What would people say if . . . ?" The argument, "Public opinion is against such a plan," is heard often in committee meetings, though no one ever knows exactly what public opinion is. The "public" is formally identified with the General Assembly, but rarely are enough members present to reveal broad opinion except about very important matters.

Public-opinion leaders emerge and supplement the formal elite, but any discrepancy between the formal and the informal elite is short-lived. Influential individuals are rather quickly proposed as candidates for important offices. In fact, officeholding itself is so important a norm that most people who avoid it gradually lose their influence. This fact and rotation in office maintain a delicate balance between formal and informal leadership.

Of course, even formal and informal social control cannot assure complete conformity; deviations exist in every sphere of life. As long as deviation remains isolated, it does not interfere with the institutional system. But if it expands, it becomes an illegitimate innovation and gradually gains legitimacy. A good example is the now legendary case of the family tea—the first occasion in which the family was the unit of consumption. It began when a man brought home an electric kettle from the Jewish Brigade after World War II. He was considered a dangerous renegade and was ordered to turn in the kettle to his kibbutz. When he refused, some people followed his example and acquired electric kettles from illegitimate sources. This expanding insubordination fueled much fervent ideological discussion in the early fifties. Later, when people realized that the kibbutz did not disintegrate (as had been prophesied) because members sipped tea in their apartments, they concluded that it was silly to give a perquisite to deviants while depriving the conformists. Kibbutz after kibbutz decided to provide electric kettles to their members. The tea ceremony became entrenched, and cakes and cookies appeared as if by magic. Thus a wicked innovation became legitimate.

To some extent, all important social changes in the kibbutz went through the same stages. The ideological literature is full of examples. Martin Buber saw in this capacity for gradual adaptation the secret of the kibbutz's success—or rather the absence of its failure—as a revolutionary social experiment (Buber 1949). How deep were these changes? To what extent do they affect the essence of the kibbutz system? These remain questions of major concern for the intellectual elite of the kibbutz movement.[21]

Chapter 4

Studying the Kibbutz

We have already pointed out that kibbutzim differ in size, seniority of settlements and of individual members, and especially in ideology, which is largely reflected by affiliation with federations. We also mentioned that every widely known book about the kibbutz was based on research in only one kibbutz (e.g., Spiro 1956; Bettelheim 1969), so that even if we accept those authors' conclusions, we cannot use them to generalize about "the kibbutz." Since our research on the division of labor between the sexes depended upon many variables (age, generation, kibbutz size, ideology), we decided not to limit our work to even one group of kibbutzim. We have sought to investigate our most important dependent variables—work, political participation, and education—in the entire adult population of two federations, the "right-wing" Ichud and the "left-wing" Kibbutz Artzi. Fortunately, this was also the most pragmatic choice.

In 1968 the statistical departments and sociological research institutes of these two federations conducted identical censuses. The third federation, the Kibbutz Meuchad, had carried out a census the previous year—limited to demographic data and not comparable to the other federations' censuses. The 1968 questionnaire was prepared by a joint team from the research institutes of the two federations, headed by their two directors, Dr. Menaham Rosner and Joseph Shepher. The chief aim, of course, was to collect basic demographic information, but the team asked additional questions to obtain data that might be needed for future research. Since 1968 the data have been adjusted periodically. The data in this volume reflect the two populations as of January 1, 1973. The information about these more than 34,000 adult members and candidates has been divided according to sex, generation, and seniority of the kibbutz. We have distinguished three subgroups within the variable "generation":

1. *Second Generation* includes all members born and raised on the kibbutz and those who, joining it with their parents before reaching age thirteen, were socialized in the kibbutz, and are therefore considered *ben meshek* (literally, "son of the farm").

2. *Kibbutz-Bred* includes all members who joined the kibbutz as students at any age, and those who were educated in it as members of a Youth Aliyah group—an organization founded in the early thirties to help refugee children reach Palestine, where most were educated in kibbutzim. They were socialized in the kibbutz but are not usually considered *ben meshek*.

3. *First Generation* includes members who joined the kibbutz after age eighteen.

We recognize that this categorization is relatively arbitrary, but it does distinguish between persons whose formative connections to the kibbutz experience differ in important ways affecting their growth and development. Thus, we are able to be rather sensitive to social patterns and individual careers as they relate to the effects of age and duration of kibbutz experience. Indeed, such a categorization is essential if we are to proceed with any confidence to assess the role of socialization in the development of kibbutz society.

We would add that North American readers in particular should note that our category "First Generation" is in a sense opposite in meaning to how the phrase is used in discussing immigration in North America. We refer only to those people who joined the kibbutz when they were adults; thus, they spent their formative years elsewhere. It does not mean that they were, or were not, the first generation to establish a kibbutz. Our focus here is on the biographies of the members, not the history of the communities.

In the variable "seniority of the kibbutz" we have distinguished:

Group I   Kibbutzim founded before 1930
Group II   Kibbutzim founded 1931-40
Group III Kibbutzim founded 1941-47
Group IV   Kibbutzim founded after 1948

The following table shows the sizes of all variables and their subgroups in each federation.

Table 2
Total Population of Members and Candidates in the Kibbutz Artzi and the Ichud Federation, by Sex, Generations and Seniority Groups as of January 2, 1973 (in absolute numbers)

Generation Group	Males				Females				Total Males and Females
	Second Generation	Kibbutz-Bred	First Generation	Total Males	Second Generation	Kibbutz-Bred	First Generation	Total Females	
Kibbutz Artzi									
I	833	338	914	2085	643	240	1076	1959	4044
II	1815	482	2368	4665	1436	338	2475	4249	8914
III	225	127	805	1157	193	90	706	989	2146
IV	87	118	620	825	72	82	542	696	1521
Total	2960	1065	4707	8732	2344	750	4799	7893	16625
Ichud									
I	1747	255	1915	3917	1277	189	2353	3819	7736
II	1045	243	1708	2996	755	198	1713	2666	5662
III	116	132	1074	1323	131	93	895	1119	2442
IV	16	26	832	874	13	18	671	702	1576
Total	2924	656	5529	9109	2176	498	5632	8306	17415

The census data gave us the necessary demographic variables, such as sex, age, marital status, number of children, age and circumstances of joining the kibbutz (what we call "generation"). We also took from the census such nondemographic data as work, education, army service, activity outside the kibbutz, and political activity (offices, committee memberships) in the kibbutz.

The census questionnaire is reproduced in Appendix A. The data have been cross-tabulated according to the associations investigated. Unfortunately, data from the tape of Kibbutz Artzi on two questions (second punch cards 52 and 63) had been accidentally erased, and we could cross-tabulate the figures with sex, age, and generation, but not with seniority of the kibbutz and with army service.

The census did not cover several variables important to our investigation, such as the division of labor within families and attitudes toward sexual division of labor. Two extensive research projects on attitudes had been carried out in 1965 (Rosner 1968; Shepher 1967), but we were not certain that the findings would still be adequate. We therefore made an additional inquiry in four kibbutzim. We investigated the adult married population of two kibbutzim of similar size and sociocultural constitution, both founded at the time of the War of Liberation; they were, however, different in ideological affiliation—one belonged to the Ichud, one to the Kibbutz Artzi. We also studied two kibbutzim founded before 1930, similar in size and sociocultural constitution, also different in affiliation; in these we used a sample of both married and single members. To conceal the identity of the kibbutzim, we will call them by these names:

	Ichud	Kibbutz Artzi
Young kibbutzim	Ofer	Ofra
Old kibbutzim	Tsvi	Tsvia

To these samples we presented a questionnaire with sixty-one items. Thirty-six of the questions were closed, requiring specific answers. The remaining twenty-five were open-ended and encouraged long replies containing attitudes and opinions as well as factual and historical material. The schedule is reproduced in Appendix B.

In Ofer and Ofra, we were able to obtain an almost total response to the self-administered questionnaires. In Tsvi and Tsvia, we were less fortunate. The Yom Kippur War broke out during the last phase of the research, and after the cease-fire we did not return to those kibbutzim; many of our male respondents had fallen in battle, and those who survived were still serving in the army reserves. Among the women, the general atmosphere of mourning and worry utterly discouraged further research. In any case, we had already procured a 25 per cent systematic sample of the adult married and single population.

The table on the following page presents the data on responses from the four kibbutzim we investigated.

We were also able to collect data on political participation according to sex, since in Ofer each person's attendance of the General Assembly had been recorded for the previous five years. Further information on participation according to sex was obtained by studying the protocols of the Assembly in detail.

Since we had reason to think that sexual division of labor had changed considerably in the kibbutz since the beginning of the movement, we wanted to learn as much as possible about the past. We interviewed the founders of the four kibbutzim about the sexual division of labor in the first years of their collectives. We conducted and recorded open group interviews lasting two and a half hours with eight older men and women in Tsvi, nine in Tsvia, six in Ofer, and six in Ofra. This gave us important material on the sexual division of labor in the early twenties for two kibbutzim, and after the War of Liberation for two others. To check this material against the early periods of other kibbutzim, we analyzed relevant literary material (memoirs, letters, articles) in Beit Trumpeldor, the Central Archives of the kibbutz movement, in Kibbutz Tel Yosef. Both sources corroborated the interview material.

This research was carried out in the course of two years of participant observation of every sphere of life in Ofer and Ofra. Special attention was devoted to work branches with all-female or mixed-sex personnel. Political activity in committees and in the General Assembly was recorded weekly. Educational activity was scrutinized, especially for signs of sex typing. Thus we were able to check questionnaire data and official records against direct observation.

Especially interesting data were gathered through observation

Table 3
Population of Respondents in Four Kibbutzim, by Sex and Generation

OFER

	First Generation		Second Generation		Total	
	M	F	M	F	M	F
Planned sample*	53	49	10	14	63	63
Number of questionnaires secured	41	40	4	9	45	49
Percentage of performed questionnaires of planned sample	77.3	81.6	40.0	64.2	71.4	77.7

OFRA

	First Generation		Second Generation		Total	
	M	F	M	F	M	F
Planned sample*	75	60	2	3	77	63
Number of questionnaires secured	48	51	/	/	48	51
Percentage of performed questionnaires of planned sample	64.0	85.0	/	/	64.0	85.0

TSVI

	First Generation		Second Generation		Total	
	M	F	M	F	M	F
Planned sample*	22	23	29	31	51	54
Number of questionnaires secured	14	15	14	20	28	35
Percentage of performed questionnaires of planned sample	63.6	65.2	48.2	64.5	54.9	64.8

TSVIA

	First Generation		Second Generation		Total	
	M	F	M	F	M	F
Planned sample*	37	33	15	12	52	45
Number of questionnaires secured	16	13	10	10	26	23
Percentage of performed questionnaires of planned sample	43.2	39.3	66.6	83.3	50.0	51.1

*In Ofer and Ofra, the planned sample was the total married population. In Tsvi and Tsvia, the planned sample was a random 25 per cent of the married population and 50 per cent of the unmarried population.

during the Yom Kippur War, when the adult kibbutz population was 80 per cent female and 20 per cent older males. We recorded how the kibbutz system adjusted to this situation in work, political activity, leisure time, education, and defense activities.

The data in the census pertaining to men's and women's army service were insufficient for understanding the different character of women's service. We had to take the following steps to complete our picture:

1. We visited the Basic Training Camp of Chen (Hebrew abbreviation of *Cheil Nashim,* the Women's Army) where two women officers showed us training, equipment, and living quarters.

2. We interviewed the commanders of the training camp about the nature of the training camp and the training and the situation of kibbutz girls in the camp.

3. We visited a Nahal [1] settlement on the Golan Heights and discussed with men and women officers the role of women in this military settlement. Shepher later visited three border settlements which, despite their civilian status, remained in military preparedness.

4. Long, intensive interviews were conducted with several women officers who were second-generation kibbutz members and had worked at a variety of army tasks.

This combination of methods and the search for consistency among sources enabled us to cover almost all topics we considered relevant. We are confident that what we will now describe and analyze is the most accurate and comprehensive collection of facts available under existing conditions.

Chapter 5

The Working Patterns of Women in the Kibbutz

There is no "they" to blame in the kibbutz, there is just "we." The work of living must be done by all the members; deficits of time and personnel are quickly felt. All of one February, after a war, it was very cold and many members of Ofer became ill. In addition, many had military duties and extra guard duties, and the remaining kibbutzniks were hard pressed to do the jobs necessary for kibbutz life. For several months many adults worked seven days a week. This was of course a terrible strain, but there was no one to complain to, no system to berate; the work had to be done. People hoped for warmer weather, and looked forward to the arrival of some young people from a settlement nearby to ease the dull, extended crisis. Meanwhile, fatigue pervaded the kibbutz as thoroughly as the cold air from the surrounding pine forest, and there was nothing to be done but what had to be done.

In a recent publication on the concept of work in modern philosophical systems, Barzel (1973) concluded that there are two predominant basic attitudes toward work. One is that work is an answer to the dictates of economic survival, a means to an end; if one can find alternative ways to live, one need not work at all. The other sees work as humanity's basic self-realization; work has value in and of itself. This latter attitude received quasi-religious elaboration in the theory of A. D. Gordon (1952), a member of the first kibbutz, who stressed the inherent value of work in helping to liberate Jews of the Diaspora from their socioeconomic past. In the Diaspora, relatively few Jews did physical labor, and even fewer worked at agriculture. As they saw it, if they implemented the will of God, others would work instead of them. Gordon maintained that in the land of

Israel the Jews would have to accommodate to nature by working the soil. This would be not only a means of survival but a path to redemption after the curse of the Diaspora. But most of the founders of the kibbutz came from East European, middle-class families and were unused to physical work. Their eventual "conquest of work" (*Kibbush Ha'avoda*) would pull them from their *petit bourgeois* socialization and sustain their efforts to develop agriculture in a new and difficult terrain and compete for markets with established local agriculturists.

"The conquest of work" became the basic ideological slogan of the early kibbutz. Despite all compromises caused by the gradual economic development and rising standard of living, the kibbutz attitude toward work has remained essentially unchanged. Not having a steady work place puts the status of the kibbutznik in jeopardy. This occurs very rarely, as a result of quarrels within a work branch, illness, or liquidation of a work branch. The kibbutz will make the greatest effort to find a new steady job for a displaced worker. Even among aged community members, reduced work loads serve to maintain morale (Wershow 1973).

The next most disagreeable fate for a kibbutznik is to have to work in a branch where he does not find satisfaction. In several research projects, a large percentage of kibbutz workers maintained that they were satisfied with their work; yet when they were asked whether they wanted to change their jobs, a large percentage said yes.

Work is connected with other basic values of kibbutz ideology: building the country, creating Jewish agriculture after 2,000 years largely without land, and establishing Jewish villages and Jewish workers. By working without direct economic reward, they were helping to build a new communistic society—the only true communism on earth because it is completely voluntary.

The kibbutz work obviously meant physical labor, and those who had to do mental work, such as managers and teachers, sought to combine their activities with occasional physical labor, to demonstrate their commitment to the basic values of the kibbutz. When Shepher told his five-year-old son that he couldn't spend time with him because he had to go to work, he answered, "Aba, you aren't working, you're only teaching." The distinction between manual and mental work is slowly disappearing because of the steady rise in the technological level, but it obviously lingers in the daily life and atmosphere of the kibbutz.

Work has been of the highest importance for women as well as for men. But what work should women do? The kibbutz had to address itself to this question from its beginnings.

Like most modern socialist movements, the kibbutz has incorporated sexual equality as a value and a goal. This aspect of its ideology developed slowly, though, and did not crystallize until the late twenties. Sexual equality was till then considered less a philosophical problem than a practical one: the only question as far as the kibbutz founders were concerned was the pragmatic one of how to bring it about. According to the *Proposal to the Constitution of the Kvutzot,* published in 1925, the social bases of the *kvutza* included "an expanding place of work for the women in the branches of the economy" and "equal duty for all members of the *kvutza* [men and women] to share housework [bakery, kitchen and laundry]" (Gadon 1958). Six years later, the council of the Kibbutz Hameuchad resolved that the units of the "kibbutz in the city"—work brigades then being sent out by the Kibbutz Meuchad to help with building and road construction in urban areas—were "obliged to care especially for the penetration of the *chaverot* [female comrades] into occupations which suit them, by founding cooperatives which will employ them and by creating such branches in the workers' economy which employ them. . . . The secretariat is required to act in such a way that *chaverot* who have been living for a long time in the country and in the kibbutz should be sent to training in the women's farms and groups" (Mibifnim 1932).[1]

Two decades later, the principle of sexual equality appeared in more crystallized form in the writings of the Kibbutz Meuchad: "Equal rights of the *chaver* and *chavera* in the economic and social creativity, in education, in defense, in public activity and in mission [Hebrew *shlichut,* the education of youth movements outside Palestine] in order to raise the ability of the *chavera* and her self-expression in the life of the kibbutz settlement, the federation, and the movement" (Gadon 1958).

An interfederation proposal, intended to be a base for kibbutz law, enumerates the aims of the kibbutz; one of them is "To advance the *chaverot* of the kibbutz toward factual equality in economic and social creativity" (Gadon 1958).

In the ideological literature, as in these formal resolutions, there is abundant material stressing the need for complete equality between the sexes, with an emphasis on work. Only the Kibbutz Artzi, however, was explicit in making such equality integral and even fundamental to kibbutz ideology. Rosner (1969) describes the Kibbutz Artzi position:

"It was evident that the kibbutz is the full solution to the question of women's liberation. It was clear—not in terms of West European ideas of emancipation but of the deepest human conviction—that the kibbutz affirms the total equality of the working woman in the kibbutz, shoulder to shoulder with man."

In its most radical form, this principle was expressed by the spiritual leader of the Kibbutz Artzi movement, Meir Ya'ari:

"There are people who find justification for the fact that the *chavera* is uninterested in politics. As though woman is not created for it. They sing hymns of praise to the *chaverot's* deep understanding in matters of education and in creating warm, friendly relations within the kibbutz. They usually distinguish between *natural qualities* of men and women. The power of men is in public relationships, as it were, and that of women in intimate, friendly relationships. Women's top achievement in the kibbutz, according to this attitude, is their conquest of some additional work branches. I have reservations about all but's and however's in this question. Just as in the agrarian problem, socialism cannot be satisfied with half solutions to women's problems. We have to demand total, uncurtailed equality. Every form of incompleteness endangers the aspiration. And just as the aspiration to abolish the difference between city and village is absolute, so is the aspiration to make the working woman equal with the working man."

Such resolutions and essays reveal that creating sexual equality in work was not easy. The statements refer not so much to women's failing to enter agriculture and construction as to men's absence from traditionally female work. Resolutions to remedy this were repeatedly introduced in congress; there were few claims of success, many complaints about failure. In the forties, in ideological essays, women frequently blamed themselves for not pursuing equality ardently enough. In 1949 the periodical of Hever Hakvutzot (vol. 6, part 3) states:

"*De jure* we achieved complete equality of rights [between the sexes], but *de facto* the idea is not sufficiently implemented. The young woman's part in the fight for realization was considerable, as was her contribution as spouse and mother. From the time of the Second Aliyah, her contribution in the process of creating agriculture and communal living was great. Those women did not know rest until they achieved their aim with full devotion—the result of a deep psychological resolution. Years passed, and the energy of our women is going to be absorbed by work in the service branches. The *chavera* has to be more active in all spheres of life, production as well as service branches, without having a feeling of inferiority because she is employed almost exclusively in service branches."

This recalls Geertz's definition (1964) of the function of ideology: "Ideology bridges the emotional gap between things as they are and as one would have them to be, thus ensuring the performance of roles that might otherwise be abandoned in despair and apathy."

There certainly has been no change in the kibbutzniks' goal of sexual equality in work. But the actual situation has been changing constantly. When we review the facts, we will see how and why ideology increasingly reflected a discrepancy between real life and ideal life.

THE "GLORIOUS PAST"

The proportion of men over women among the founders of the first kibbutzim was very high, as it was in the rest of Palestine's Jewish population. Some of the early settlements consisted of a dozen young men and one or two women. Later more women arrived, but a disproportionate ratio persisted almost until the establishment of the state.

The first kibbutzniks lived in old, abandoned Arab buildings, later in tents and barracks. The standard of living was very low, food scarce, garments few. There were no children. Service work was therefore limited to some cooking and laundry. It was generally accepted that the few women had to do it. Atara Sturman, one of the founders of Ein Harod, writes in her memoir about their group in Merchavia—four women and thirty-one men:

"The work of the *chaverot* in Merchavia was very heavy, but we didn't realize that then. We were working joyfully and in high spirits; we didn't pay attention to the difficulties because we had only one worry—how to facilitate the situation of the *chaverim,* what to do and how to behave to keep the *chaverim* from feeling the poverty, how to improve the taste of the bad food."

Nevertheless, when more women came, they all wanted to share in the pioneer work. They understood that some women had to do the limited service work of the collective, while the rest worked in the fields, in road construction—everywhere the men were working. It was also accepted that the men had to do at least some of the service work. One of the founders of Tsvi said in our group interview:

"I didn't agree to work only at cooking and laundering. I went working in the fields and plowed. I didn't agree that only boys should do that work. I also carried water from the spring, which was very heavy work. And I went there alone, even though there were Arabs around us. I was seventeen and a half then, and I had been working that way for quite a long time."

Another *chavera* from the same kibbutz had this to say:

"When we were in Shomria, there were girls who worked in road construction. I think they were deeply respected. They prepared pebbles for the coating of the road, and in the evening they talked a lot about their efficiency in this work. Some girls even worked in the quarry, carrying baskets full of stones. The service work was limited to the kitchen and the communal store. The laundry was very primitive. Boys helped in the laundry—they collected and cut wood for boiling the water and carried the wet laundry back to the camp."

Conditions were similar in Tsvia, which was founded in 1923 by two groups that had been engaged in public work. One group had contained fifteen boys and three girls; the girls were all busy with kitchen work, and as the group grew, a boy sometimes assisted them. The second group had consisted of sixteen boys and four girls; it was part of a larger work brigade for which the British Mandatorial government had established a kitchen; so all the girls, like the boys, worked in road construction, mostly leveling and making pebbles.

The pattern was similar in both groups: to the extent that there was service work, the girls did it, sometimes assisted by the boys. When there was a surplus of girls, some of them worked with the boys, and the tasks were subdivided to give the girls the easiest jobs.

This was the rule, not the exception; a survey of material in the archives of Beit Trumpeldor reveals the same pattern in hundreds of workers' groups during the Third Aliyah period (1921-24). For instance, from a woman, Hasia Dror:

"Educational work, which had been the ideal of my life for years in Russia, faded away in contrast to work in the fields, raising crops and animals" (Dossier, Reshimot).

Both men and women who witnessed women working at road construction reported that "along the road you could see groups of youngsters, boys digging ditches and girls riding on heaps of pebbles" (Ish-Shalom: From Koln to Mizra, Reshimot, part 15), and that "on all the roads, especially on the roads from Haifa to Nazareth and from Nazareth to Afula, there were a lot of female workers. They shared all the heavy work except quarrying, digging and hewing" (A. Avatichi, part 24).

The kitchen and "sick bay" remained the realm of the women: "The kitchen was the girls' place. They cooked and washed the dishes. When malaria came, they set up special rooms for the ill and cared for them" (David Ofer: On the road Tsemach-Tveria-Dossier, Memoirs, item 44).

"When I came to Tel Yosef, I was charged with organizing the laundry. I had a tent, some tubs, and boilers, and that was all. A boy brought me water on the back of a donkey" (Stefa Reiss; Dossier: Memoirs, item 49).

Even this partial change in women's work pattern was considered a major revolution: "There was a strong will to revolutionize women's work-life, to change their nature. We felt that in public work we were able to be as productive as the boys. It seemed to us that here everything was different, that the meaning of Eretz Israel was something new, revolutionary. We came here to work, to conquer the new life and the country. I refused to learn the job of nurse because it would have removed me from the people with whom I wanted to build the country, to conquer it with my own hands" (Malka Kimmelman; Dossier: The First Days, item 56).

Characteristically, work in the kitchen, laundry, communal store, and tending the sick were not considered "building the country" by most women. The idea that caring for those who "really" build the country also contributed to the building was only gradually accepted.

Nevertheless, there were girls who accepted the necessity of doing service work and did not rebel against it constantly. And those who made major efforts to "get out of the kitchen" still did their kitchen work efficiently and well.

As long as service work remained very limited, two or three girls could do it and still have some time left over for working outside the house. Interestingly, there seems to have been no serious challenge to the notion that service work should be done mostly by women. True, men helped them in the kitchen and with the laundry, but always on a temporary basis. We did not find a single proposal to completely abolish the sexual division of work permanently and assign males to the kitchen or laundry. In the words of one of the male founders of Tsvi:

"Boys worked in the kitchen bringing wood, washing dishes, waiting, but we never contemplated the possibility of boys working permanently in the kitchen and girls going out to work on the road."

However, women did significantly enter agriculture and construction. In a collection of memoirs, stories, and poems called *Chaverot Bakibbutz* (Poznansky and Shkhoury 1944), we find a long list of jobs done by females in the Second and Third Aliyah, including vegetable gardening, tending plant nurseries and seed beds, honey production, raising poultry and cows and sheep, citrus growing, tractor-driving, fishery, construction, shoemaking, carpentry, plumbing, tin-can manufacture, weaving, and baking. Unfortunately, we do not know how many women did these jobs or for how long. Much of this labor may have been exceptional or temporary; even so, it contrasted strongly with the life of a "good Jewish girl" from an East European *shtetl* (Jewish town or part of one). And it was revolutionary in terms of social roles linked to gender.

The groups that pioneered the kibbutzim lived nomadically during their first years in Palestine. They set up temporary camps along roads under construction, spent months in the *moshavot*—agricultural communities with nuclear families; they are not communist farming villages, though there is some sharing of equipment. There they did wage work for farmers, or labored in training cooperatives. Some people changed groups and locations as many as ten times before joining a new kibbutz. Life was unstable. The sexual division of labor was rudimentary. When groups finally consolidated and settled, two important changes took place: more women joined kibbutzim, and work possibilities became more diversified for both sexes. Now the sexual division of labor became even less polarized than during the years of wandering, as group interviews in Tsvi and Tsvia show.

Of Tsvia's twenty-five founders, seven were women. These women started three agricultural branches—vegetable gardening, dairy farming, and poultry-raising. They also ran the service branches—the kitchen, communal store, laundry, health care and, with the advent of children, child care. There were, nevertheless, distinctions; when women worked in dry farming, they sowed the corn, walking funnel in hand behind the men who did the plowing with a mule. Had the woman ever worked with the mule, and the man with the funnel? A male founder of Tsvia said, "For that to happen it wouldn't have been enough to convince the man to give up his place. You'd also have had to convince the mule."

Of Tsvi's fifty founders, twenty were women. These women ran the poultry and dairy branches (a hundred chickens and five cows) and worked in the vegetable garden. There were already seven families and some children, so that service work was more extensive than in Tsvia. Women ran the kitchen, communal store, laundry, and children's house. One of the first *chaverot* told us:

"Only a few *chaverot* were inclined to work in the kitchen. The communal store was obviously in their hands. The laundry was very primitive; boys worked there, but on a rotation basis. Boys did the heavy work of cleaning showers and latrines. So there was a rather natural division of labor. All that continued while the economy was small."

Founders of both kibbutzim unanimously estimated that 50 to 60 per cent of the women worked in production branches during the first five years of their settlements. The participation of men in service work was considerable, but on a temporary, *corvée* basis. Even at this early stage, some problems appeared. Here is the testimony of a female founder of Tsvi:

"I worked in the cowshed, as did my husband. I had a small child, and often I worked on Shabbat, so I always had a headache about where my child was [on Saturday morning the children's houses were closed]. My child hated the cowshed, so he never came there, but other children did. When my turn came to work in the cowshed in the evening shift, I wasn't able to put him to bed for two or three months."

Such problems may have been exceptional during the early years. After a decade the situation changed considerably.

THE TRANSITION PERIOD

We have noted that the birth rate was very low in the early years of kibbutzim founded in the Third Aliyah. But after a decade, more and more children were being born. The Ichud Federation is the only one for which we have figures, but there is no reason to assume there were different trends in the other federations. In the Ichud kibbutzim, 201 children were born between 1910 and 1932; 668 between 1932 and 1942, and 2,645 between 1943 and 1952 (Sikumei Ohlosia 1973). The adult population did not expand similarly during the second of these decades, and the task of education was faced by a relatively small adult population. This and the sex ratio were probably the major factors in the sexual division of labor. The sex ratio equalized gradually. In the earliest years the ratio was about 400, at the end of the first decade about 150, and at the end of the second decade about 120. (This estimate of the able-bodied adult population is based on Kibbutz Artzi information, found in Mimoetza Lemoetza 1974.) Since there were 20 to 50 per cent more men than women during the transition period, and it was evidently unacceptable for men to care for small children, the only solution was to transfer women from production to child care. This is amply confirmed in our interviews. For instance, in Tsvi:

Chavera A: A fight started. Women who were already tied to their work because they had been at it for years didn't want to leave it and lose their status.

Interviewer: Do you remember any case of a woman who was required to leave her work and go to child care appealing to the Assembly?

Chavera A: I do remember that people went to talk with a woman to convince her. And I remember Z. and T.

Chavera B: There were *chaverot* who didn't want to work with children. They said they didn't have the temperament for it.

Chavera C: Not all the *chaverot* were like that. Some saw child care as a primary task. They conceded the great importance of expanding production, but they felt they contributed to the common cause by rearing our children.

The following exchanges, in Tsvia, make similar points:

Interviewer: When did the service branches start expanding? How did the expansion affect the division of labor between the sexes?

Chavera A: The division came to be girls in service work, boys in agriculture. But it wasn't complete; there were still girls in the cowshed and girls who raised poultry and worked in the orchard and the vegetable garden. And the girls had a strong desire not to go to work in the service branches. They fought against it.

Interviewer: Were men ever sent to work with small children?

Chavera B: Only once, when there was an epidemic.

A strong desire on the part of some women to stay in agriculture had different sources in these two kibbutzim. Tsvi belongs to the Ichud, Tsvia to Kibbutz Artzi. In Kibbutz Artzi, graduates of the Hashomer Hatsair Youth Movement felt strongly about the issue of sexual equality. One woman said:

"That's how we had been educated: We were taught that boys and girls were equal. When we came to this country, we even learned to tile floors. Later we went to work in agriculture because we'd been taught to believe boys and girls are equal."

But in Tsvi, we heard quite a different story:

"We had been educated to see the building of the country as our most important aim and task. To us that meant construction or agriculture. Nobody would have accepted that working in the kitchen meant building the country. That's why we girls wanted to work in agriculture and then didn't want to leave it."

But whatever the argument, women succumbed to the same course of events. Under the demand for expanded services for a growing population, they gradually left the agricultural branches; they fought hard, but succeeded only in delaying the change for a while. The total kibbutz-movement population expanded steadily, from 4,391 in 1931 to 27,738 in 1941 to 54,208 in 1948.[2] Not only was the sex ratio still high and service work more in demand than ever before, but the standard of living was rising as well. Food was no nger limited to bread and olives; clothing improved, and the com-ıunal store now had more to do than add a new patch to an old patch. And there were children. Food and clothing could be treated casually, even neglected, but children could not be. In fact, they needed the best possible care; these endlessly intriguing but demanding creatures would people the kibbutzniks' dreams of the future.

The effect of the new demands for service is set out clearly in Talmon's study (1956) of eight kibbutzim in the Ichud Federation, which reconstructs the division of labor in 1948.

Table 4
Division of Labor Between the Sexes in 1948 (in percentages)

	Agriculture	Non Agricultural Production	Production Services	Services to Adults	Child Care and Education	Management, Public Activity and Various Other Work	Total
Men	27.6	3.9	26.7	11.3	5.4	25.7	100.0
Women	11.1	2.8	1.3	38.3	40.0	6.6	100.0

By 1948 only 15.2 per cent of the women in this federation worked in its production branches, compared to some 50 per cent in the early twenties, a 35 per cent decrease over twenty-five years. In 1954 Talmon found only 10.4 per cent of the females in production branches. The process still continues.

The atmosphere of work life is important, and not all data are statistical. Before examining figures on the present work situation, we will describe a normal workday in one of the kibbutzim we studied.

A WORKDAY IN OFER

Ofer is an unexceptional kibbutz in northern Israel, with several agricultural branches and one industrial plant. Its 200 adults and eighty children are all immigrants from Central Europe (40 per cent) and sabras, or native Israelis (60 per cent). The mean age of the male founders is fifty, of female founders forty-seven; the mean age of the entire adult male population is about thirty-five, for the entire adult female population thirty-two.

This socialist town is richer than most, and physically very agreeable. In fact, it is almost luxurious. As the sun falls, sprays of water douse the extravagant flora, and children and parents move along the generous grounds. A visiting British politician once said that the kibbutz was apparently the Israeli social form closest to the landed aristocracy. It is certainly delightful here; the inhabitants lounge on the porches of their comfortable apartments, where each addition to the housing is larger and more comfortable than the last. As for the nurseries, perhaps only Swiss ones are cleaner and better supplied.

Work never stops in Ofer, day or night. The Jewish day starts with what the West considers early evening. Let us conform to the local rule and start with an evening—say, during summer.[3]

At about 9:30 P.M., the night watchmen (*shomrim*) go to work. In peacetime, one man (*shomer*) and one woman (*shomeret*) are on guard. On the way, they may stop at the clubhouse for an espresso; there they find groups of *chaverim* reading newspapers, playing chess or *shesh-besh* (a popular Middle Eastern game), or just sitting and chatting over coffee or orange juice. From the clubhouse, the *shomeret* goes to the babies' house, her station for the night, to sit before an electronic babysitter consisting of microphones leading to a central amplifier. If a child cries, she will go to comfort it.

The *shomer* goes to the room of the work assigner (*sadran avoda*) who is negotiating with the branch managers about dividing the chronically insufficient work power for tomorrow's tasks. Finally the *sadran* closes the work list; now the *shomer* has a list of people he will have to awaken for work during his shift. His next stop is the kitchen, where the kitchen manager (*ekonomith*) closes up the stores, gives him provisions for the night, and turns over her keys. He takes an Uzi submachine gun from the kibbutz arsenal. He then returns to the kitchen and boils water for coffee in case any of the cowmen (*raftanim*) whose work shifts begin at 11 P.M. should feel too sleepy to start work.

By 11 P.M. the clubhouse is empty. So is the dining hall, where the last television viewers have finished watching the news.[3] In the houses the lights slowly go out. When the *shomer* starts his first round, it is silent, except perhaps for some angry dog or amorous cat. It takes him a half-hour to go around the whole kibbutz. Then he picks up empty milk cans at the babies' house and heads for the cowshed. The mooing of the cows and rattle of the milking machine tell him that the *raftanim* are busy. He takes the big cans of foamy fresh milk from the cowshed back to the kitchen. There he boils the milk and starts preparing the night meal for himself, the *shomeret,* and the *raftanim.* At about 2:30, after he has made another round of the kibbutz, he eats with the *raftanim* and prepares coffee for the early risers. The *shomeret* cannot leave her post, where she is reading and knitting between demands for her attention. The *shomer* brings her food and milk for the babies. On the way, he listens to the call of the muezzin in the neighboring Arab village. It is about 3 in the morning.

Then comes the heavy work. Between 3:30 and 4:30 he knocks on many doors, awakening the tractor drivers, orchard workers, and factory laborers—*"Boker tov"* (good morning), he says, and waits for the sleepy *"Toda raba"* (thank you). A few lights go on. At about 4:00, around the coffeepot in the kitchen, a group of still figures sips coffee before piling into trucks bound for the fields and factory. Now the *shomer* goes to awaken the nursing mothers. On the way he meets the *ekonomith,* who is already heading toward the kitchen. After the *shomeret* has given the mothers news about their babies, she goes home with slow, tired steps. At 5:30 the *shomer* as well has finished his work. The people he meets on the way home jokingly greet him with *"Layla tov"* (good night) as sunlight filters down through the branches of the pines.

The general manager and the work assigner give orders by radio to those who started work at 4:00 A.M., and in person to those preparing to leave at 6:00 A.M. By this time almost everyone who works within the kibbutz is at his job. The babies' nurse will have already started to help the nursing mothers; the other nurses start at 6, when they wake the children to get them ready for the seven o'clock school bus. By that hour most people who work outside the kibbutz will have left as well: two university professors, the treasurers of a district factory and of a national marketing organization, and an agriculture expert in the service of the Ministry of Agriculture—all men. The women who work outside the kibbutz are a primary-school teacher, a kindergarten teacher, and four bookkeepers at the factory.

Meanwhile, work proceeds all over the kibbutz, from cowshed to carpentry shop. Most of the men work in the fields (dry farming, orchard, citrus) and in the factory. Some work in the administration office—the general manager, the construction engineer, the treasurer (who spends part of his time in Haifa and Tel Aviv), the work co-ordinator, the secretary, and an accountant; the women there are the head accountant, a second accountant, the postmaster, and two typists.

Most women work in the kitchen, the communal stores, and the children's houses. There may be one man in the kitchen, usually called "the male of the kitchen," who does such heavy work as carrying boxes and cans. Occasionally one or two men wash dishes.

At about 8:00, people come to the dining hall for breakfast. Waiters have been preparing since 6:00, and now they serve eggs, sausage, cheese, plenty of vegetables, and coffee or tea. Service then becomes almost continuous: the *raftanim* come at 9:30, the end of the second cowshed shift; at noon lunch is served, a hot meal corresponding to Euro-American dinner. Around 1:00 adults start returning from the fields and factory, and children from school. The dining hall is very busy at 2:00, when the afternoon kitchen shift takes over, and it remains so till almost 4:00. But by 4:30 only two people are still at work in the kibbutz, the afternoon cook and a dishwasher (except at certain periods when dry farming requires a three-shift system). Now it is the children's time; the sidewalks, lawns, and playing fields are full of children and their parents. By 6:30 almost everyone has returned home, showered, changed into after-work (Shabbat) clothes, and gone to the dining hall for dinner. When the meal is over, usually by 8:30, the afternoon cook, assisted by waiters who work on a *corvée* system, cleans the dining hall and the last dishes. By the time they have finished, three other people have already started their work: the clubhouse keeper, a woman, who turns on the espresso machine and prepares cold drinks and cookies; the general manager, already busy negotiating with the branch managers about tomorrow's work; and the *sadran*, preparing the work assignments. Soon the *shomrim* appear, and their rounds begin again.

DIVISION OF LABOR TODAY

Let us now examine the overall division of labor according to sex in all the kibbutzim of our two federations. In the following table, 34,040 men and women are divided according to their permanent occupations as of January 1, 1973 (temporary jobs assigned through the *toranut*, or *corvée* system, have been disregarded).

Table 5
Last Work Branch, by Sex and Federation (vertical and horizontal percentages)

	ICHUD			K.A.				Male Percentage	Female Percentage	Total
	N = 9109 Male	N = 8306 Female	N = 17415 Total	N = 8732 Male	N = 7893 Female	N = 16625 Total				
Agriculture	39.0	5.9	23.0	32.8	6.2	19.7	Ichud	88	12	100.0
							K.A.	87	13	100.0
Industry	8.4	3.7	6.1	14.7	5.0	9.9	Ichud	82	18	100.0
							K.A.	77	23	100.0
Construction and Auxiliary Shops	16.9	0.1	8.8	14.5	0.2	7.4	Ichud	99	1	100.0
							K.A.	99	1	100.0
Service Consumption	7.6	42.7	24.6	8.1	43.8	25.7	Ichud	18	82	100.0
							K.A.	16	84	100.0
Management	8.2	3.7	6.0	7.1	4.5	5.8	Ichud	71	29	100.0
							K.A.	64	36	100.0
Education, Teaching	4.0	36.3	19.6	6.2	32.5	19.2	Ichud	12	88	100.0
							K.A.	16	84	100.0

(Continued)

Table 5 (Continued)

	ICHUD			K.A.					Male Percentage	Female Percentage	Total
	N = 9109 Male	N = 8306 Female	N = 17415 Total	N = 8732 Male	N = 7893 Female	N = 16625 Total					
Economic Public Service	7.7	2.6	5.2	6.9	1.6	4.3		Ichud	77	23	100.0
								K.A.	84	16	100.0
Movement Activity	3.1	1.8	2.5	4.2	1.9	3.1		Ichud	64	36	100.0
								K.A.	71	29	100.0
Political Activity	1.0	0.3	0.6	1.8	0.5	1.2		Ichud	87	13	100.0
								K.A.	78	22	100.0
Military and Third-Year Service	1.2	0.2	0.8	0.5	0.2	0.3		Ichud	58	42	100.0
								K.A.	72	28	100.0
Further Education, Illness, etc.	2.8	2.6	2.7	3.2	3.5	3.3		Ichud	54	46	100.0
								K.A.	50	50	100.0
Art	0.1	0.0	0.0	0.2	0.0	0.1		Ichud	100	0	100.0
								K.A.	100	0	100.0
TOTAL	100.0	100.0	100.0	100.0	100.0	100.0		Ichud			
								K.A.			

The sex typing of labor is obvious. Agriculture, industry, construction and auxiliary shops (plumbing, electrical, carpentry, etc.), management, economic and political activity, and movement or outside work are predominantly male. Service, consumption, and education are predominantly female. The remaining categories—military service (predominantly male), third-year service, movement activity, further education, illness, artistic work—represent not work but sanctioned exemptions from ordinary work in the kibbutz. (Third-year service is kibbutz-raised youngsters' duty toward their federation. It began when obligatory military service lasted two years, and a third year had to be devoted to the kibbutz movement. The youngsters worked as leaders in the youth movements affiliated with the federation or helped in new kibbutzim. Later, when military service increased to three years, a fourth year was given to the movement, but the name of the service remained the same—*Shnat Sherut Shlishit*.) Art is rarely full-time work; a federation committee classifies artists by their achievements and allots a certain number of workdays for artistic activities, usually two to four days a week. The last three categories in the table—military and third-year service, further education and illness, and art—contain only 1,224 people, or 3.7 per cent of the Kibbutz Artzi population, and an even smaller proportion of the Ichud.

The predominantly male branches contain only 18.1 per cent of the women in the Ichud Federation and 19.9 per cent of the women in the Kibbutz Artzi. In the predominantly female branches, we find only 11.6 per cent of the men in the Ichud and 14.3 per cent in the Kibbutz Artzi.

We must be cautious in calling agriculture a man's job and education a woman's, since the sexual division of labor varies from place to place; one can only say that in X society, Y is considered male or female work. Should "male work" mean work done exclusively or only predominantly by men? And how broad should work categories be? The narrower the categories, the greater the chance of finding tasks done exclusively by one sex. (For the best review of this problem, see D'Andrade in Maccoby 1966.)

In such broad categories as agriculture, which include both men and women, we will have to speak of predominance. But what constitutes predominance? One measure might be deviation from the sex ratio of the entire population. The sex ratio is almost the same in the two federations we have studied—110 in the Ichud and 109 in the Kibbutz Artzi. Any significant deviation from this range in a work category could be considered a sign of preponderance. Another measure might be the comparison of the division of labor in kibbutzim to that in Israeli society. This would not be easy, though; much of what the kibbutzim consider service and consumption work is done by housewives in the broader Israeli society and therefore remains unrepresented in statistics.[4] The latest Israeli Labor Force Survey shows that in April-June 1972, 33.6 per cent of all Israeli females (including kibbutzniks) older than fourteen belong to the labor force (Statistical Abstracts 1973). In the kibbutz, however, 88.5 per cent of all women over fourteen belong to the labor force, since in the kibbutz domestic tasks are predominantly completed by persons in the labor force, not by private citizens whose actions are unrecorded.

The alternatives, then, are these: to accept the traditional concept of men doing production and women doing housework, which is the norm in Israel, or to define male and female work according to data about kibbutz society. We believe the latter would be more useful and accurate. We define as sex-typed every occupation that shows at least a 20 per cent deviation from the sex ratio of the total population. This is an arbitrary figure, and a high one; we deliberately made our requirements very severe, so that any defined deviation would be unequivocally significant.

In fact, it has turned out that by either measure, the results are the same: agriculture, industry, construction, management, and outside work are predominantly male, and service work and education predominantly female. We regard the remaining categories as neutral.

There are differences between the two federations—more sex typing of agriculture, management, and education in the Ichud, more sex typing of industry, outside work, and service branches in the Kibbutz Artzi. There is a slight tendency to somewhat less sex typing in the Kibbutz Artzi, which is nonetheless significant since we are dealing with a total population. We will return to this variable later.

We have presented here a single perspective at a given time. May some unknown factor have influenced the picture? Let us use some other data and try another perspective. Every person inter-

Table 6
Work Branch of Longest Occupation, by Sex and Federation (vertical and horizontal percentages)

	ICHUD			KIBBUTZ ARTZI				Male Percentage	Female Percentage	Total
	N = 9109 Male	N = 8306 Female	N = 17415 Total	N = 8732 Male	N = 7893 Female	N = 16625 Total				
Agriculture	49.8	8.1	29.6	46.4	9.9	28.4	I	87	13	100.0
							K	84	16	100.0
Industry	6.0	2.6	4.4	9.8	2.9	6.4	I	72	28	100.0
							K	72	28	100.0
Construction and Auxiliary Shops	18.2	0.2	9.5	18.2	0.3	9.4	I	99	1	100.0
							K	98	2	100.0
Service Consumption	6.2	37.2	21.2	5.5	36.6	20.9	I	15	85	100.0
							K	14	86	100.0
Management	5.4	2.4	4.0	3.8	2.8	3.3	I	71	29	100.0
							K	60	40	100.0
Education, Teaching	4.0	44.9	23.8	7.1	43.3	24.9	I	10	90	100.0
							K	15	85	100.0
Economic, Public Service	5.9	1.8	3.9	4.5	1.1	2.8	I	78	22	100.0
							K	71	29	100.0

(Continued)

Table 6 (Continued)

	ICHUD N=9109 Male	ICHUD N=8306 Female	ICHUD N=17415 Total	K.A. N=8732 Male	K.A. N=7893 Female	K.A. N=16625 Total		Male Percentage	Female Percentage	Total
Movement Activity	1.6	0.6	1.1	2.2	1.1	1.7	I	74	26	100.0
							K	69	31	100.0
Political Activity	0.7	0.2	0.5	1.3	0.2	0.8	I	79	21	100.0
							K	88	12	100.0
Military and Third-Year Service	1.1	0.2	0.6	0.4	0.1	0.2	I	85	15	100.0
							K	81	19	100.0
Further Education, Illness, etc.	1.0	1.8	1.4	0.7	1.7	1.2	I	38	62	100.0
							K	18	82	100.0
Art	0.1	0.0	0.0	0.1	0.0	0.1	I	100	–	100.0
							K	100	–	100.0
TOTAL	100.0	100.0	100.0	100.0	100.0	100.0	I			
							K			

Table 7
First Work Branch, by Sex and Federation (vertical and horizontal percentages)

	ICHUD			K.A.			Male Percentage		Female Percentage		Total
	N = 9109 Male	N = 8306 Female	N = 17415 Total	N = 8732 Male	N = 7893 Female	N = 16625 Total	I	K	I	K	
Agriculture	55.7	12.6	34.9	49.9	16.8	33.5	83	77	17	23	100.0 100.0
Industry	4.0	2.1	3.1	6.6	1.5	4.1	68	83	32	17	100.0 100.0
Construction and Auxiliary Shops	17.4	0.3	9.1	17.3	0.2	8.9	98	99	2	1	100.0 100.0
Service Consumption	5.4	34.9	19.7	7.0	37.0	21.8	14	17	86	83	100.0 100.0
Management	4.7	1.6	3.2	4.4	1.7	3.0	76	74	24	26	100.0 100.0
Education, Teaching	3.5	43.1	22.7	4.1	36.4	20.0	8	11	92	89	100.0 100.0

(Continued)

Table 7 (Continued)

	ICHUD			K.A.				Male Percentage	Female Percentage	Total
	N = 9109 Male	N = 8306 Female	N = 17415 Total	N = 8732 Male	N = 7893 Female	N = 16625 Total				
Economic, Public Service	3.6	1.3	2.5	3.1	0.7	1.9	I	75	25	100.0
							K	83	17	100.0
Movement Activity	2.9	1.4	2.2	3.2	1.8	2.5	I	69	31	100.0
							K	66	34	100.0
Political Activity	0.6	0.2	0.4	1.3	0.2	0.8	I	76	24	100.0
							K	88	12	100.0
Military and Third-Year Service	1.5	0.5	1.0	1.7	0.9	1.3	I	77	23	100.0
							K	68	32	100.0
Further Education, Illness, etc.	0.7	1.9	1.3	1.4	2.7	2.0	I	28	72	100.0
							K	36	64	100.0
Art	0.0	0.0	0.0	0.1	0.0	0.0	I	–	–	100.0
							K	100	–	100.0
TOTAL	100.0	100.0	100.0	100.0	100.0	100.0	I			
							K			

viewed in the census was asked to name his or her first work branch, last work branch, and branch of longest work during the period 1952-68. First- and last-work branches may have been influenced by random factors, but branch of longest occupation is certainly significant for the whole population.

We find little difference in sex typing when we compare longest work (Table 6) with last work (Table 5). This is more easily seen in a summary table of first, longest, and last work.

Table 8
Women Working in Male Jobs, and Men in Female Jobs, by Federation (in percentages)

		Last Work	First Work	Longest Work
ICHUD	Women in Male Work	18.1	19.5	15.9
	Men in Female Work	11.6	8.9	10.2
K.A.	Women in Male Work	19.9	22.9	18.3
	Men in Female Work	14.3	11.1	12.6

In the Ichud, only 15.9 per cent of the women worked longest in male tasks, compared to 18.1 per cent in their last work. In Kibbutz Artzi, the respective numbers are 18.3 per cent and 19.9 per cent. If anything, longest work shows even more sex typing than last work. If we examine sex typing by branches, we again see that agriculture, industry, construction, management, and outside public activities are predominantly male, service and education predominantly female. Patterns of sex typing in the various work branches are similar in both federations and in the frequency distributions according to different variables of time. The last work figures, then, fairly represent the realities of working life.

Let us also compare last work with first work. To be sure, our picture of first-work branch is not consistent; some people first took jobs in 1954, others as late as 1967. Nevertheless, it is the best approximation we have of such experience during the fifteen-year period. Table 7 shows that in first work, as compared to last, there is less sex typing in agriculture, but more in education. In the Ichud Federation, 19.5 per cent of the women did male jobs for their first work; in Kibbutz Artzi the figure was 22.9 per cent.

Our summary in Table 8 shows a tendency over time to increased sex typing of women: in both last work and longest work, fewer women have male occupations than in first work. There is a tendency to less sex typing of men: more men work in female occupations in last and longest work than in first work.

This shift over the years is not really surprising. We have already noted that during the fifteen years under review, services (both consumption and education) expanded much more than production—a general tendency in modern welfare societies. Production has become much more effective in Israel, and about 3 per cent of kibbutz men have moved to the expanding service branches, where the 2-3 per cent increase in women service workers was insufficient to cope with the expanded array and quality of tasks.

WORK AND GENERATION

We described in Chapter 4 how we divided our population into three groups called generations. The second generation are people whose parents are or were members of the kibbutz, and who were themselves socialized in the kibbutz for at least six years of childhood and adolescence. The kibbutz-bred are people whose parents are not and were not kibbutzniks, and who were socialized in the kibbutz for less than six years during adolescence. The first generation includes all others—those who were socialized outside the kibbutz and joined it as adults. These three groups largely overlap with age groups, as Table 9 shows.

In both federations men and women of the second generation are concentrated in the youngest age groups; about 80 per cent are under thirty. Most of the first generation are over forty, and about a third are over fifty-five. The kibbutz-bred group is similar to the second generation, but older. Later we will look further at the impact of age. But now let us look at the second generation. Table 10 gives data of sex distribution in sex-typed work categories.

Table 9
Generations by Sex, Age, and Federation (in percentages)

		Males				Females			
		Second Generation	Kibbutz-Bred	First Generation	Total	Second Generation	Kibbutz-Bred	First Generation	Total
55+	I	0.5	1.4	31.8	19.6	0.4	0.2	30.9	21.1
	K.A.	0.2	0.1	41.6	22.5	0.4	0.7	37.8	23.1
41-54	I	3.9	24.1	22.3	16.6	4.3	30.3	22.7	18.3
	K.A.	1.5	19.5	32.2	20.3	1.4	20.5	31.7	21.6
31-40	I	16.4	27.9	20.7	19.8	13.2	26.4	18.3	17.4
	K.A.	14.9	38.3	17.1	18.9	12.7	37.9	18.7	18.8
-30	I	79.1	46.6	25.2	44.0	82.1	43.1	28.2	43.2
	K.A.	83.4	42.1	9.0	38.3	85.5	40.9	11.8	36.5
Total	I	32.1	7.2	60.7	100.0	26.2	6.0	67.8	100.0
	K.A.	33.9	12.2	53.9	100.0	29.7	9.5	60.7	100.0

Table 10
Women in Male Jobs and Men in Female Jobs in the Second Generation,
by Work Categories and Federation (in percentages)

		Last Work	First Work	Longest Work
Ichud	Percentage of Women in Male Work	17.0	22.0	16.0
	Percentage of Men in Female Work	5.4	3.5	4.8
Kibbutz Artzi	Percentage of Women in Male Work	22.0	26.0	21.0
	Percentage of Men in Female Work	6.7	7.6	5.2

From these data we can draw the following conclusions about the second generation:

1. In both federations, a relatively large percentage of women start out doing male work (Ichud, 22 per cent; Kibbutz Artzi, 26 per cent), certainly more than in the whole population (compare to Table 8).

2. In the Ichud Federation, the difference between the women of the second generation and all other women disappears in the categories of longest work and last work. In the Kibbutz Artzi, the difference is smaller.

3. In both federations, considerably fewer men start and continue in female work than in the total population.

4. In the Ichud there is less sex typing of men in last and longest work than in first work; in the Kibbutz Artzi, the tendency is to more sex typing.

5. The Ichud again is more sex-typed than the Kibbutz Artzi.

We can summarize the work characteristics of the second generation along the following patterns:

1. Most kibbutz women return from military service at age twenty, still single. Most go directly into female work, especially work

with children, where they are eagerly welcomed. Some, however, try to reenter the agricultural branches where they worked as adolescents. In some kibbutzim, a regulation obliges girls returning from the army to work at least one year in agriculture, especially in the dairy.

2. The mean age at marriage of second-generation women is 21.23 (Shepher 1971); first birth usually follows within two years. Pregnancy, birth, and nursing are generally considered incompatible with agricultural work except in the case of exceedingly strong women. These and other women who do not marry young remain in male branches—and constitute about 20 per cent of all women. Since more than 80 per cent of the second-generation are under thirty, this 20 per cent will doubtless dwindle, moving gradually from agriculture to industry, management, and outside work.

3. Boys serve in the army for at least three years; officers serve six months or a year longer than that, and 36 per cent of all second-generation men are officers (Shepher 1971). When they return to the kibbutz at age twenty-one or twenty-two, they are keenly awaited in production, especially agriculture. They are the best-trained workers and must replace older, first-generation members approaching retirement—especially in kibbutzim where, for historical reasons, there is no intermediate age group between the first and second generations. None of the boys were trained during adolescence in female work, as some girls were in male work. The result is that very few men enter female occupations, and the few who do usually spend only a one-year *corvée* in the kitchen (especially in Kibbutz Artzi) and as youth leaders and Youth Aliyah leaders.

Table 11 describes the small kibbutz-bred generation.

The picture basically resembles that of the second generation:

1. More women do male jobs as first work than as last or longest work; this difference exists in both federations but is slightly greater in Kibbutz Artzi.

2. The tendency of men is the reverse: in both federations, fewer men begin employment in female branches than enter them as longest or last work.

3. Kibbutz-bred women enter more sex-typed work than second-generation women. The same is true for men.

4. As in the whole population, women as a group move to more sex typing, men to less.

Table 11
Women in Male Work and Men in Female Work Among the Kibbutz-Bred,
by Work Categories and Federation (in percentages)

		Last Work	First Work	Longest Work
Ichud	Percentage of Women in Male Work	14.1	14.6	10.2
	Percentage of Men in Female Work	9.8	6.8	8.5
Kibbutz Artzi	Percentage of Women in Male Work	16.9	23.1	16.6
	Percentage of Men in Female Work	13.9	9	10.7

The kibbutz-bred generation's reference group is the second generation, whom they try to imitate. But because of their scantier education in the kibbutz, kibbutz-bred men and women are less able than the second generation to enter the prestigious agricultural branches. As a result, fewer of this generation's women do male work, and more of the men do nonagricultural male work and female work.

Finally, here is the first generation:

Table 12
Women in Male Work and Men in Female Work in the First Generation,
by Work Category and Federation (in percentages)

		Last Work	First Work	Longest Work
Ichud	Percentage of Women in Male Work	18.2	18.9	15.8
	Percentage of Men in Female Work	13.4	10.5	11.8
Kibbutz Artzi	Percentage of Women in Male Work	19.7	22.0	17.6
	Percentage of Men in Female Work	16.0	12.2	14.6

The first generation resembles the population as a whole (Table 8). This is not surprising, since about 60 per cent of the whole population are first generation. The main characteristics of this group are

1. In both federations, many more first-generation men than other men do female work. This is true at all stages of their work career.

2. Fewer women do male work than in the second generation, but more than in the kibbutz-bred.

3. As in the whole population, women tend to more sex typing, men to less.

The first generation is a mixed-age group, but about 60 per cent are over forty-one. This explains the comparatively large percentage of men in female work, particularly in high-school education. Age also explains the comparatively low percentage of women in male occupations. About 15 per cent of the first-generation women are under thirty—about the same percentage of women as work in male occupations. Again, we find more women in sex-typed work in the Ichud than in the Kibbutz Artzi. In the Ichud, 28.2 per cent of the first-generation females are under thirty, but only 16 per cent of the women did male work as their longest work. In the Kibbutz Artzi, the respective figures are 11.8 and 17.6 per cent.

SENIORITY OF KIBBUTZIM

Just as generation is important in terms of the individual, seniority is important in terms of the kibbutz. Most senior kibbutzim have these characteristics:

1. A full range of ages, but less than a third of its members over fifty-five and more than a third under thirty.

2. A sex ratio close to 100, and sometimes even lower.

3. A rather high total population. In the thirty-three kibbutzim in the highest seniority group, twenty-four have more than 500 members, seven have 301-500, only two have fewer than 300. In general, the correlation between seniority and population size is 0.70 in the kibbutz movement (Shepher 1971).

4. A well-developed and well-differentiated economy based on several branches of agriculture and industry.

5. A high standard of living, highly differentiated service branches, and many workers involved in service and education.

Seniority is a continuous variable, and the characteristics it gives rise to form a diminishing pattern. Therefore it should be sufficient to describe the least senior group, which includes the kibbutzim founded from 1949 on. They have the following characteristics:

1. A very young population; 80 per cent or more are under forty.

2. A rather high sex ratio, approximately 118.

3. A small total population. Of thirty-two young kibbutzim, twenty-nine have fewer than 300 members, and only three have 301-500 (Shepher 1971).

4. An economy based mainly on mixed agriculture, with one factory or none.

5. A comparatively low standard of living, and limited service branches employing no more than 25-30 per cent of the manpower, most of it in child care.

The oldest kibbutzim present a pattern rather like that of the total population (Table 8). The only difference is that in the Ichud, somewhat more men work in women's occupations in the older col-

Table 13
Group I: Women in Male Work and Men in Female Work,
by Federation and Stage of Work (in percentages)

		Last Work Branch	First Work Branch	Longest Work Branch
Ichud	Percentage of Women in Male Work	19	22	18
	Percentage of Men in Female Work	14	11	12
Kibbutz Artzi	Percentage of Women in Male Work	21	25	18
	Percentage of Men in Female Work	14	12	13

lectives than in the total population—not surprising, since this seniority group includes more than a third of the total population. The tendency to more sex typing for women and less for men across the years is also apparent: fewer women do men's jobs as last and longest work than as first work, and the opposite is true for men.

Table 14
Group II: Women in Male Work and Men in Female Work,
by Federation and Stage of Work (in percentages)

		Last Work Branch	First Work Branch	Longest Work Branch
Ichud	Percentage of Women in Male Work	18	16	15
	Percentage of Men in Female Work	10	10	10
Kibbutz Artzi	Percentage of Women in Male Work	22	21	18
	Percentage of Men in Female Work	15	13	14

Group II is more sex-typed than Group I. In both federations, fewer of these women work in men's occupations in almost all work categories. In the Ichud, fewer Group II than Group I men work in women's jobs; in the Kibbutz Artzi, somewhat more do.

The tendency to greater sex typing for women is somewhat blurred here: fewer women do men's jobs as longest work than as first work. In the Ichud, the same percentage of men do women's jobs in all three categories; in Kibbutz Artzi, somewhat more men do women's jobs in last and longest work than in first work.

The two youngest groups show a great difference in sex typing of women in first work compared to longest and last work. This is especially true in the Kibbutz Artzi: in Group II, the difference is 15 per cent; in Group IV, it is 10-12 per cent. A higher percentage of Kibbutz Artzi men do women's jobs as last and longest work than as first work. Group III seems slightly more sex-typed than Group IV.

Some general tendencies emerge from our analysis of generations and seniority groups, but other variables must be considered, such as

Table 15
Group III: Women in Male Work and Men in Female Work,
by Federation and Stage of Work (in percentages)

		Last Work	First Work	Longest Work
Ichud	Percentage of Women in Male Work	16	20	13
	Percentage of Men in Female Work	11	6	8
Kibbutz Artzi	Percentage of Women in Male Work	15	30	15
	Percentage of Men in Female Work	15	7	10

Table 16
Group IV: Women in Male Work and Men in Female Work,
by Federation and Stage of Work (in percentages)

		Last Work Branch	First Work Branch	Longest Work Branch
Ichud	Percentage of Women in Male Work	17	26	19
	Percentage of Men in Female Work	9	5	5
Kibbutz Artzi	Percentage of Women in Male Work	19	29	17
	Percentage of Men in Female Work	12	8	9

sex ratio in the working population and the availability of men's and
women's work. After we examine these, we will have a clearer picture.

POLARIZATION

Complete absence of polarization, or absolute equality, would mean
that in every work category the sexes participate according to the

sex ratio of the working population. This would result from completely ignoring gender in dividing labor. Complete polarization would mean that all men work in occupations defined as men's, all women in jobs defined as women's. We have seen that in the kibbutz all permanent jobs are sex-typed. Only such categories as higher education and army service can be called neutral; they are temporary and involve less than 4 per cent of the population.

We are categorizing permanent occupations very broadly; for instance, agriculture includes at least twelve work branches. Consequently the working population tends to seem mixed-sex, with a strong preponderance of one sex. A continuum between absolute equality and absolute polarization exists, and any work category, large or small, can be placed on it. As we defined it earlier, sex typing is a 20 per cent deviation from the sex ratio of the entire population. We further describe an entire society as having sexually polarized division of labor if at least 50 per cent of its working population is in sex-typed occupations. We can place a society on the equality-polarization continuum by pooling all male-typed and then all female-typed work and finding the deviations of these two groups from the sex ratio.

The kibbutz obviously has sexually polarized division of labor; almost all its population works in sex-typed jobs. How great is this polarization? In Appendix C we proposed two measurements of polarization. One takes into account only the sex ratio of the working population: $\dfrac{D1 + D2}{2}$, the Specific Polarization Index (SPI). We use this only for populations whose population unit is *not* also a unit of division of labor—generation, for instance, which is never a basis for division of labor. The other measure is the General Polarization Index (GPI), which takes into account both the sex ratio and the supply of men's and women's jobs. We use this for population units that *are* units of division of labor. For instance, we assume that young kibbutzim have a different supply of women's jobs than older kibbutzim, since in the latter services are more extensive and varied, and because there are more children. We can also assume that each federation's ideology influences the supply of men's and women's jobs.

The two indices will enable us to present a broad and accurate picture of sex polarization in labor in our many population categories, with time expressed by the categories first work, longest work, and last work. Note that we can omit here the distinction between men's and women's work; we have already summarized the deviations from sex ratio and work supply that are created by men in women's jobs and by women in men's jobs. We are aware that these two deviations do not have the same significance, but at this point in our analysis we need a general picture. We will return to the significance of the two deviations in our conclusions:

Table 17
Specific Polarization Index (SPI) of the Sexes
by Generation, Federation, and Categories of Work

| | Ichud | | | |
	Second Generation	Kibbutz-Bred	First Generation	Total Population
First Work	0.744	0.790	0.707	0.715
Last Work	0.751	0.752	0.685	0.695
Longest Work	0.778	0.806	0.721	0.737
	Kibbutz Artzi			
First Work	0.681	0.682	0.681	0.681
Last Work	0.696	0.674	0.634	0.645
Longest Work	0.832	0.724	0.677	0.690

These data can be summarized by the following points:

1. The range of indices shows rather high polarization: the lowest is 0.634 (Kibbutz Artzi, first generation, last work), the highest 0.832 (Kibbutz Artzi, second generation, longest work). Most of the indices are twenty-five to thirty points from absolute polarization.

2. The groups socialized inside the kibbutz (second generation and kibbutz-bred) are more polarized than the group socialized outside the kibbutz (first generation).

3. In the Ichud Federation, the kibbutz-bred generation is more polarized than the second generation. In the Kibbutz Artzi, the opposite is true.

4. In all generations, longest work is more polarized than last work, and in all groups except the first generation of the Kibbutz Artzi, longest work is more polarized than first work.

5. In the second generation of both federations, the indices in-

crease from first work to last work to longest work. In the two other generations, last work has a lower index than first work.

6. In eleven of the twelve parts of the table, all Ichud indices are higher than Kibbutz Artzi indices; the exception is Kibbutz Artzi, second generation, longest work.

Let us refrain from drawing conclusions until we have analyzed the seniority groups. Here we can use the generalized index.

Table 18
Generalized Polarization Index (GPI) of the Sexes
by Seniority Groups, Federations, and Categories of Work

	Ichud				
	I	II	III	IV	Total
First Work	0.795	0.849	0.849	0.819	0.823
Last Work	0.784	0.819	0.832	0.847	0.807
Longest Work	0.810	0.833	0.881	0.861	0.827
	Kibbutz Artzi				
First Work	0.753	0.786	0.785	0.754	0.775
Last Work	0.765	0.752	0.810	0.833	0.768
Longest Work	0.785	0.792	0.848	0.844	0.813

These data can be summarized as follows:

1. The indices range from 0.752 (Kibbutz Artzi, Group II, last work) to 0.881 (Ichud, Group III, longest work). The indices are all high, showing 80 per cent polarization.

2. In both federations, the most polarized seniority group is Group III, followed by Group IV. The younger kibbutzim are more polarized than the older ones.

3. Longest work is more polarized than last work in all groups of both federations, and higher than first work in all except one (Ichud, Group II). Last work is less polarized than first work in three of the four groups.

4. In all parts of the table, Ichud indices are higher than those of Kibbutz Artzi. The range of differences is 6.7 per cent to 1.4 per

cent. The smallest differences are in longest work, the largest in first work.

Finally, let us compare the two indices in the two federations:

Table 19
Polarization, Measured by SPI and GPI, in the Two Federations

	First Work		Last Work		Longest Work	
	SPI	GPI	SPI	GPI	SPI	GPI
Ichud	0.715	0.823	0.695	0.807	0.737	0.827
Kibbutz Artzi	0.681	0.775	0.645	0.768	0.690	0.813
Difference	0.034	0.048	0.050	0.039	0.047	0.014

The GPI shows higher polarization in both federations than the SPI, for it takes into account both sex ratio and work supply.

The Ichud indices are only slightly higher than those of the Kibbutz Artzi, and the differences tend to disappear with time.

We can now draw some conclusions:

1. The sexual division of labor is highly polarized in the kibbutz, ranging from 70-80 per cent, depending on the method of measurement.

2. Polarization is greater among people socialized on the kibbutz than among those socialized outside it.

3. Younger kibbutzim are more polarized than older ones.

4. Ideology makes only a very small difference, and it tends to disappear when people go from first to longest work.

5. If we measure the effect of time by comparing first and last work, we find that the second generation and the youngest kibbutzim tend to become more polarized, other kibbutzim and kibbutzniks less polarized. But if we compare first with longest work, we see that all generations and groups but one become more polarized with time.

In fact, polarization is even greater than these numbers suggest. This is clear when we see precisely where men and women have such opposite sex-typed jobs that do exist. We have used broad work categories; but when people enter into opposite-sex work, they do not enter into all its subdivisions. These subcategories reveal more refined but quite definite sex typing. To avoid reviewing all three time categories again, we will focus only on longest work in certain representative branches.

1. *Agriculture*. Women in both federations are concentrated in three branches—hothouse culture, vegetable farming, and poultry-raising. No other agricultural branch is more than 14 per cent female. The few women who work in industrial crops usually turn to insect control for cotton cultivation, an exclusively female subcategory.

2. *Industry*. In both federations, women are concentrated in ceramics, plastics, printing, textiles, and arts and crafts. Women in other industries, especially heavy industries, work almost exclusively in administration.

3. *Management*. Almost all the women do clerical work. They comprise the large majority of typists, accountants, and technical secretaries. In the higher echelons they are heavily underrepresented, as we shall see in the chapter on the political system.

2. *Public Activity and Outside Work*. Most women in this category work in three departments of the federations' administration—social, cultural, and especially education—where they are the majority in both federations. They are also the majority in "outside work," which usually means teaching in outside schools and kindergartens. In political activity, central economic activity, and central kibbutz-movement activity, they are severely underrepresented.

5. *Service and Consumption*. Most men are concentrated in general maintenance and general storeroom, shoemaking, gardening, sanitation, library, archives, and clubhouses. In all these subcategories except the last, they are the majority.

6. *Education*. Virtually no men work with preschoolers. They constitute less than 18 per cent of the personnel in elementary schools, about 40 per cent in high schools, and 35 per cent in the Youth Aliyah. In all these subcategories, they are exclusively teachers, never nurses.

ATTRACTION TO SEX-TYPED WORK

Up to this point, we have surveyed the sexual division of labor at the group level. But obviously, net balances do not tell us about individuals. *Who* has moved from men's work to women's and vice versa?

If we have three categories of work (male (1), female (2), and neutral (3)) and three time phases (first work a, longest work b, and last work c), we have twenty-seven possible combinations of factors. Not all the combinations can be equally frequent—for instance, neutral work is usually temporary and can hardly be longest work except for professional army officers and younger people in very long educational programs, such as medical school. The most frequent patterns are summarized in the following table:

Table 20
Most Frequent Combinations of First Work, Longest Work, and Last Work, by Sex and Federation (in percentages)

Ichud Men		Kibbutz Artzi		Ichud Women		Kibbutz Artzi	
$a_1b_1c_1$	79.44	$a_1b_1c_1$	74.49	$a_2b_2c_2$	69.61	$a_2b_2c_2$	64.24
$a_2b_2c_2$	6.02	$a_1b_1c_2$	5.52	$a_1b_1c_1$	9.51	$a_1b_1c_1$	8.84
$a_1b_1c_2$	3.88	$a_2b_2c_2$	5.36	$a_1b_2c_2$	6.21	$a_1b_2c_2$	8.30
$a_1b_2c_2$	2.95	$a_2b_1c_1$	4.52	$a_2b_2c_1$	5.23	$a_2b_2c_1$	6.62
$a_2b_1c_1$	2.95	$a_1b_2c_2$	3.42	$a_2b_1c_1$	3.72	$a_2b_1c_1$	4.49
$a_1b_2c_1$	1.38	$a_2b_2c_1$	2.0	$a_1b_2c_2$	2.5	$a_1b_1c_2$	3.81
$a_2b_2c_1$	1.11	$a_1b_2c_1$	1.92	$a_3b_2c_2$	0.25	$a_2b_1c_2$	1.32
$a_3b_1c_1$	0.76	$a_3b_1c_1$	1.55	$a_2b_1c_2$	0.14	$a_1b_2c_1$	1.08
Total	98.49	Total	98.70	$a_1b_2c_1$	0.10	$a_3b_2c_2$	0.84
				Total	97.27	Total	99.54

Spearman Rank Order Correlation between two federations:

$$r_s = 0.962 \qquad r_s = 0.950$$
$$p = 0.001 \qquad p = 0.0001$$

This table shows that virtually all men and women in both federations use only about a third of the possible combinations. The most frequent pattern is continuous work in a job typed to one's own sex ($a_1b_1c_1$ for men, and $a_2b_2c_2$ for women). The second most frequent pattern is the opposite—continuous work in an opposite-sex-typed job ($a_2b_2c_2$ for men, $a_1b_1c_1$ for women); for Kibbutz Artzi men, this pattern is third in rank order, but beneath the second by only 0.16 per cent. The rest choose different patterns in which longest work is one's own sex-typed work (Ichud men 58 per cent, Kibbutz Artzi men 61 per cent, Ichud women 79 per cent, Kibbutz Artzi women 64 per cent of all patterns except the first two).

The individual's experience reflects the group situation: about two-thirds of the women and three-quarters of the men work in jobs typed to their own sex in all time phases. Less than 10 per cent of women and about 6 per cent of men do work typed in the opposite sex. The similarity of the federations can be seen in the very high rank-order correlation.

Comparing first work and last work, we see that more than 85 per cent of men who started in men's jobs ended in men's jobs. About 75 per cent of women who started in women's jobs remained in them. But of women who started in men's work, more than half went over to women's last work, showing movement toward greater polarization.

Comparing longest work and last work, we see that 94 per cent of all men whose longest work was men's work remained in men's jobs as last work. More than 91 per cent of all women whose longest work was women's work went into women's last work, which suggests the consistency of the patterns.

Table 21 summarizes the movements of men and women between men's jobs and women's.

We see once more that both men and women move from men's work to women's between first and last jobs. *The movement of the women is toward more polarization, that of the men toward less polarization.* There is no great difference between men in the two federations, but the women of the Kibbutz Artzi become more polarized than those of the Ichud. In the comparison of longest and last work, there is a marked difference between federations: men of the Ichud become *more* polarized, men of the Kibbutz Artzi *less* polarized. In both federations, women become more polarized.

The coefficients of sex typing in generations and seniority groups confirm that polarization tendencies are stronger in the younger generations and the younger kibbutzim.

Trying now to summarize this part of our investigation, we must point out that sex-typed work is widely "attractive" for both sexes, especially for women. We say attractive not in a psychological sense but in a sociological one. We did not know at this stage of our analysis whether women were really attracted to women's work or were pushed toward it by circumstances, public opinion, or formal decisions of kibbutz institutions. We will have more to say about this in Chapter 10, on attitudes toward sex typing in work.

Whatever the reasons for the surprising data we have presented,

Table 21
Coefficients of Sex Typing (Am* and Af*) and Polarization Balance,* by Sex and Federation

		First Work, Last Work				Longest Work, Last Work			
		Ichud	Kibbutz Artzi	Polarization Balance, Ichud	Polarization Balance, Kibbutz Artzi	Ichud	Kibbutz Artzi	Polarization Balance, Ichud	Polarization Balance Kibbutz Artzi
Men	Am	−3.5	−3.9	−6.2	−7.2	+3.4	−3.9	+4.8	−7.2
	Af	+2.8	+3.3			−1.4	+3.3		
Women	Am	−1.2	−2.9	+2.0	+5.8	−2.0	−2.9	+4.9	+5.8
	Af	+0.8	+2.9			+2.9	+2.9		

*Am = per cent of those in men's last work minus per cent of those in men's first work or longest work

*Af = per cent of those in women's last work minus per cent of those in women's first or longest work

*Polarization Balance: arithmetic sum of Am and Af

Am is negative for men and Af negative for women in terms of causing less polarization. Am is positive for men and Af positive for women in terms of causing more polarization.

the conclusion is inescapable: some powerful pervasive force or forces intervene between the intentions of kibbutz ideology and the reality of kibbutz social structure. Since we have been focusing on women in this study, we have gathered little systematic information about the behavior of men as work assigners, managers, and citizens, and the extent to which their attitudes and bonds with one another may prevent or dissuade women from keenly seeking men's work. For example, a woman who had had the unusual experience of being her kibbutz's general manager told us that when she, the only woman in the community's senior management at the time, engaged in lively, absorbing discussion about work with her male colleagues, they began occasionally referring to her as "he." Does such a bizarre event symptomize a larger, more general process? We cannot say, just as we cannot comment on women's readiness to accept men in their own work environments. Whatever the personal processes are, they cause a significantly asymmetrical division of labor that fails to manifest the ideology of the kibbutz founders. This asymmetry calls into question the proposed remedies for sexism of many writers who foresaw in communism of property, food preparation, and child care a structural antidote to centuries of differences in men's and women's work. (For an early, prescient, and classic statement, see Schreiner 1911.)

Nevertheless, we must remark on the changes the kibbutz system has achieved in women's work and activities. As we have seen, kibbutz life has been devoted to production, not consumption, and work originally had a redemptive aspect. Even preparing and enjoying food and choosing and caring for clothing were considered productive. It was unthinkable that women would not work; the stereotypical *shtetl* woman was replaced by the road builder, poultry manager, and cook-for-hundreds. Even if men's and women's work still differ considerably, the opportunity to take issue with or accept this pattern rests on a radical change of women's circumstances, particularly the balance of public obligations and private options.

One should bear this in mind when assessing criticisms that the kibbutz movement is now too prosperous, that its members no longer work as long and hard as before, that its original purity has given way to such softening luxuries as baking at home, enjoying stereos and televisions, and even hiring outside labor for successful enterprises that the limited work force of the kibbutzim can no longer maintain.

There are several replies. First, besides work's redemptive value, one reason for the early kibbutzniks' earnest efforts was precisely to establish enough economic security to permit a relaxation of their strenuous, austere existence. Second, one of the important ideological aims of the movement has been to fulfill its members' cultural and emotional needs, and to a limited extent this is now increasingly possible. Third—and this is so obvious it requires mentioning—things change, and there is no reason for ideologically based movements to be exempt from the course of human unpredictability.

It is pertinent to our concern with women's work to note that the changes form a general pattern. We must ask whether men's work is generally accorded higher status than women's on the kibbutz. And if it is, as some evidence suggests (Blumberg 1974), it must be asked why this is so. Does it reflect the general social practice marked by paying more for jobs done primarily by men? Since no one on the kibbutz is paid for his or her work, the frequently heard argument of higher pay leading to higher prestige cannot apply. Or is the alleged higher prestige really a male delusion? And do women express their real opinion of these primarily male jobs by avoiding them? Have kibbutz women emancipated themselves from the assumption that men's work is more important work, and that men's standards, values, and enthusiasm are more central to human communities than their own?

Chapter 6

The Politics of Women in the Kibbutz

When Golda Meir was prime minister of Israel, some people were horrified and others were charmed by the rumor that she conducted important policy discussions in her kitchen. Indeed, her "kitchen cabinet" was said to be composed of the most influential members of the government. Perhaps the prime minister grew accustomed to mixing eating with power during the years she lived in a kibbutz. Many of the political assemblies in the kibbutzim are held in dining halls, often the largest rooms available and almost always free in the evenings when assemblies are usually called. Thus the integration of different social functions in the kibbutz is reflected in the use of space; there is no formal political place, no ceremonial chamber. And those who customarily take political promises with a grain of salt will find an ample supply on each table.

We begin this chapter with the life history of a kibbutz woman who has had an outstanding political career. There are very few kibbutz women like her. But her achievements approach the kibbutz ideal and provide a sense of possibility for others. Only a few minor details have been altered, to protect her privacy.

Batya was born in 1916 in Germany. Her parents divorced, and she lived with her mother, a brother, and a sister, under difficult conditions. When Batya was sixteen, the family moved to Berlin. Although she was an excellent student and tried to finance her studies by giving private French and English lessons, she was not able to continue her studies; at seventeen, she left school and joined the Zionist Youth Movement. Batya had already learned to speak Hebrew and had studied dancing, and she could ride a horse. In the Youth Movement she quickly became a leader.

In 1935, at the age of nineteen, she emigrated to Palestine. When she reached her kibbutz, she was unusual—one of those few people who did not want to speak a word in her native language, only in Hebrew. Along with most of the other girls, she would have been sent to work in the kitchen or the children's houses, but she contracted paratyphoid fever and was forbidden to labor in either. When she recovered, she was sent to the vegetable garden, where she became quickly and completely involved.

At twenty-one she married, at twenty-five she bore her first child, a girl. A year later she became the branch manager of the vegetable garden, then the largest agricultural branch of the kibbutz. She was considered by the other women to be not a feminine character but a "sportive" one. For instance, she worked until the last day of her pregnancy, and she rode to and from the fields on a horse to nurse her child. She never made use of the privileges usually given pregnant women.

With the deterioration of the security situation after World War II, Batya was sent to the Commanders' Course of the Haganah, where she became an officer and trained both women and men in her own and other kibbutzim in the then illegal use of weapons. In 1946 she was recruited by her federation's security committee. During the hot days of the illegal war against the English and the Arabs, she went to kibbutzim from the north to the south of Israel, organizing training courses and illegal defense units. After a year, she acquired a driver's license, which created a stir at the time. She continued her work until she bore her third child at the end of the War of Liberation.

In 1949 she returned to the vegetable garden; shortly afterward she was elected general manager of her kibbutz. She profited from her connections from her work in the security committee and became a successful organizer and agricultural expert. Her kibbutz belonged to the Kibbutz Meuchad Federation, which split in 1951; Batya belonged to the minority that moved to a new place. She took command of the rebuilding of the kibbutz. In 1952 she returned to the vegetable garden, but in 1954 she was sent as a student to the first general managers' course. Upon returning from the course, she was reelected general manager. After two years, she was recruited by the economic committee of the Ichud Federation as an agricultural and economic expert. She then returned for a third time to the general managership of her kibbutz, only to leave again for the Ichud Federation, now as a major figure in the powerful economic committee.

When asked how people around her reacted to this career, which is exceptional for a woman, she acknowledged that most of the women did not favor it, but that most of the men appreciated her and supported her throughout her career. Some men considered her a competitor—one, she said, was jealous of her quick rise in the military sphere in her own kibbutz; and another, a central figure in the Kibbutz Meuchad movement, had been jealous of her using the car in her work in the security committee. But most of the men had been very kind to her and very encouraging—especially her husband, who had willingly shared the care of their three children. He was able to accept his wife's career without renouncing his own; at the time of the split in the Kibbutz Meuchad, he was the kibbutz secretary, and he was so strongly against the split that he declared that he would renounce his membership in both kibbutzim if the split took place. He did exactly that, and although he continued living with his wife and children, he had the status of inhabitant rather than member. An expert in cattle breeding, he began work in the National Organization of Cattle Breeders. Two of the children have left the kibbutz and are successful outside it. The third is a fighter pilot.

In many modern societies, politics is kept separate from private life, and the distinction between the public and private realms is usually clear. Politics is concerned with such public problems as defense, national economy, welfare, and justice. The private realm is the concern of the individual and the family. Politics may decide what a person's or family's minimum income will be, but the recipient is free to decide how to spend it. Politics may decide what every child's minimum education is to be, but the family is free to decide to give the child ballet lessons or to apprentice him in a carpentry shop. Politics decides which food products are medically acceptable and sometimes fixes their prices, but the individual and family are free to determine their food budget and daily menu.

In the kibbutz, most of the matters that elsewhere are considered of individual concern are of public concern, and are therefore matters of politics. The "income" of an individual or family is set by the collective in its General Assembly, which also decides how much income will be provided in kind—given directly as food, health care, housing, education, recreation, etc., with no opportunity to exchange it for something else—and how much will be given as comprehensive budget and spent at the person's or family's discretion. If a person chooses to work especially long or hard, this will not increase his "income," only the esteem in which he is held.

A situation in Ofer demonstrates this basic characteristic of the kibbutz system. M. is seventeen years old and has been permitted by the education committee to study the piano for seven years. His musical taste has developed in two directions; he is a devotee both of baroque music, especially Bach, and of jazz. His great dream is to play the organ. The smallest electric organ in Israel costs about $1,500, a vast sum even for a well-to-do Israeli—about five times the average monthly salary. The only way for M. to get an organ would be for him to apply to the education committee for one. That committee would have to decide whether to recommend the case to the economic committee, which in turn would decide whether to include the organ in the next year's investment budget. But M. and his parents know that it is futile to apply; considering the economic situation of the kibbutz and the nation, especially after the Yom Kippur War, the organ would be a luxury, and many more important purchases have had to be delayed.

Theoretically, M. and his parents could have bought the organ by foregoing about four years of their comprehensive budget for clothing, shoes, drugstore articles, coffee or liquor, and vacations. In actuality, living in utter austerity would not get them the organ, which is defined as an "exceptional commodity" and therefore not personal property. So the organ remains a dream. The boy is not bitter; he understands the situation and the system of which he feels very much a part.

Such transformations of private problems to public decisions have a powerful impact on every kibbutznik's political involvement. Although most women work in the kitchen, communal store, and child-care centers, many of the problems they face there are not individual but public, political matters. The selection of kitchen equipment is not a housewife's option but a community's economic and social decision. This situation *predestines* men and women to considerable political involvement.

One would therefore expect a great deal of formal political participation on the part of the women of the kibbutz. But is this in fact the case? We will approach the question as we did the question of women's participation in work, by giving an historical account, a picture of political life today, and data about women in politics. Political life, of course, requires different units of measure than work. We must distinguish the various arenas of political activity such as the General Assembly and its many committees, each of which has a different political significance and function. For instance, we shall have to see whether women concentrate in committees that have what Jessie Bernard calls "stroking functions," such as education, health, and social affairs. Whether they also participate in committees dealing with economy, work organization, finance, and overall coordination of political activity. Whether they share proportionately in all levels of political organization. And given the peculiar intimacy of kibbutz life and politics, and the legal and economic equality of the sexes, whether any differences can be explained.

THE POLITICAL ACTIVITY OF WOMEN IN THE PAST

Political life was very rudimentary and informal in the early days of the kibbutz. The small solidary group of a dozen or so youngsters decided everything directly, and the participation of each individual was taken for granted. The economy was simple and undifferentiated, requiring little or no organization and no specialized administration. Ideologically and practically, there was no problem about including women. They were part of the group, they were always present, and they shared the discussion and decision-making. The formal General Assembly was established early, chiefly to make decisions about external political matters. Daily life was still directed informally, and work was still far more important than political activity. The political participation of women as such is rarely mentioned in early kibbutz documents—though neither is the political participation of men.

Nevertheless, people with strong personalities quickly emerged in political activity. Golda Meir describes her early days in Kibbutz Merchavia:

"I was not received well in Merchavia because I was married, and as an American I was considered 'spoiled' and incapable of physical work. First, I had to get used to physical work, which was not very difficult, because I was in fact not spoiled. I was sent to harvest almonds. I had a backache and my hands were yellow, but it wasn't terrible. Then I was sent to dig pits; that was crushingly difficult work but I overcame it. I became an expert in poultry and bread-baking. I requested that the tables be covered with linoleum and that the waiters not smoke while waiting on tables. I was considered a 'witch' (*mehashefa,* literally, 'witch,' meaning a nagging, dominant female—roughly 'bitch'). As a side job, I taught English. Since I had a child, I became the nurse of all the children. That was a twenty-four-hour-a-day work. After six months of membership I was elected to the economic committee and the committee of social affairs" (Dossier: Settlement item 35).

Despite a bad start, this woman paved her road to political prominence by energy, devotion, and decisiveness.

Our group interviews suggest that women were politically active in the early days of the kibbutz for several reasons. They joined the men in formal and informal gatherings, though they seem to have taken the floor less often; they were otherwise equal partners at the general level of political activity. In the first decade, a number of agricultural branches were founded and run by women; as branch managers, they belonged to the important economic and work committees (the first committees established in most kibbutzim). The women who managed the kitchen and communal store occupied important political positions. When child care was incorporated in the kibbutz system, women became active in—and eventually dominated—the education committee.

The social affairs committee of the Kibbutz Artzi carried out a survey on public activity in its kibbutzim during 1943-44 and reported the results to the federation council in 1945 (Table 22).

Their findings led to serious criticism in the Kibbutz Artzi. The report of the secretariat of the federation to its council stated:

"Even after the resolutions of the Council in Maabaroth, no change for the better had taken place in the status and political activity of the *chavera,* especially in the institutions of the federation. As a result of the rising birth rate and the absorption of youth and

Table 22
Political Participation Among 3,400 Members of 24 Kibbutzim* of the
Kibbutz Artzi Federation, 1943-44

	Men	Women	Percentage of Women
In Committees and Executive Jobs	944	385	29
Branch Management in Agriculture, Industry, and Service	292	176	37.6
In External Activity and Movement Jobs	437	105	19.4

*This is about 53 per cent of the kibbutzim and about 57 per cent of the membership of the Federation.
Source: Mimoetza Lemoetza, 1947.

children of Youth Aliyah, the extraction of *chaverot* from production branches continues, and the percentage of service work rises. There are worrisome signs of declining political consciousness and alertness among the *chaverot,* and many resolutions are awaiting implementation" (Mimoetza Lemoetza 1947).

The situation was similar in the two other federations. In 1941 the thirteenth Conference of the Kibbutz Meuchad in Ashdot Yaakov had passed three resolutions on the status of women. The third resolution reads: "The Conference repeats the resolution of (at least) 33 per cent representation of women in every institution governing the federation and each kibbutz" (Protocol of the Conference).

In the Hever Hakvutzot, a special Women's Convention was called in Haifa in 1949 to deal with the situation of women. Resolutions 2 and 3 read:

"The Convention emphasizes woman's activity in all spheres of our life, and it requires appropriate representation of the women in the institutions of the federation and the *kvutza.* We must especially emphasize woman's participation in the economic committee, the secretariat, and the social affairs committee.

"The convention finds it absolutely necessary to establish a central committee of social affairs of the federations, one of whose tasks would be handling of the problem of the *chavera"* (Niv Hakvutza, vol. 6, issue 3, 1949).

We can assume from the great volume of complaints about the

inactivity of women in the forties that the gap between ideology and reality was steadily becoming wider. Talmon (1965), who investigated the political activity of women in twelve kibbutzim in 1954-56, concluded that "examination of the membership of committees in the last ten years indicates that in most kibbutzim there is a gradual yet cumulative trend toward growing sex role differentiation."

From the similarity of the complaints in all federations, we can infer that less than a third of the women in the kibbutz system was politically active. Talmon (1965) points out that there was balanced male-female membership in the committees dealing with work, social affairs, culture, housing, and absorption. Women predominated in the committees on education, health, consumption, soldiers' care, and old parents' care, but such central public offices as the secretariat, the economic committee, the planning committee, and the youth activities committee were predominantly held by men. Only 6.6 per cent of the women Talmon studied held central public offices (see Table 4), or central managerial positions. The more important the job, the more likely it was to be held by a man.

We have already seen that while the growing population and economy stimulated a more elaborate formal organization with more managerial positions, women gradually moved out of production to education and consumption—perhaps curtailing their interest in and knowledge about economic matters. It has further been suggested that, for instance, kibbutzim were becoming economy-oriented and therefore "importance" and "economy" were analogous (Blumberg 1974). However, Talmon's work does not confirm this.

Talmon (1972) distinguished three types of kibbutzim: pioneering kibbutzim, economy-oriented kibbutzim, and consumption-oriented kibbutzim. The consumption-oriented kibbutzim did not show lower sexual polarization in political activity. In fact, Shepher (1967) found that in familistic, consumption-oriented kibbutzim, polarization is significantly *greater* than in the collectivist, economy-oriented kibbutzim, and that there is no significant difference in the percentage of women in the central elite (6.34 per cent of women in the familistic kibbutzim, 6.93 per cent in the collectivist ones). Some other factors must then be responsible for the sexual polarization, and we shall discuss those later.

Before we describe the present situation, let us sketch the political atmosphere of the kibbutz. We described work in a twenty-four-hour cycle; the best unit of time for political activity is a week.

POLITICAL LIFE IN OFER

Every Sunday morning, the secretary of Ofer fixes the weekly program on the bulletin board in the anteroom of the dining hall. It looks something like this:

	Assemblies	Committees	Circles	Cultural Activities	Sports	Club-house
Weekly Program in Ofer						
Sunday		Economic, Education				Open
Monday		Work, Culture	Educators		Ping Pong Training	Closed
Tuesday				Film		Closed
Wednesday		Social Affairs			Basketball Training	Open
Thursday		Health, Absorption	Photographers			Open
Friday		Secretariat 1 P.M.		Concert		Closed
Shabbat	General Assembly				Basketball Match 6 P.M.	Open at 1 P.M.

Political life begins with the General Assembly on Saturday evening, the beginning of the Jewish week. People going to the Assembly greet one another with *"Shavua tov"* (good week). The Assembly is supposed to start at 9:30 P.M., but there is a persistent punctuality problem because Israeli television's broadcast of *Ironside* ends at 9:50. (The kibbutz federations asked the Israeli Broadcasting Corporation for a rescheduling of the program but were turned down.)

But the fifty-odd members finally do arrive at the dining hall, alone or with their spouses, having read the agenda posted the previous Friday.

The members do not seat themselves randomly around the dining tables; most have fixed places, which sometimes are mockingly and irrelevantly called "right" and "left." Senior members usually sit closer to the chairman than do younger members. On rare occasions, a motion to add to the agenda or a challenge to it is handed in by a member; this extraordinary measure always takes precedence over the published agenda. Normally the chairman opens the Assembly by giving information about the first point—each item must be prepared by a committee, usually the secretariat. After the chairman gives the background and other relevant information, he opens the floor to the members. He notes the sequence in which people request the floor by raising their hands. Most of the speakers are men and usually each talks for three to five minutes. (The speaker generally represents only himself, but sometimes a committee chairman represents his committee.) Discussion may be quiet or fervent or even angry. When there is no one else who wishes to speak, the chairman summarizes the discussion and proposes a motion. Sometimes his proposal is rejected and an alternative approved. Most voting is by show of hands, most elections by secret ballot.

Whenever an Assembly has been particularly exciting, people remain in the dining hall long afterward. Occasionally, a family invites those still in the hall to have a cup of tea at their home, where the discussion may continue well beyond midnight, and only the prospect of rising early for work brings the session to a reluctant end.

The secretary records the Assembly's decisions, and the following morning contacts the kibbutz officers and committees to ask them all to carry out any new resolutions.

One or another committee meets almost every day except Tuesday evening, when the weekly film is shown (only an extraordinary issue can compel kibbutzniks to attend a meeting instead). Friday evening is the beginning of Shabbat and is devoted exclusively to cultural and social activities. On Shabbat itself, the day of rest, no committee work is done until evening, when the ritual sabbath is ended. There are more committees than weekdays, and some kibbutz members belong to more than one committee. The secretary takes care to create a schedule free of time conflicts. A pattern has gradually developed wherein certain major committees meet on the same day every week. The only committee that gathers during the workday is the secretariat; the traditional time is one o'clock on Friday afternoon. The secretariat meets in the clubhouse, usually over coffee, and the chairman presents the issues for discussion. The gender composition of committees is a factor in planning; for instance, the predominantly male economic committee and the predominantly female education committee are both scheduled for Sunday evening.

Committees meet in one of the rooms of the administration building or in the apartment of one of the members. Attendance is usually 100 per cent; one must have a serious reason for skipping a meeting. Committees usually start between 9:00 and 9:30 in the evening and last till midnight. When we consider that they follow a long, demanding workday, we can understand why some members indulge in furtive napping if the discussion is not very lively. Decisions are usually by consensus, but occasionally votes are cast. Only the committees of health and social affairs are enjoined from publishing minutes, because of the personal nature of many of their decisions.

Some central officers have exhausting work schedules. The treasurer's week includes trips to Tel Aviv, Jerusalem, and Haifa; he is also an *ex-officio* member of the economic committee. Although the secretary (like the general manager and the work coordinator) is not formally a member of any committee except the secretariat, he is invited to attend many committee meetings.

About 40 per cent of the population belong to committees, which are the community's informal lines of communication. The day after a meeting, the committee members are frequently asked what went on in the committee. This happens especially in the case of members of the two central committees, the secretariat and the economic committee. They are sometimes jokingly called, with respect and perhaps a touch of envy, "close to the power" (*mekoravim leshlon*).

The everyday activity of the executive is carried on in the administration building, an old barracks containing four small rooms and the pinned-up products of socialist groups' mandatory mimeograph machines. The secretary, general manager, and work coordinator consult one another, give orders, receive requests, and always, of course, hear complaints. They also represent the kibbutz to other authorities of the district, municipal, and national administration.

One of the most striking traits of kibbutz life is the almost complete absence of formal political groups. They simply do not exist as power levers. True, groups of like-minded people crystallize during the General Assembly, but this is almost always spontaneous. It is not acceptable to organize a lobby to convince people to support one's request in the General Assembly or in committees. Even approaching an officer to request something of personal importance is only semilegitimate. The only legitimate procedure is to go to the Assembly and try to convince the people there through open discussion, without prior negotiation or persuasion.

Another characteristic of the kibbutz atmosphere is the relative scarcity of judicial procedures. Deviations, personal clashes, and quarrels are responded to formally and informally through "clarification" (*beirur*). The informal approach consists of asking an influential person to talk to the deviant person or quarreling parties; the formal approach is inviting people to the social affairs committee for *beirur*. The aim of clarification is to solve problems by consensus. The intervening person or committee tries hard to avoid the role of arbitrator, let alone that of judge. Only if no consensus is reached does *beirur* turn into arbitration. Any decision by an officer or committee can be appealed to the General Assembly, but it is rare for disputes to reach that stage. (When they do, there is much tension in the Assembly— and high attendance.)

During formal or informal clarification, from the lower level of a committee to the General Assembly, public opinion is lively, active, and multifaceted. Since the resolutions of the mediators, committees, and arbitrators are not published, the community's curiosity is fed only by gossip. People communicate their attitudes informally, except in the rare and delectable cases that reach the General Assembly.

Political life in Ofer is intense, but not everyone participates. About 10-15 per cent of the members are never elected to a committee and never go to the General Assembly. This retreat from political life may be caused by an unresolved conflict with some members in the past, real or imagined personal offenses, shyness, or simple lack of inclination. This political periphery, however, is not completely ineffective. Its members do not directly influence formal political decisions, but they comment privately, with some effect, on the decisions made by others through political institutions. Another 25-30 per cent of the members are only slightly active in the political process. These people may be members of committees, but they take the floor very rarely; they attend the General Assembly only "when there is something interesting," and it is unusual indeed for them to speak there. They are politically more informed than those on the periphery, but they, too, are commentators more than active participants and express their opinions largely through informal channels.

THE GENERAL ASSEMBLY

Shepher (1967) found in a study of eighteen kibbutzim that women in every community attended the General Assembly much less often than men did. Comparing the nine collectivist kibbutzim in his sample with the nine familistic ones, he found the gap between the sexes somewhat wider in the familistic ones. In our own questionnaire in four kibbutzim, we asked about attendance at the General Assembly and obtained the results in Tables 23a and 23b.

These four kibbutzim may or may not be representative, but the findings are strongly suggestive. Whether we pair the kibbutzim by ideology or seniority for purposes of comparison, we find that more men than women attend half to all the assemblies and that more women than men attend rarely or not at all. The male-female differences are all in the same direction, although they are statistically significant only in the senior kibbutzim and Ichud kibbutzim. These data are based on interviewees' accounts of their behavior, and we can assume that they were trying to give a positive picture of their behavior. (We must remember that attending the Assembly is considered a social virtue.) Fortunately, we were able to find in Ofer very detailed attendance data on the General Assembly between the years 1968-73. The elaborate minutes of the General Assembly also enabled us to distinguish the extent of active participation.

In these five years there were 167 meetings, an average of 33.4 a year.[1] The population of the kibbutz can be roughly divided into two large age groups. The senior members are Ofer's founders and the few people over forty who joined the kibbutz before 1958. The

Table 23a
Attendance of General Assembly in Four Kibbutzim,
by Sex and Seniority of Kibbutz

	Younger Kibbutzim		Older Kibbutzim	
	Men	Women	Men	Women
Attended All or Most Assemblies	52.4	44.6	46.5	19.4
Attended Approximately Half the Assemblies	19.0	17.8	16.3	13.9
Rarely Attended	22.6	19.8	11.6	41.7
Never Attended	6.0	17.8	25.6	25.0
Total	100	100	100	100

$\chi^2 = 5.98$, df = 3 p = n.s. $\chi^2 = 11.29$, df = 3 p = 0.01

Table 23b
Attendance of General Assembly in Four Kibbutzim,
by Sex and Kibbutz Federation

	Kibbutz Artzi		Kibbutz Ichud	
	Men	Women	Men	Women
Attended All or Most Assemblies	62.82	47.3	48.5	37.9
Attended Approximately Half the Assemblies	18.6	21.6	20.6	13.9
Rarely Attended	14.3	23.0	22.1	24.1
Never Attended	4.3	8.1	8.8	24.1
Total	100	100	100	100

$\chi^2 = 4.04$, df = 3 p = n.s. $\chi^2 = 7.32$, df = 3 p = 0.025

junior members are the entire second generation and those younger people, most of them under thirty, who joined the kibbutz after 1963 as members of an organized youth group (*garin*) or as spouses of second-generation members. Table 24 gives the numbers of men and women in each age group who attended the General Assembly.

Table 24
Attendance of General Assembly of Ofer, 1968-73 (in absolute numbers)

	1968–69	1969–70	1970-71	1971-72	1972-73
Number of Assemblies per Year	40	29	26	40	32
Average Attendance, Young Men	15.32	18.27	17.80	17.55	19.15
Senior Men	18.0	21.41	12.19	14.52	12.09
All Men	33.32	39.68	29.99	32.07	31.24
Young Women	10.47	10.89	10.96	10.3	9.53
Senior Women	12.37	10.34	10.61	13.12	10.15
All Women	22.84	21.23	21.57	23.42	19.68
All Young	25.79	29.16	28.76	27.85	28.68
All Senior	30.37	31.75	22.80	27.64	22.24
Variance by Sex (F)	41.77***	39.34***	10.77**	76.82***	57.13***
Variance by Age (F)	7.96**	18.13***	5.40*	1.09 n.s.	17.70***
Interaction (F)	0.23 n.s.	92.10***	4.21*	92.10***	49.14***
Average Total Attending	56.17	51.92	50.41	55.49	50.93

***P = 0.001
 **P = 0.01
  *P = 0.05
 n.s. = nonsignificant

The following conclusions can be drawn:

1. The average attendance of each Assembly was about fifty (out of 130-150) during all five years.

2. In both age groups, an average of ten more men than women was present at the Assembly.

3. The difference between the sexes in the senior group is small and tends to diminish with time. By contrast, the difference between younger men and women is higher and increases with time.

4. Except for the first year, more young members of both sexes attended the Assembly than older members.

A factorial analysis of variance shows that the differences between the sexes are always greater than the differences between age groups. This is striking, given the historical turbulence of the kibbutzniks' histories. In 1971-72 the difference between age groups is not significant. The F ratio in 1968-69 shows that more senior than young members attended; in the other years with significant F ratios, the differences are reversed. Significant interaction F ratios indicate that proportionately more older women and younger men attended the Assembly than young women and older men.

Usually about 60 per cent of the people at the Assembly are male, 40 per cent female. Table 25 shows what percentage of the total male and female membership these figures represent.

This table shows that:

1. In all years, a higher percentage of kibbutz men than women attended the Assembly.

2. The differences between men and women were again greater than between junior and senior members.

3. The senior group had higher average attendance than the junior group in the first year; the reverse was true in the four succeeding years.

4. Factorial analysis of variance also reveals that the differences between sexes are always higher than those between age groups. There were, in fact, statistically significant differences between the age groups only in 1969 and 1972-73. Observation as well reveals greater activity by young men and older women. The peak of political activity for women seems to be around the age range normally associated with menopause (most of Ofer's senior women are about forty-five). The peak of political activity for men is between ages twenty-five and thirty-five. Older men remain in the Assembly only if they reached an active level of political status during their prime years.

5. The overall average attendance varies from 33.75 per cent in 1970-71 to 38.7 per cent in 1968-69.

Noting the fact that more older women than younger ones attend the Assembly might prompt the guess that it is nursing babies and

Table 25
Presence in General Assembly of Ofer, 1968–73 (in percentages)

	1968–69	1969–70	1970–71	1971–72	1972–73
Number of Assemblies per Year	40	29	26	40	32
Average Attendance, Young Men	38.12	46.66	35.88	44.57	48.51
Senior Men	47.33	34.31	34.84	38.70	32.18
All Men	42.75	40.48	35.57	41.65	40.51
Young Women	36.1	35.0	31.26	35.0	32.12
Senior Women	32.48	29.52	30.42	33.22	25.21
All Women	33.8	32.0	30.73	33.92	28.12
All Young	37.38	42.13	34.23	41.5	41.09
All Senior	39.9	30.48	32.5	36.0	28.87
Variance by Sex (F)	12.94***	6.53*	6.57*	19.03***	44.73***
Variance by Age (F)	1.41 n.s.	7.67**	3.75 n.s.	4.92 n.s.	44.27***
Interaction (F)	7.46***	1.13 n.s.	0.3 n.s.	1.07 n.s.	6.97**
Average Total Attending	38.7	36.03	33.73	37.32	34.54

***$P = 0.001$
**$P = 0.01$
*$P = 0.025$
n.s. = nonsignificant

putting children to bed that curtails the participation of young women, but this is rarely the case. Are kibbutz women of childbearing age especially uninterested in politics?

Attendance at the Assembly is not in itself an accurate measure of political activity. The Assembly is three-fifths male, but activity there is less balanced than that figure implies. And if we look at what people do in the Assembly, we find an even greater sex difference.

Every member may ask for the floor as many times as he wants, and there is no restriction on duration of comments. The following data describe active participation in Ofer's General Assembly during two years, 1971-73.

Table 26
Indices of Activity in the General Assembly of Ofer, 1971-72 and 1972-73, by Sex

	1971-72		1972-73	
	Men	Women	Men	Women
Average Number of People Addressing Assembly (1)	9.17	1.45	9.79	1.69
Average Number of Times Assembly Was Addressed (2)	14.82	1.88	19.61	1.82
(2) : (1)	1.61	1.29	2.00	1.07
Percentage of Active Members of All Attendants	28.59	6.19	31.32	8.58
Range max-min (1)	2-17	0-4	1-23	0-6
Range max-min (2)	2-32	0-10	1-47	0-7
Percentage of Assemblies Women Did Not Take the Floor		33.3		35.0

The following conclusions are evident:

1. In both years, about six times as many men as women were active in the Assembly.

2. Since more men are present at the Assembly, the percentage of *active* men and women is a good measure of participation. In 1971-72, 4.6 times more men than women were active. In 1972-73 the figure was 3.6.

3. More men than women asked for the floor, and they did so more frequently.

4. More men than women addressed an Assembly.

5. During the two years under study, only on one occasion did more women than men take the floor—on the issue of the kibbutz making or buying apartment curtains. There was never a time when there was no man who asked for the floor, but in about a third of the assemblies in each year, there was no woman who spoke.

One qualification of these data must be made. In Ofer, for both years in question, the chairman of the Assembly was a man, and the chairman takes the floor at least once on every issue on the agenda. This inflates the statistics for both the number of men who asked for the floor and the number of times a man addressed the Assembly. Even so, the disparity between the sexes is very great; the women are quite passive in the General Assembly.

However quiet women may be in the Assembly, they express their opinions freely and abundantly in informal situations—in conversation after the Assembly, in the places where they work, on the lawns adjoining their houses. This discrepancy between formal passivity and informal energy is characteristic of the political behavior of women in the kibbutz. The importance of informal social control in the kibbutz has already been discussed (Chapter 3); the political influence of women is most likely greater than their formal participation suggests.

We can add from participant observation that when women do take the floor in formal situations, they talk briefly and to the point. Whether this economy is effective we cannot say. It is men who often repeat themselves and argue ponderously and bombastically. We have mentioned a meeting in which more women than men took the floor. It was an uncommonly short meeting in which two women each took the floor once—but one man talked three times. We have also observed that at least in Ofer, it is almost always the same women who speak in the Assembly, most of whom are in charge of institutions of consumption or education. As we saw in Table 25, younger women address the Assembly very rarely (whereas younger men are more active than their seniors).

We noted the idea that women's formal inactivity may stem from their comparative lack of knowledge about and interest in economic matters, as compared to their interest in consumption. It is pertinent, then, to know whether women's attendance varies with the topics on the agenda. This is difficult to study because most Assemblies have mixed agendas. A very few, though, are devoted entirely to problems of production; the attendance of women at these is indeed significantly lower than at all other Assemblies. Some women frankly acknowledge that they do not attend Assemblies devoted mainly to matters of production. Are women more likely to attend Assemblies devoted to matters other than production? A special general meeting called a Members' Assembly (*assefat chaverim*) deals with problems of individuals—admission to membership, interaction of members, arbitration of conflicts between members and between members and committees. Another kind of assembly, the Annual Assembly, is a series of meetings held once a year, usually around the High Holidays in the spring or fall, to elect kibbutz officers and committees and to discuss general planning and policy. This Annual Assembly is usually festive, intended to set the pace and tone for the following year. Since Members' Assemblies and Annual Assemblies are extraordinary events from which production problems are largely absent, one would assume that they attract more members, especially women (Table 27).

Annual and Members' Assemblies do attract more women than regular Assemblies, in both the total population and in the seniority groups. But they also attract more men. Do the Annual and Members' Assemblies draw a different *ratio* of men and women? (See Table 28.)

In 1968-69 the Members' Assemblies drew a lower ratio of men to women than did the regular Assemblies, but the Annual Assemblies showed a higher ratio. In 1972-73 both Annual and Members' Assemblies brought a lower ratio. If we examine seniority groups, we again find that senior members' ratio in 1968-69 was lower than in the regular Assemblies, but in Members' Assemblies it was higher. In 1972-73 that pattern was reversed. Among young members, the Members' Assembly had a lower and the Annual Assembly had a higher ratio than the General Assemblies in 1968-69. In 1972-73 both kinds of special assemblies showed a higher ratio.

We can conclude that Annual Assemblies and Members' Assemblies do generally attract more women than regular assemblies do. But at least in 1968-69, Annual Assemblies attracted even more men than usual, so that the ratio did not change considerably. We therefore cannot say that women are especially attracted by festive As-

Table 27
Average Attendance of Various General Assemblies in Ofer, 1968–69 and
1972–73, by Sex and Age (in percentages)

	1968-1969			1972-1973		
	Regular	Annual	Members'	Regular	Annual	Members'
Total Men	35.08	49.46	50.44	36.97	41.50	53.25
Total Women	28.08	38.26	43.38	24.34	35.10	39.16
Young Men	31.83	45.00	48.00	44.04	52.60	61.50
Young Women	29.38	43.46	43.00	26.18	40.8	46.66
Older Men	38.33	53.92	52.88	29.90	30.4	45.0
Older Women	26.77	33.07	43.77	22.50	29.4	31.66

Table 28
Ratios of Percentages of Men and Women Attending Various Assemblies in Ofer,
by Seniority Groups, 1968–69 and 1972–73

	1968-69			1972-73		
	Regular	Annual	Members'	Regular	Annual	Members'
Total Population	1.24	1.29	1.16	1.51	1.18	1.35
Senior Members	1.43	1.63	1.20	1.32	1.03	1.42
Young Members	1.08	1.03	1.11	1.68	1.28	1.31

semblies or by more personal and dramatic agendas; more women than usual asked for the floor, but even more men did than usual; the characteristic ratio of male-female activity became even less.

Shepher, who has attended General Assemblies in dozens of kibbutzim in his more than twenty years of scientific work, has been impressed by the recurrent picture of women attending the Assembly less and, when present, participating less than men do. The periodical literature of the kibbutz movement frequently complains of just this situation. We noted earlier that our interviewees in the four kibbutzim stated that in older kibbutzim and the kibbutzim of the Kibbutz Artzi, the differences between the sexes are not significant. Nevertheless, we have good reason to assume that the situation in most of the 230 kibbutzim in Israel is not much different from the one we describe in Ofer, judging from the frequently repeated universal complaints about the situation and proposals to change it at the federation level, and by the virtually complete absence of contrary data.

Participation in the General Assembly is quite different from the next level of political activity—activity in a committee to which only somewhat less than half the population is elected by the Annual Assembly at any given time.

COMMITTEES AND OFFICERS

The executive consists of elected officers and committees, and it manages the everyday affairs of the kibbutz. More than 40 per cent of the kibbutz population are involved as officers or committee members. What role do women play in the executive? To what extent do they take political responsibility, especially in work where they predominate, such as education, consumption, and social services? Are they at all active in work where they are a minority? Table 29 shows detailed census data on the two federations.

We divided the members of the many committees that are active in most kibbutzim into several groups. We put in our first group people not elected to any committee in the year of the census or the year before. In the second group we pooled members of committees whose activities are mostly or exclusively economic (economic, finance, work, planning, agriculture, industry, etc.). In the third group are members of committees dealing with service (education, social affairs, health, housing, absorption, youth, parents' care, soldiers' care, etc.). The fourth group includes the secretariat and committees such as the security and the political; except for the secretariat, these function only occasionally and involve very few members.

First let us look at the total population. In the economic sphere, the percentage of men is three to four times higher than that of women. In social, cultural, and educational work, we find a significantly larger percentage of women than men in both federations. In the general category, the percentage of men is about twice that of women. Overall, a larger proportion of women than men are politically inactive

Table 29
Sphere of Committee Activity, by Sex, Generation, and Federation (horizontal and vertical percentages)

| Sphere of Activity | Sex and Generation | Vertical Percentages | | | | | | | |
| | | Second Generation | | Kibbutz-Bred | | First Generation | | Total | |
		M	F	M	F	M	F	M	F
No Activity	K.A.	57.8	58.4	33.0	36.2	20.6	28.9	30.8	35.9
	I.	60.6	59.0	36.6	41.9	29.1	45.1	38.1	48.2
Economic	K.A.	8.7	3.0	16.0	5.0	21.4	6.3	17.7	5.5
	I.	12.3	2.8	20.5	5.6	21.1	5.0	18.7	4.4
Social, Cultural, Educational, Service	K.A.	20.7	31.0	34.1	51.6	42.2	57.6	36.2	51.3
	I.	18.0	32.9	32.1	43.8	35.5	41.9	30.7	40.1
General	K.A.	12.8	7.6	16.9	7.2	15.8	7.2	15.3	7.3
	I.	9.1	5.3	10.8	8.6	14.3	8.0	12.5	7.3
Total	K.A.	100	100	100	100	100	100	100	100
	I.	100	100	100	100	100	100	100	100

in both federations—five per cent more in the Kibbutz Artzi, ten per cent more in the Ichud.

What this means is that distribution of the sexes in political activity closely resembles that in division of labor. Most of the women are concentrated in social, cultural, and educational activities; the men are about equally divided between the general and economic activities and the social-cultural-educational spheres. The service

Table 29 (Continued)

Horizontal Percentages

Second Generation			Kibbutz-Bred			First Generation			Total		
M	F	T	M	F	T	M	F	T	M	F	T
55.6	44.4	N = 3080	56.5	43.5	N = 623	41.2	58.8	N = 2357	48.7	51.3	100
58.0	42.0	N = 3056	53.4	46.6	N = 449	38.8	61.2	N = 4149	46.4	53.6	100
78.6	21.4	N = 327	81.7	18.3	N = 208	76.9	23.1	N = 1309	78.1	21.9	100
85.5	14.5	N = 421	82.7	17.3	N = 162	80.5	19.5	N = 1449	82.3	17.7	100
45.75	54.25	N = 1340	48.4	51.6	N = 750	41.8	58.2	N = 4750	43.8	56.2	100
42.3	57.7	N = 1242	49.2	50.8	N = 429	45.4	54.6	N = 4322	45.6	54.4	100
68.0	32.0	N = 557	76.9	23.1	N = 234	68.3	31.7	N = 1090	69.9	30.1	100
69.8	30.2	N = 381	62.3	37.7	N = 114	63.7	36.3	N = 1241	65.3	34.7	100
55.8	44.2	N = 5304	58.7	41.3	N = 1815	49.5	50.5	N = 9506	52.5	47.5	100
57.3	42.7	N = 5100	56.8	43.2	N = 1154	49.5	50.5	N = 11161	52.3	47.7	100

sphere contains a great number of committees, and we will have a clearer picture if we analyze the horizontal percentages. These show that the economic category is about 80 per cent male; the social, educational, and service categories are more than half female. Almost 70 per cent of those active in the general category are male. The inactive category contains more females.

If we look at the generations, we find the same pattern, with slight modifications, in both federations. The only exception is the second generation of the Ichud, where more men than women are inactive. Turning again to horizontal percentages, we see that in both federations among the younger members (second generation and kibbutz-bred), the inactive group contains relatively more men, whereas in the first generation this group contains relatively more women.

Hierarchy is always. of course, an important factor in political activity. Scope of action is also important in kibbutz politics, as elsewhere. In a committee, the chairman is the initiator; he prepares its agenda, leads the meeting, summarizes discussion, and occasionally represents the committee in the General Assembly. There is also hierarchical order among committees. The secretariat, economic committee, and social affairs committee are to some extent synthesizing committees. All committees must report to the secretariat, and often to one another. The central officers of the kibbutz coordinate the whole administration—secretary, treasurer, economic manager, work coordinator.

Table 30 shows how authority is distributed between the sexes in this very apparent functional hierarchy.

These general conclusions may be deduced:

1. The lowest level of authority contains a larger percentage of women than men, but among committee chairmen the proportion of men is higher. Men also predominate in the membership of central committees. The higher the level of authority, the wider the gap between men and women. Six to eight per cent of men reach the highest levels of authority, but only 0.6 per cent of women.

2. When we analyze the horizontal percentages, we see that the lowest level of authority is female-dominated, the three higher ones male-dominated. The highest group is most polarized; more than 90 per cent of the central officers in the Kibbutz Artzi and about 85 per cent in the Ichud are men.

3. Generations follow the same pattern as the general population. The one exception is the second generation of the Kibbutz Artzi, whose lowest level of authority contains more men than women. At the highest level of authority, this group is more polarized than the general population.

Even though these data show political polarization, as do those on division of labor, they indicate a very high extent of female activity. In what other society are 40-50 per cent of the women politically active? To understand the full significance of our data, we must discount the influence of the overall sex ratio. To do this we reworked the Specific Polarization Index we had used to analyze data on work. Social, educational, and service activity were characteristically female, economic and general activity, generally male. The lowest level of authority was disproportionately female, the three higher levels disproportionately male—a classification justified by the horizontal percentages in Table 30. The indices of polarization in political activity are presented in Table 31.

The indices are much lower than in division of labor, showing about 30 per cent of maximum possible polarization. In both federations, spheres of activity are more polarized than levels of activity, though the differences are not great. The generations show different patterns in the two federations: the Ichud second generation is more polarized in sphere of activity than the rest of the Ichud population; in the Kibbutz Artzi it is less polarized, and the kibbutz-bred are the highly polarized group. In level of activity, the second generation is more polarized in both federations than the total population.

We have no certain explanation for the low polarization in sphere of activity of the Kibbutz Artzi's second generation. But we do have a guess: the Kibbutz Artzi is the most polarized of the federations in longest work (see Table 17); some balancing mechanism may be at work. For instance, there may be somewhat ritualistic election of women to economic and political positions and of men to predominantly female committees as a compensatory gesture of political equality. The analysis of our two intensively studied kibbutzim from the Kibbutz Artzi seems to support this theory. Let us now return briefly to all four of those kibbutzim where we relied less on macrodata in our analysis.

We shall begin with Tsvia, the older kibbutz of the Kibbutz Artzi, on which we have data for the years 1960-71. The sex ratio in offices and committees resembles that of the total census population. In only four of the twelve years we studied was there a woman among the central officers; in every case, four central officers had been elected instead of three, after the community decided to have a woman as well as a man as secretary. Not once during the twelve years was a

Table 30
Level of Activity Ever Carried Out, by Sex and Generation (in percentages)

Level of Activity	Sex and Generation	Second Generation		Kibbutz-Bred		First Generation		Total	
		M	F	M	F	M	F	M	F
No Activity	K.A.	58.0	58.7	33.2	36.0	20.0	29.0	30.8	36.0
	I.	62.2	61.7	38.7	45.5	30.6	46.9	39.9	50.4
Member of Committee	K.A.	26.7	32.2	39.7	51.4	41.8	50.9	38.0	47.0
	I.	20.2	30.2	32.7	38.5	31.6	37.2	28.5	35.3
Chairman of Committee	K.A.	8.1	5.6	14.3	7.3	20.5	12.7	16.7	10.6
	I.	5.6	5.1	13.8	9.8	16.8	8.2	13.5	7.7
Member of Central Committee	K.A.	6.1	3.5	8.7	5.0	9.5	6.6	8.6	5.8
	I.	8.9	2.9	10.6	5.7	10.7	7.0	10.1	6.0
Full-Time Central Job	K.A.	0.1	0.02	4.1	0.3	8.2	0.8	5.9	0.6
	I.	3.1	0.1	4.2	0.5	8.5	0.7	8.0	0.6
Total	K.A.	100	100	100	100	100	100	100	100
	I.	100	100	100	100	100	100	100	100

woman elected general manager or treasurer. In 1971 the secretariat had four women out of twelve members—the maximum number of women in any year. In most years, the secretariat had ten to eleven members, two of them women. The economic committee had from one to five women members out of sixteen. There were five women

Second Generation			Kibbutz-Bred			First Generation			Total		
M	F	T	M	F	T	M	F	T	M	F	T
54.0	46.0	N = 3092	56.7	43.3	N = 624	40.3	59.7	N = 2333	48.6	51.4	N = 5531
57.3	42.7	N = 3101	52.3	47.7	N = 461	38.6	61.4	N = 4182	46.0	54.0	N = 7576
51.1	48.9	N = 1545	52.3	47.7	N = 808	44.6	55.4	N = 4411	47.2	52.8	N = 7028
47.2	52.8	N = 1249	52.7	47.3	N = 406	45.4	54.6	N = 3848	46.9	53.1	N = 5528
64.7	35.3	N = 371	73.4	26.6	N = 207	61.3	38.7	N = 1574	63.5	36.5	N = 2295
59.6	40.4	N = 275	64.7	35.3	N = 139	66.8	33.2	N = 1391	65.8	34.2	N = 1870
68.8	31.2	N = 263	71.0	29.0	N = 131	58.5	41.5	N = 764	62.1	37.9	N = 1209
80.5	19.5	N = 323	71.4	28.6	N = 98	60.0	40.0	N = 986	64.9	35.1	N = 1418
97.0	3.0	N = 33	95.5	4.5	N = 45	91.0	9.0	N = 424	91.6	8.4	N = 562
86.8	13.2	N = 152	82.0	18.0	N = 50	85.8	14.5	N = 754	85.4	14.6	N = 1023
55.8	44.2	N = 5304	58.7	41.3	N = 1815	49.5	50.5	N = 9506	52.5	47.5	N = 16625
57.3	42.7	N = 5100	56.8	43.2	N = 1154	49.5	50.5	N = 11161	52.3	47.7	N = 17415

elected in 1960 and 1962, but for most years the number was one to three. In the work committee of seven, there were one to three women. When a woman was elected to chair the work committee, it was only as a result of a decision to elect two leaders, one man and one woman. During the twelve years, from 33 to 40 per cent of all elected officials consisted of women.

Table 31
Specific Polarization Index in Spheres of Activity and Levels of Activity, by Generation and Federation

	ICHUD				KIBBUTZ ARTZI			
	Second Generation	Kibbutz-Bred	First Generation	Total	Second Generation	Kibbutz-Bred	First Generation	Total
Spheres of Activity	0.373	0.236	0.266	0.296	0.273	0.335	0.310	0.309
Level of Activity	0.354	0.234	0.210	0.283	0.261	0.302	0.256	0.258

In Ofra, for which we have data from 1964-72 (except for 1968-69), the situation was somewhat different. During those eight years, Ofra had a woman secretary for one year, a woman treasurer for two years, and a woman general manager for one year. Once there were four women in a secretariat of seven; during the other years, there were usually two women in a secretariat of eight. In the economic committee, there were two to three women in a committee of ten to twelve. About 40 per cent of all elected officials consisted of women.

In Tsvi, the older kibbutz of the Ichud, we have data from 1959 to 1973. There, all central positions were filled by men except in 1971, when a woman was elected secretary. In the secretariat, the usual number of women was two to seven in a committee of nine to fifteen. In the economic committee, the number of women never exceeded two; in over fifteen years there were three three-year periods when there were no women at all. The percentage of women in all elected positions ranged from 25 to 39 per cent.

In Ofer we have data for 1960-73, during which years no woman ever held a central position. In the secretariat, there were one to two women out of nine to ten members. In 1969 the secretariat of ten contained no women. The economic committee, which usually had nine members, had no women for three years; in the other years there was one. The percentage of women in offices varied from 31 to 40 per cent.

Our data on these four kibbutzim support our hypothesis about lip service being paid to sexual equality in political participation. In both kibbutzim of the Kibbutz Artzi, additional central positions were forthrightly created in order to elect women. We do not know whether these women belong to the second generation, but the theory of compensatory lip service in that generation seems to be somewhat confirmed by events in the four kibbutzim.

FEMALE HIERARCHIES

Since division of work by sex is extremely polarized in the kibbutz, there are all-woman work groups. We devoted special study to the presence of hierarchy and the use of authority in such groups as a case of the political behavior of women of one kibbutz. While kibbutz ideology seriously limits the use of authority, authority nevertheless exists in large branches with differentiated tasks. A graded division of authority creates a hierarchy, however it may differ from openly authoritarian patterns. And since work hierarchies are eventually reflected in political activity, hierarchies of women are bound to tell us something about kibbutz women politically.

We found at least six work branches in Ofer that were predominantly or exclusively made up of women.

Table 32
Female-Dominated Work Branches in Ofer

Name of Branch	Usual Number of Women	Usual Number of Men
Kitchen	9	1
Dining Room	3	occasionally several
Laundry	2	occasionally several
Communal Store	15	0
Health Care	2	0
Child Care	17	0
Total	48	1–3

All these jobs are filled by kibbutz members. Nonmembers (parents, volunteers, training-group members) work mainly in the kitchen, dining room, and children's house and do not change the sexual constitution of those work branches. The branch managers of the kitchen and the two storerooms are elected—unlike the managers of production branches, who are appointed by the economic committee

—because they are responsible for distribution and are therefore felt to require wide social support.

In the kitchen, the dominant figure is the *ekonomith,* who as the branch manager decides upon the distribution of goods and organizes and assigns the work. In a sense, she dominates the whole kibbutz. She allocates food not only for the communal meals but for every individual and family as well (afternoon tea, materials for baking cakes for Shabbat and other festive occasions). She also allocates work to the volunteer workers and the "male of the kitchen." She stands at the center of attention; everyone in the kitchen seeks her out, and if she is not there to make a decision, they must wait until she returns.

Second in the kitchen hierarchy are the two permanent cooks who, like the *ekonomith,* are women of about fifty. Once the *ekonomith* has decided on the menu, she usually gives them a free hand in its preparation. The cooks give orders to the preparation room, and sometimes to the dishwashers and a young kitchen assistant. The preparation room is somewhat hierarchical; there is an older woman in charge, assisted by three or four women, usually older parents and temporary workers. One woman works half of each day, subordinate only to the *ekonomith,* preparing the baby food in the separate children's kitchen and sweets for festive occasions.

The organization of the kitchen staff is represented in Figure 4.

This is certainly no typical bureaucratic structure, even for a kibbutz. At all levels, authority is accepted somewhat reluctantly, and people constantly worry about their personal independence, to the extent that personal relations are usually strained. The only man in the kitchen is more or less subordinate to almost everyone, yet men and women frequently express a desire to be led by a man. Examples of other kibbutzim with a male *ekonom* are often mentioned during the elections and in the nomination committees that prepare annual elections.

People may be privately very critical of kitchen workers; the structure is maintained by constant compromise between real opinions of others and the wish to maintain permanent jobs for older women and a few older men—possibilities for new work are very limited for a woman who has to abandon her permanent work around the age

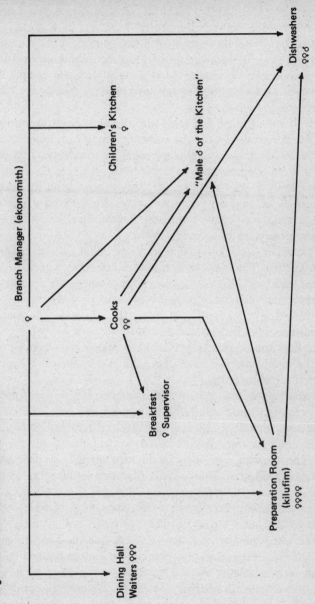

Figure 4
Organization Chart of the Kitchen in Ofer

of disruptive physical decline. Almost all the permanent kitchen workers criticize one another frequently; however, as a group they are criticized by those they serve, and this outside criticism helps maintain the system by motivating the permanent workers to defend one another publicly, no matter what their private views are. Permanent kitchen workers almost never have primary relationships with one another outside work.

In an all-male branch the same size, acceptance of authority is much readier, personal relations are smoother, mutual criticism is more open, and there is less worry about personal independence. In a male branch with a few women, such as dry farming, the men do not seem domineering toward the woman; rather, they appear to set them apart with some show of courtesy, even gallantry. We shall return to this difference in male and female branches after we finish examining the other major hierarchies of women in Ofer.

The hierarchy in the communal storeroom differs somewhat from that of the kitchen. There are two separate storerooms, one for adults and one for children. The first employs ten women, the second five (this figure includes two nonmembers). Both sections do ironing and mending, sort finished laundry, organize the purchase of clothing, produce curtains and bed covers, and do budget bookkeeping. The adult store does the additional service of women's tailoring; work is done to a limited extent for adolescent girls in the children's store by two old mothers of members.[2]

The adult-store manager (*machsanait chaverim*) is formally responsible for the whole store and in part for the laundry. She organizes ironing, mending, sorting, purchasing, and budgeting, but has almost nothing to say about the independent dressmaking establishment. The dressmakers' illegitimate separateness, a product of very old kibbutz disputes, is emphasized by the closed doors to their rooms.

The storeroom workers are in three rooms, each of which opens to another. The place is overcrowded with part-time workers and with women who can work nowhere else because they are pregnant, ill, or aged. Nevertheless, the atmosphere there is more relaxed than in the kitchen, largely because there is less stress in the work; meals must be briskly and unfailingly ready at specific times under all conditions, but the adult storeroom meets only weekly schedules. The storeroom women are critical of the dressmakers, not only because they are independent, but because they themselves are part of the dressmakers' clientele. It is interesting to note that the atmosphere is not cordial among the three women within the dressmakers' shop. The first assistant is highly critical both of the head dressmaker and of the second assistant, who is a relative of the head dressmaker.

The children's storeroom is in one large room and has, in effect, two departments: one for sorting (small children receive laundry daily, adults once a week), the other for ironing and mending. Two old women work in a separate room far from the storeroom; there is no interference with their work, but they are told what to do. The *machsanait* maintains hierarchical order in the entire storeroom—though in a way locally called "sugar-coated." The women who work with her are very quick to take offense; if any step of the *machsanait* or of a worker seems to deviate from work norms, it is commented on in detail. Long-strained relations between workers are frequent. There are no primary relationships outside work hours in either of the storerooms.[3]

Work in child care is organized so that it prevents the emergence of a firm hierarchy. Children are divided into age groups (*kitah*), presided over by a responsible nurse, who has an assistant for half to three-quarters of the day. For children up to age four, there are three to four such units. The one kindergarten group consists of ten to twenty children of ages four to seven. The kindergarten teacher works with a trained nurse and one or two assistants. In all, eight to ten women work with the kindergarten-age children (*hagil harach*); five to six are professionally trained, and two to five are untrained assistants. Within the *kitah,* the trained nurse (*metapelet*) gives orders to the assistant, who usually helps in such nonprofessional work as cleaning. In kindergarten the system is more differentiated, with the teacher deciding educational matters and the *metapelet* matters of nurture.

The head nurse has undisputed authority over all questions of education and nurture for preschool children. She is about fifty, older than the other nurses and much more experienced. The kindergarten teacher is also an older woman of undisputed authority, but she accepts the head nurse's authority over her work with her preschool children. The authority of the head nurse is also formally supported; she is usually a member of the education committee and has the title

Head Nurse of Preschool Children (*Merakezet Hagil Harach*). The head nurse does not use her authority during a routine workday. In emergencies such as serious illness or quarrels between parents and nurses, she is called on to make decisions. She is also involved in parents' particular concerns about their children.

Work with school-age children requires almost no system: the primary-school children go to the school of a neighboring kibbutz; the *metapelet* works for only an hour before the children leave for school and for two hours after their return. There are two classes in the elementary-school age group, each attended by a nurse. The high-school-age group consists of two sections, attended by two half-time nurses. Except during these nurses' planning of activities, no organized activity exists between them; since they work independently, they cannot be considered work branches.

In summary, we can point out that in the three work branches described above, we found hierarchical systems of different scope and intensity. In the kitchen, the hierarchy is highly developed and involves all workers. In the communal storerooms, workers are less subject to hierarchical relations. In child care, a hierarchy arises only in emergency situations.

We know of two recent, extraordinary situations in which temporary hierarchies of women developed. They deserve brief mention.

Some years ago, a kibbutz adaptation of Mother's Day appeared in several kibbutzim—*Yom Hachaverah,* or Day of the *Chavera*. It is not surprising that Mother's Day assumed a special form in the kibbutz, focusing less on individual mothering and more on the overall services provided by women in the community. It is the kibbutz rather than the family that rewards the *chaverot*. All the women in the kibbutz are relieved of their responsibilities for the day. Men who work in the kitchen serve the festively dressed women a rich breakfast in the dining hall. A sightseeing bus takes them on a day-long trip for a variety of recreations and amusements. Meanwhile, men care for the kitchen and children (including the babies—which causes the mothers no little worry). The communal storeroom is usually closed, for the men are useless at needlework. The day's recreation program is organized by the women on the culture committee, but this does not create a hierarchy—unless something goes wrong. On one occasion spirits were very low because of a delayed and disagreeable lunch in a Jerusalem restaurant. The *chaverot* were all complaining and quarreling among themselves. Two of the women in the group took the initiative, managed to rapidly change the atmosphere, and dictated the steps to be taken for the rest of the subsequently successful trip.

A very different temporary hierarchy of women appeared in the first days of the Yom Kippur War, when the district where Ofer lies was shelled by Syrian Frog missiles. All the people had to stay in bunkers at night for almost two weeks. Most of the bunkers were mixed-sex, but the best one had been allocated to the babies and youngest toddlers, with their nurses and mothers—about twenty-five people in all. A hierarchy quickly developed: at the top was the head nurse, under her the other nurses, and then the mothers. The babies had beds, but the women had to sleep on the floor and even on the steps. A watch was organized, and the cooperation and discipline were extraordinary. The head nurse said afterward, "In spite of the constant fear and worry, it was a great experience. So many women together without quarreling and so fully disciplined. Everyone really gave her best."

This brief look at hierarchies of women in Ofer shows what the larger studies suggest—that the most prominent trait is the marked centralization of authority. In almost all the groups, authority is concentrated in one woman, with little or no downward gradation. Marret (1971) found the same pattern in female-dominated organizations and ascribed it to the following factors:

1. Women usually show more need for close personal relations than men, so are reluctant to accept tasks that involve impersonal authority. They leave decision-making to a few people, whose hierarchical positions entail the consequences of command.

2. Women are more concerned than men are with providing personal services to individuals rather than groups; therefore they tend to have a greater commitment to practice than to policy-making. Policy decisions are left to the woman at the top.

3. Since women have higher turnover rates at work than men do, those who do remain at their jobs are invested with a near-monopoly of power.

4. Most all-female and female-dominated organizations are semi-professional (teaching, nursing, etc.). In such organizations, profes-

sionalism—a formalized independence—does not counterbalance centralization, as it does in professional organizations.

All four points seem to apply to the kibbutz situation, though no direct evidence can be presented here except for the third point. All the really dominant women are now approaching or past menopause and without young children. If we compare the present situation with the past, when the now-dominant women were of childbearing age, we see that the hierarchical system was less developed and that more women were involved in decision-making.

Two other traits of hierarchies of women are strained personal relations and reluctance to accept the authority of other women. We have already said that we cannot risk an explanation at this stage of our research because we do not have an all-male service branch for comparison. We can, however, state that in Ofer there is no reluctance among the women to accept the authority of the men. In all mixed branches, authority is in the hands of the men, and there seem to be no discipline problems. This has also been found to be true by Simpson and Simpson (1969); they do not, however, seem to see any difference in whether the authority of a woman is exercised over men or women.

We have not yet made explicit the personality type of the dominant women. For the most part, they are in their fifties and the mothers of from two to four children. They are respected by men as well as by other women. Compared to nondominant women, they are austere, serious, and somewhat moralistic. An interesting sidelight is that while dominant men tend to have many extramarital affairs, dominant women tend to refrain from any extramarital activity. This stands in opposition to the usual pattern; women, as a group, have had more extramarital affairs than men. True, half the dominant women are wives of dominant men—but then the other half are not. The most common extramarital pairing is a dominant man with a younger, nondominant woman, but some nondominant women the same age as the dominant women also have extramarital affairs.

The limited possibility of comparison with all-male groups, and the absence of all-female groups outside the service sphere, preclude our coming to an unambiguous conclusion about whether the peculiar traits of hierarchies of women in the kibbutz can be attributed significantly to their being women. Etzioni (1957) attributes the male-female differences between work branches to women's branches being in service and therefore under the constant social control of a wide clientele, while men's branches, doing production work, have an anonymous market. Also, the service branches demand comparatively unspecialized training, the production branches more highly specialized training. The first usually have no institutional backing except in child care; the economic committee always gives the production branches strong institutional backing.[4] It is difficult to refute the possibility that factors other than sexual differences (such as those discussed by Etzioni) are decisive because of the difficulty of finding a control group—an all-female production branch. However, our observations of mixed groups do, we feel, support our hypothesis.[5]

THE POLITICAL SYSTEM

We have seen that most women work in all-female groups, yet we are hard put to find any of these in the political system, at least officially. There has never been an all-female elected committee in Ofer. However, in one year the few men elected to the education committee were almost completely inactive on it; they had conflicting demands on their time and attended very infrequently. While all-male committees are uncommon, a number have been elected, despite warnings at election time from various members of the Assembly about the unfairness of electing one-sex committees. There is a gradation: while an all-male committee is regarded as inappropriate, a formally elected all-female committee has been almost unthinkable up to the present time. Even where there is an unbalanced ratio, men normally take disproportionate part. For instance, the education committee often has seven women and two men, but one of the men is likely to be the chairman. By contrast, the economic committee usually contains eight men and one woman, but some years there have been no women at all, and no woman has ever chaired this committee.

The official argument against all-male committees is that women should be represented on every committee. Women have recurrently proposed allocating at least one or two seats in each committee to women. These motions have always been turned down; the formal argument for having a man as chairman of a female-dominated committee has been that since the main executive power is *de facto* all male, men must be elected to the chairmanship, because only they can get along (*lehistader*) with the male executives and thus ensure efficiency. This argument, though circular, is to some extent true; women may very effectively extract performance benefiting their own homes, but several politically active women told us privately that they felt an all-female committee would not work as well as a mixed-sex one. Men openly say that women are not objective and energetic enough to pursue important tasks in any sphere of kibbutz life.

The few *de facto* all-female committees that have existed in Ofer were not very successful. But unsuccessful committees are hardly exceptional in Ofer, so we cannot conclude that an all-female group has less chance of success than an all-male or mixed one. In the absence of comparative material, we can only note the ethnographic fact that there is a consensus against all-female committees.

This basic asymmetry is made clear in Table 33, which summarizes the gender of committee chairmen and members over several years.

We can see that during six years, fifty-four committees were elected in Ofer, of which five were all-male and none all-female. Only three committees usually had a majority of women—education, housing, and health care. However, only the education committee had a strong majority of women (1:2.6), and it had a man for a chairman for three of the six years. On the health-care committee, a major focus of women's activity, a man presided for five years, though he was the only man on the committee. Total membership in committees present a male-over-female ratio of 1.777, but the chairmanship ratio is 2.6.

SUMMARY

The political rights of women have always been much more clearly acknowledged than their right to similar work. The implementation of these political rights, however, was impaired as early as the forties. We have found that today women attend the General Assembly less than men do, both in absolute numbers and in per-

Table 33
Sex Composition of Nine Major Committees in Ofer, 1968–73 (asterisks indicate sex of chairman)

Years/Sex — Name of Committee	1968 Men	1968 Women	1969 Men	1969 Women	1970 Men	1970 Women	1971 Men	1971 Women	1972 Men	1972 Women	1973 Men	1973 Women	6-Year Average Men	6-Year Average Women
Secretariat	7*	2	10*	—	7*	2	6*	2	6*	2	8*	1	7.33	1.5
Economy	9*	1	9*	1	8*	—	9*	—	8*	—	8*	1	8.5	0.5
Work	5*	2	7*	2	7*	2	5*	1	5*	1	5*	1	5.66	1.5
Social Affairs	4*	3	3*	4	4	3*	4	3*	4	3*	5*	3	4.0	3.16
Education	3*	5	2*	5	2	7*	2	7*	2	7*	3*	5	2.33	6.0
Housing	2	5*	4	3*	3*	3	3	3*	3	2*	1	4*	2.66	3.33
Health Care	2*	3	2*	3	1*	3	1*	3	2*	3	2	3*	1.66	3.0
Higher Education	7*	1	7*	—	7*	1	7*	1	7*	1	7*	1	7.0	0.83
Culture	6*	3	5*	4	5*	3	4	7*	4	7*	3	5*	4.50	4.83
Total	45	25	49	22	43	23	41	27	41	26	42	24	43.5	24.5
Total Chairmen	8	1	8	1	7	2	5	4	5	4	6	3	6.5	2.5

centages. Older women attend more often than younger ones do (especially those between the ages of twenty-two and thirty-five). When women do attend Assemblies, they are much less active than men are; they take the floor less often and more briefly. Even special Assemblies do not attract relatively more women than men.

We have found considerable sexual polarization of interest in elected offices and committee members. Higher offices, committees dealing with overall management, work, economy, finance, and planning are male-dominated. Among all the kibbutzim, committees dealing with education, social affairs, health, and various aspects of social welfare have a slight majority of women, but are not dominated by them, except perhaps the education committee. Generally, the higher the level of authority of an office or committee, the lower the percentage of women in its personnel—a finding similar to the one of Duverger in Europe (1955) for a variety of political and economic bodies. In the highest echelons of authority, kibbutz women are severely underrepresented. The younger adult population is more polarized than the general population—in both sphere and level of activity—except for what seems to be adjustive tokenism, or lip service to equality; this is shown by nominating women to central political positions created especially for them. Still, there is a great deal less sexual polarization in political activity than in work, as the SPI indicates.

The authority of women is concentrated in a few dominant women with marked characteristics: they are very equable and somewhat puritanical; they are approaching or past menopause; they are usually respected by both men and other women; their authority and influence tend to be more specific than the dominant men's.

Both work and political activity may, of course, be influenced by that sphere of kibbutz life we are about to examine—education.

Chapter 7

The Education of Women in the Kibbutz

It is widely acknowledged that the educational system of the kibbutz is the best in Israel. The public one is widely criticized; there are always controversies among proponents of technical, linguistic, religious, humanitarian, and professional emphases. It is a measure of both human adaptation and the ephemeral role of cultural patterns that the unwarlike Jews of Europe, draft dodgers and scholars alike, should settle a new country and there produce a brilliant military, but an indifferent educational, system.

In her book *Commitment and Community,* Rosabeth Moss Kanter (1972) undertakes to make a distinction between successful and unsuccessful communes in nineteenth-century America (her criterion is whether the community lasted more than twenty-five years, "the sociological definition of a generation"). Kanter does not go on to say whether the twenty-five years add up to anything more than longevity—that is, whether the commune succeeded in socializing a new generation, for just as procreation assures biological continuity, socialization assures social continuity.

In a society with a long history, continuity is usually taken for granted. In a planned, revolutionary, utopian community, the values, norms, and role system must all be transmitted to the second generation or the experiment will end with the founders. The founders, socialized in their country of origin, must assume that their own personality is not ideally adapted to the society they seek to create. They themselves must be resocialized through revolutionary fervor, commitment, and deep solidarity (Lifton 1968). But this process can never be as effective as the socialization of a child "uncontaminated" by the prerevolutionary value system. Socialization and education, then, are expected to create a new personality completely adapted to the exigencies of the new society. This assumption is itself utopian, and it makes heavy demands on education.

The kibbutz is no exception. Authors who have studied kibbutz socialization (e.g., Spiro, Rabin, Bettelheim, Liegle) stress the almost holy attitude with which educational work is done there. The ideologists of kibbutz education (Golan, Messinger, etc.) have repeatedly stated that the aim of collective education is to create a new personality adapted to the kibbutz social structure, inculcated with its basic aims and values, and the specific norms that result from those values. Since sexual equality is part of the value system, it should be an important component of the new personality, and the founders spent a great deal of time considering the question. Women were certainly to have the same rights, duties, and socialization as men. And as we shall see, this assumption has been almost completely implemented. But did equality really mean sameness in everything but gender-linked activities such as pregnancy, childbirth, and nursing?

As hard as they tried, the founders of the kibbutz could not quite escape their own cultural background. Most of them came from small, traditional East European Jewish communities. This society had enormous respect for education, which was religious and intellectual rather than practical. The study of the Torah and Talmud gave a youngster far more prestige than wealth ever could. But extensive education was for boys only. Girls' education was limited to basic reading and writing in Yiddish and to knowing the Hebrew prayers. Women were thought to need no more, for they were not part of the religious community; they were not initiated by the traditional bar mitzvah ceremony and were forbidden a role in the *minyan,* the basic quorum for religious rites. But sexual inequality went beyond religion. A Jewish woman was supposed to devote herself to the care of her children and her home. And those few women who were active in the family's economic enterprise were also held responsible for the house and children.

Given this background of theirs, the founders of the kibbutzim brought about a great revolution indeed. The kibbutz assumed women's equal status with men. It transferred responsibility for child care and consumption from the housewife to the community. It gave women an equal share in creating and legitimizing values and in attending cultural activities and ceremonies. A fundamental, symbolic indicator of the change is the reformed bar mitzvah ceremony for girls. In Jewish Orthodox religious law, the concept bat mitzvah (daughter of the commandments) is senseless, but in the kibbutz it is completely accepted. Since most kibbutzim are not religious, the concept *mitzvah* (religious commandment) has been transformed into kibbutz *mitzvah,* which includes working effectively, doing night watch, learning the environment, etc. Both boys and girls must perform such tasks at age thirteen. Unlike its counterpart in North America, for example, which only superficially resembles the male ceremony, the bat mitzvah in the kibbutz is the same as the bar mitzvah.

We have said that education may influence the sexual division of labor and of political activity on the kibbutz. And education keeps changing; as generations come and go, education may cease to be an independent variable and become a dependent one. The sexual division of work and political activity in the first generation certainly did influence education. We must investigate the adults who teach and the children who are taught. We have a great deal of information about the adults, but very little about children in the early days of the kibbutz.

In his autobiography, *A Village by the Jordan,* Joseph Baratz (1960) recounts that when his first child was born—the first baby of the first *kvutza*— ". . . everybody fussed about him and nobody knew what to do with him. Our women did not know how to look after babies. There was nobody whose advice Miriam [the mother] could ask. The other women were still younger than she was. She found her own methods . . . wherever she went, she took the baby with her. She took him to the vegetable plots, to the kitchen and to the poultry run. If she was in the cowshed she put him down on the straw and the cow licked him. The whole of Degania cried over the baby: they cried because they thought he would die of dirt . . . when another child was born in the colony, she proposed to its mother that each of them should take it in turn to look after both of the babies, but the other mother only wanted to look after her own, so both of them went on overworking . . . it was a difficult problem. How were the women both to work and to look after their children? Should each mother look after her own family and do nothing else? But the women wouldn't hear of giving up their share of the communal work and life.

Should one woman look after all the children? It seemed strange at first. How could a mother hand over her child to another? Somebody proposed that the colony should hire a nurse. But Joseph Bussell [1] said the children must belong to their parents but the responsibilities for them must be shared by all. In this sense they are the children of the *kvutza*. All the women, whether single or married, should take part in looking after them, then the mothers could do other work as well. And the cost of the education of the children must be borne by the community as a whole. So we didn't hire nurses, but we chose one girl to look after the lot of them, and we put aside a house where they could spend the day while the mothers were at work."

To a great extent, collective education answered the problem of women's work. If women were to work in agriculture and thus be unavailable to their children during the day, education had to be collectivized. Significantly, no one suggested that men look after the children. From the first, women were less reluctant to care for their own children than to work in the kitchen, laundry, or communal store. This emerged clearly in our group interviews. One of the female founders of Tsvi told us:

"We saw education as one of the central tasks of our collective creation. It wasn't something inferior. To the contrary, rearing children brought into relief our identification with the group. We felt that by rearing children we were working for the collective as much as someone who worked in the cowshed. I was the first kindergarten teacher in the *kvutza*. There was very intense interaction between the parents and educators."

In the first kibbutzim founded in the Second Aliyah, children's housing had not become a problem. Child care was collectivized, but the children spent afternoons and nights in their parents' rooms. Only in the Third Aliyah, probably under the impact of still more radical socialist ideology, did children spend their nights in dormitories that were part of the comprehensive house (see page 304). Some kibbutzim of the Second Aliyah did not change their original housing system; others did. Until 1954 only four kibbutzim had familistic housing (Degania Alef, Degania Bet, Kiryat Anavim, and Ein Harod). After 1954 some of the Ichud kibbutzim changed back to the familistic system, and today about twenty Ichud kibbutzim—about 9 per cent of all kibbutzim—have familistic housing.

The theory and practice of collective education crystallized slowly, becoming organized only in the late thirties and early forties. A detailed account of this process would be disproportionate in this book,[2] but a brief, general description of everyday life of the education system in Ofer is in order.

DAILY LIFE IN THE CHILDREN'S QUARTER OF OFER

At five o'clock in the morning, the first nursing mothers come to the babies' house, take them from the cribs, and feed them, by breast or by bottle. By that time the nurse has arrived and prepared the babies' baths. She chats with the mothers about their babies' development. The cheerful work of bathing the babies is shared by the mothers and the nurse. The babies are diapered and dressed, and the sleepy mothers leave one by one. The nurse puts the babies back in the crib. When it is warmer outside, she puts them in playpens in a shaded part of the yard.

The babies' schedule is organized around the nursing times, 5:00 A.M., 9:00 A.M., noon, 4:00 P.M., and 9:00 P.M. The nurse cares for the babies between the nursing periods. She cleans them, brings them back into the house when it is too hot outside, prepares their bottles, and scrupulously cleans the house. Her workday is from 5:30 A.M. to 1:00 P.M., when the second nursing period is over. Then she rests while an assistant watches the sleeping babies. At four o'clock the nurse returns to give the babies to their parents, who will bring them back at about seven o'clock and prepare for the last nursing. At 9:00 P.M. the night watch arrives and assumes responsibility for the babies during the night.

Older babies constitute a new unit, called *gemulon* (literally, "the weaned"), with the same nurse and house. They are fed by the nurse and have more space for crawling and playing. Their apartment is decorated with more pictures and toys. They have more contact with one another as well as with the nurse. A mother may visit in the morning before work, to take a quick glance at her sleeping baby or, if it is awake, to greet it with a kiss. She returns to spend half an hour with the baby between 9:00 and 10:00 A.M. when she may take it out for a short walk. At about 4:00, parents take the babies to their apartments, returning them at about 7:30 to put them to bed. Between this time and the arrival of the night watch, one of the parents arrives to watch the children. The nurse, assisted by a younger girl during the early afternoon, brings food from the kitchen, feeds the babies, cleans them, dresses them, and watches them play.

The next unit, the *peuton* (literally, "small ones"), consists of children from two to three and a half years old. Now the toddlers receive their main meal and hygiene training. They have many toys to play with and a large, fenced playground where they can expend their energy in the morning. Occasionally the nurse takes them on short trips to the kitchen or to the children's store.

Between the age of three and a half and four, the children change their nurse and house for the first time. They go to the kindergarten, a big house with five bedrooms, a large dining room, two playrooms, lavatories, a kitchen corner, and a large playground. A kindergarten teacher and two nurses share the work for each multiage group of twelve to fifteen children. The daily program varies with the age of the children. The younger ones spend most of their time at play and on trips. The older ones are gradually taught to read and write by the kindergarten teacher. The afternoon rest period is now shorter, and the children spend more time listening to stories and music and playing games. They also begin to help with the work. They clean the tables, dry the dishes, sweep the floors, and make their beds.

When they leave kindergarten at the age of seven, the children reenter a one-age group, called a class (*kita*), and move to another house with a new nurse. Since 1970 the children of Ofer have gone to the district school in a kibbutz eight miles away. They are awakened at 6:30 A.M. by the nurse, who helps them dress themselves and prepare for their school day. At 7:15, after a quick breakfast in the dining room, they leave for school. The school bus brings them back at 12:30. The nurse is waiting with a hot lunch, which they consume in their own dining room. They spend the early afternoon in rest and play and go to their parents' rooms at about 4:30. The nurse cleans the house while they are gone. The children spend part of this time doing homework in their parents' apartment or in their own study room. From kindergarten age on, the children eat dinner with their parents in the general dining room.

At the age of thirteen, the children change to another district school, which is divided into a junior and senior high. They wake up earlier, leave at seven o'clock and return at 1:00 and 2:30 on alternate days. They spend the afternoon playing and studying. Late in the afternoon, they may attend the activities of the Children's Society: sports, trips to places near the kibbutz, educational activities, musical and cultural activities such as preparing for the Shabbat or writing for the Children's Society bulletin. The older they are, the more they work—from one and a half hours every other day in the seventh grade, up to four or five hours daily in the twelfth grade.

The children's day is a busy one. They see their parents only at afternoon tea or coffee in their parents' apartments and at dinner. At thirteen, the children put themselves to bed, though the parents still come to say good night. The nurse's job becomes more and more limited. When children reach the higher grades, the nurse works only half a day, and her main task is supervising their schedule, ensuring that they awake in time for school, bringing and fetching their laundry, and keeping in contact with the school about their academic development.

The peer group is very important in the children's education from their earliest years, but its impact becomes decisive in late childhood and adolescence when the children spend most of their time with their peers, who become their ultimate and unrivaled focus of attention and source of prestige. By the time they are seventeen, they have assumed responsibilities in the work of the kibbutz as a whole and are attending the General Assembly.

The entire system is supervised by the education committee, which nominates nurses, elects candidates for teachers' training, arranges refresher courses for its personnel, coordinates the efforts of parents, nurses, teachers, and youth leaders, deals with the needs of retarded and talented children, and with security and discipline. Once a week the personnel of a wider age group such as of junior high school meet a clinical psychologist to discuss the problems of the age group. Sometimes the psychologist lectures all the educational personnel and the parents on specific problems, such as bed-wetting and sex education.

KIBBUTZ WOMEN'S EDUCATION

Does the educational system of the kibbutz encourage sex differences in work and political activity? Surely not by intention. If anything, early socialization in educational institutions disregards sex differences. Naturally, the children are aware of sexual dimorphism because they see each other naked. And as we have already noted, the Hebrew language, being extremely gender-oriented, contributes to gender awareness. But great conscious effort is made to avoid accentuating sex differences in normative behavior. All children are dressed in the same "work clothes" in the children's house. There is no sex difference in the style of haircut. Children take whatever they want from the pool of toys; girls are not encouraged to play with dolls, boys are not encouraged to play with cars and trucks. The children do not hear such sex-typed injunctions as "It isn't nice for girls to . . ." and "Boys shouldn't . . ." Girls often climb trees, play very energetic ball games, and engage in fights. Boys cry without shame, handle dolls, learn to cook, and sometimes knit.

But the children also spend part of each day in their parents' apartments, where they quickly become aware of the sexual division of labor. Their fathers return from the fields in oily, dirty overalls, and their mothers return from the children's houses or the kitchen. Children learn that problems of food and clothing are their mothers' concern; problems of electricity, garden water pipes, and repairs are their fathers'. They see differences between their fathers' and their mothers' clothes and hair styles. Visiting relatives, especially grandparents, introduce more evidence of sex differences, including gifts of sex-typed toys and clothes.

Sex typing in the parents' homes is still less than in individualistic socialization; child care is very egalitarian. Compared to the task-oriented nurses, both parents are expressive and warm (Bar Yosef 1959). Using a psychoanalytic perspective, Rabin (1965) has stated that Oedipal factors are much weaker in kibbutz children than in children of the same ages in the moshav, the cooperative settlement system. Rabin's explanation for this is that the male child has less intense contact with his mother and that the division of authority between the father and mother is comparatively egalitarian. Kugelmass and Breznitz (1965, 1966) have found that fourteen-year-old kibbutz girls see their mothers as instrumental-achievement-oriented and their fathers as "expressive," or emotional, and that city girls do not. Lifschitz (1973) compared preferential attitudes toward parents in kibbutz and city children aged six to fifteen. She found that kibbutz girls preferred their fathers to their mothers, whereas city girls made no distinction, and that city boys explicitly preferred their fathers, whereas kibbutz boys made no distinction.

So despite the sex typing impact of the parents' home, kibbutz adolescents appear to have a markedly lower level of polar gender classification than their moshav or city peers. From this we can conclude that early socialization has at the very least a considerable equalizing effect on the basic attitudes of children toward sexual division of labor.

During adolescence, the equalizing effect of socialization continues. The Children's Society is the main vehicle of education at this age and is conceived as a small-scale blueprint ideal of kibbutz life (Golan 1961). Socializing by anticipation, it tries to translate kibbutz values into everyday reality for the youngsters. Dar (1974) points out that the social structure of the Children's Society is close to the Bund type of the kibbutz—that is, the revolutionary communion in which the commitment to and the implementation of communal values is almost complete. The Children's Society tries to counteract any "anti-revolutionary" influence of the parents' home and of daily life in the kibbutz. It has its own political system, complete with Assembly, committees, and officers. Girls are very active, frequently filling the highest posts in the very task-oriented system. The youngsters emphasize performance, not personal indulgence or hedonism. Gerson (1968) found that the attitude toward work of girls in the Kibbutz Artzi is much more egalitarian than that of the girls in Kibbutz Meuchad: the Kibbutz Artzi emphasizes the Children's Society much more than the Kibbutz Meuchad does.

In recent years Western youth culture has penetrated the kibbutz. Pop music, clothing fads, sexual experimentation, and other components of "having a good time" and "living in the present" have had their effect on kibbutz youngsters, to the extent that there is hidden but real conflict between the new influences and the Children's Society ideologies of action, performance, and creativity. The former are slowly prevailing because of their apparent attractiveness to young people and because of support from the parallel familization of the kibbutz (see Chapter 9). One indication of this is the new relative permissiveness in early heterosexual relations (homosexuality in the kibbutz appears to be virtually nonexistent). Shepher (1971) found that girls in Kibbutz Yaara start their sexual activity at the age of fifteen, boys about two years later. Natan and Schnabel (1972) compared the attitudes of seventeen- and eighteen-year-old kibbutz adolescents to those of a city control group as to the acceptable age of starting sexual intercourse. Table 34 shows the results:

Table 34
Attitudes of City and Kibbutz Adolescents Toward Acceptable Age of Starting Heterosexual Relationships (in percentages)

	Boys		Girls	
Acceptable Age for Beginning Heterosexual Relationships	City	Kibbutz	City	Kibbutz
By Age 16	25.0	20.5	4.0	20.7
Ages 17–18	42.0	48.3	16.0	53.1
Total By Age 18	67.0	68.8	20.0	73.8

Almost three-quarters of the kibbutz girls find heterosexual relationships acceptable by the age of eighteen, as do a somewhat lower percentage of kibbutz boys. Fewer kibbutz adolescents than city adolescents claim they accept the "double standard." (There is no difference in attitudes between kibbutz boys and city boys in this regard, but an enormous difference between kibbutz girls and city girls, though what specific effects these attitudes may have in actual behavior is certainly open to serious question.) Establishing a sense of personal dignity and skill in the conduct of sexual relations is widely felt to be central to adult competence; the egalitarian attitudes of kibbutz men and women indicate the far-reaching consequences of kibbutz socialization in this area. While attitudes may not reflect behavior (they do not, for instance, in kibbutz sexual politics), the data of Natan and Schnabel agree with what information there is on the sexual behavior of kibbutz youth. The earlier maturation of girls than of boys—the normal pattern in the human species—is manifested, however marginally, in their sexual behavior and attitudes. In any event, the men and women of the kibbutz clearly did not learn about sex as a transaction between older, manipulative, or importuning men and younger, resisting, quasi-virginal women—and this is a major difference between socialization in the kibbutz and socialization both elsewhere in Israel and in most of Western society.

Let us now turn to male-female differences in academic achievement and number of years of education. In the kibbutz, girls and boys receive the same primary and secondary educations. Some district schools offer elective courses to students of sixteen and seventeen that may have sex-typing connotations, such as cooking, nursing, tailoring, agrotechniques,and aviation. The first three are offered only to girls, the last two predominantly, but not exclusively, to boys. Many other elective courses are not significantly sex-typed (foreign languages, art, biochemistry, agriculture, physics, mathematics, sociology, and psychology). There are only two district schools with a professional department where most courses are not coeducational. The overwhelming majority of kibbutz children receive the same education for eighteen years.

Dar (1974) analyzed sex differences in achievement in a group of 700 boys and girls of the kibbutz who in 1970 studied in forty-eight classes of the tenth, eleventh, and twelfth grades in six district schools in northern Israel. The study used the grades of the National Examination (*seker,* literally, "review"), given in the eighth grade and similar to the Eleven Plus in England. Dar also used teachers' evaluations of the students' abilities and achievements, and added two tests of ability, the Milta (Other and Morcialli 1966) and the Raven (1956). He found that:

1. In all five subdivisions of the National Examination, boys scored higher than girls; in four of the five, the differences were statistically significant (the nonsignificant difference was in vocabulary, the greatest difference in mathematics).

2. In all subdivisions of both ability tests, boys scored higher than girls. In five of the six subdivisions of the ability tests, the differences were significant; again the nonsignificant difference was in vocabulary, the greatest difference in mathematics.

3. Teachers evaluated girls significantly superior to boys in literature and languages. In history and sociology, there were no differences between the sexes. In biology and mathematics, boys were rated significantly superior to girls. In overall *ability* or "potential," boys were rated significantly superior, but there was no difference in ratings of *achievement*.

Dar felt that boys began senior high school with an advantage, so he weighed the achievement and ability results by using tests of covariance. He found that:

4. In the two ability tests boys scored significantly higher than girls in sociology, biology, and overall achievement, but that in literature there were no differences. Teachers' evaluations of students' abilities again resulted in higher ratings for boys. Evaluations of achievement resulted in statistically nonsignificant higher ratings for girls.

5. To eliminate the possible impact of "native ability," the author held ability constant by dividing the entire sample into four quartiles. Again, boys scored higher in all tests except for language achievement in the highest quartile.

The results greatly surprised the author. Despite technical difficulty, he was able to compare series of results of similar studies in Israel and elsewhere. He concluded that his results generally resemble those in Israel and the Western world—the higher linguistic achievement of girls in lower grades, the gradual disappearance of this advantage, the advantage enjoyed by girls in teachers' evaluations compared to objective tests, etc. *Nevertheless, differences between the sexes were found to be greater in the kibbutz than outside it.* The boys are superior not only in mathematics and biology but in sociology and sometimes even in history and languages. And although the boys' superiority is almost always statistically significant, the girls' usually is not.

Why, despite an equalizing socialization system of the kibbutz, is there a greater difference in achievement and ability between the sexes than there is in more traditional sex-typed socialization? Not because of the system of socialization, Dar believes, but in spite of it. He concludes that the reasons are anticipation of the actual division of labor in the adult world and the intrusion of "Western youth culture." Anticipating their work in the adult world, from contact with their mothers and from a gradual introduction to adult female roles during adolescence, girls do not bother much with studies of minor occupational relevance. The conflict between egalitarian socialization and polarized division of adult labor predisposes them to retreat from academic achievement into expressive, erotic, and familistic orientations. The results are early sexual activity, early marriage, and rising birth rate.

The only problem with Dar's ingenious analysis is that the boys' secondary education is just as irrelevant to future occupations as the girls' is.[3] High schools give both sexes a wide, basic education, not a narrowly vocational one. Most of the boys will work as farmers, electricians, industrial workers, etc., yet there are few preparatory courses for these jobs. Few kibbutz high schools teach agriculture; those that do make it an elective, which not many boys choose. The boys study physics, chemistry, etc., but usually on a theoretical rather than on a practical level. One could even argue that the general curriculum is occupationally more relevant to girls since a larger percentage of them become teachers.

Kibbutz youngsters are prepared for their occupations by gradual introduction to various jobs in the kibbutz from the sixth grade on. By the time they are seventeen or eighteen, most boys and girls are already filling very important roles in work branches—boys in agriculture or artisan shops, girls in the children's houses. After army service, kibbutzniks join their permanent work branches and may then be sent to school for one or more professional courses that add theoretical background to their practical skills.

The great difference between boys' and girls' academic ability and achievement, then, may be not vocational relevance but rather girls' anticipation of the family role and maternity. Why this should result in relatively low academic ability and achievement is difficult to understand; examining boys' and girls' educational level and the kinds of education they receive may be helpful. Data are plentiful, and we can compare the two federations according to generations and seniority groups. We have distinguished seven levels of education: eight years or less of school; partial secondary education (less than twelve years); full secondary education (twelve complete years); higher nonacademic education; academic education short of a bachelor's degree; baccalaureate completed; graduate and postgraduate studies.

The category "higher nonacademic," which needs special explanation, involves many women. It includes all courses of higher education that do not end in an academic degree but that require on the average two years of study. It prepares one to be a kindergarten teacher, primary-school teacher, nurse, medical assistant, artist, or technician. Until 1967 it prepared one to be a high-school teacher, but now all high-school teachers are required to obtain at least a bachelor's degree.

The following table shows the level of education by sex and by generation. For comparison, one can keep in mind that Israeli Jews had an average 8.62 years of education in 1972—8.95 for men and 8.10 for women.

Table 35
Educational Level, by Sex and Generation (in percentages)

Sex and Generation / Educational Level		Second Generation		Kibbutz-Bred		First Generation		Total	
		M	F	M	F	M	F	M	F
Elementary (8 years or less)	K.A.	0.5	0.8	41.5	43.2	14.1	14.2	13.4	13.4
	I.	2.2	1.0	31.5	36.9	15.5	14.6	13.0	12.9
Partial Secondary (9–11 years)	K.A.	1.6	0.9	13.2	13.0	33.5	31.5	20.7	21.2
	I.	12.3	7.2	28.8	25.9	25.1	24.8	21.6	20.7
Full Secondary (12 years)	K.A.	91.2	85.1	32.9	27.5	28.6	25.8	49.1	42.3
	I.	77.2	76.1	30.5	26.4	38.1	35.0	48.9	44.4
Higher Nonacademic	K.A.	3.4	11.8	8.6	15.0	7.7	19.7	6.3	16.9
	I.	2.9	13.0	2.7	8.8	5.9	15.7	4.8	14.4
College (less than Bachelor's Degree)	K.A.	1.8	0.9	2.3	0.8	11.6	6.6	7.3	4.5
	I.	2.2	1.7	1.9	0.9	7.8	5.8	5.7	4.5
College (B.A., B.S.)	K.A.	1.5	0.4	1.3	0.5	3.4	1.6	2.5	1.2
	I.	2.6	0.9	3.4	1.1	5.8	3.4	4.5	2.6
Post–graduate	K.A.	0.1	0	0.3	0	1.1	0.6	0.7	0.4
	I.	0.7	0.1	1.2	0	1.9	0.8	1.5	0.6
Total	K.A.	100	100	100	100	100	100	100	100
	I.	100	100	100	100	100	100	100	100
Average Number of Years of Education	K.A.	12.10	12.19	9.53	9.48	10.03	11.12	11.16	11.24
	I.	11.85	12.12	9.79	9.49	11.12	11.21	11.16	11.31

The following conclusions can be drawn:

1. There are great differences between the three generations. The second generation has the highest average educational level, more than complete secondary education. The kibbutz-bred group has the lowest level, nine and a half years of education; this group consists mainly of Youth Aliyah groups composed of many refugees whose education had been interrupted or curtailed by their or their parents' movement. The first generation has an average education of about eleven years; many of the founders could not complete their secondary education in their countries of origin or preferred to immigrate to Israel, even at the cost of interrupted schooling. The comparatively high percentage of academic education in this generation results from the fact that in a number of kibbutzim people joined the kibbutz with an academic degree from abroad. In one kibbutz thirty-nine members had Ph.D.'s from Germany.

2. There is a very slight difference between the sexes in average years of education: in both federations, women receive a little more education than men. In the first and second generations, the difference is marginal. In the kibbutz-bred group, men have somewhat more education. If, moreover, we examine the form of education, we see significant differences between the sexes. In both federations, more men than women have full secondary educations. At least three times as many women as men have higher nonacademic education, but more men than women obtain a baccalaureate degree (the ratio of men to women is 1.5 in the Ichud, 1.73 in the Kibbutz Artzi). In short, both sexes go to school for about the same number of years, but more men have academic higher education and more women have nonacademic higher education.

3. There is no difference between the federations in average years of education.

Table 36 represents the seniority groups.

We can conclude that:

1. There are almost no differences between the seniority groups. Almost all male and female seniority groups have an average education of about eleven years. This is probably because the different generation groups within each seniority group equalize one another.

2. In each group the average educational level of the women

Table 36
Educational Level, by Sex and Seniority (in percentages)

Education Level	Sex and Group	Group I		Group II		Group III		Group IV		Total	
		M	F	M	F	M	F	M	F	M	F
Elementary (8 years or less)	K.A.	8.4	8.2	14.1	14.7	18.8	18.7	14.6	13.0	13.4	13.4
	I.	16.9	16.2	9.6	8.1	10.6	11.4	8.5	7.7	13.0	12.9
Partial Secondary (9–11 years)	K.A.	17.8	19.9	20.8	22.5	24.0	21.2	22.5	17.0	20.7	21.2
	I.	19.5	19.5	18.1	16.1	25.4	25.7	23.4	14.8	21.6	20.7
Full Secondary (12 years)	K.A.	56.1	47.8	49.1	41.9	41.0	35.0	42.6	39.5	49.1	42.3
	I.	50.9	46.5	47.3	42.3	46.8	40.4	49.6	51.4	48.9	44.4
Higher Nonacademic	K.A.	6.0	17.3	6.2	15.5	5.6	17.7	8.7	23.7	6.3	16.9
	I.	4.2	11.9	5.8	21.3	5.2	14.6	4.3	16.9	4.8	14.4
College (less than Bachelor's Degree)	K.A.	7.7	5.0	7.0	4.0	7.6	5.8	7.7	4.7	7.3	4.5
	I.	4.3	3.6	8.6	6.9	6.3	4.5	6.1	3.1	5.7	4.5
College (B.A., B.S.)	K.A.	2.8	1.4	2.2	1.0	2.5	1.3	3.3	1.8	2.5	1.2
	I.	2.9	1.6	8.8	4.5	4.1	2.9	7.0	4.0	4.5	2.6
Postgraduate	K.A.	1.0	0.4	0.6	0.4	0.4	0.3	0.6	1.8	0.7	0.4
	I.	1.5	0.6	1.8	1.0	1.6	0.5	1.0	0.2	1.5	0.6
Total	K.A.	100	100	100	100	100	100	100	100	100	100
	I.	100	100	100	100	100	100	100	100	100	100
Average Number of Years of Education	K.A.	11.52	11.61	11.09	11.1	10.73	10.97	11.13	11.77	11.16	11.24
	I.	10.95	11.01	11.70	11.96	11.28	11.29	11.47	11.82	11.16	11.31

is very slightly higher than that of the men; the greatest difference, in Group IV of the Kibbutz Artzi, is a bit more than a half-year.

3. In all seniority groups, a considerably higher percentage of women receive higher nonacademic education, and a higher percentage of men receive higher academic training.

4. The overall differences between the federations are again very small, but they vary according to seniority group. In the first seniority group, the Kibbutz Artzi has a higher average; in Groups II to IV, the Ichud.

We noted above that there are three forms of postsecondary education in the kibbutz: professional courses, higher nonacademic training, and higher academic education. Because the professional courses are closely involved with kibbutz work branches, we can classify them as we did the branches and their work—"masculine," "feminine," and neutral courses. Agriculture, industry, and artisanship are masculine courses, and medical workers, feminine. The third category consists mostly of courses in arts and crafts and cultural activity (see Table 37).

The following facts are obvious from this table:

1. The second generation is very underrepresented in professional courses—mainly because a larger percentage of them has an academic education.

2. In all generations, the courses are sexually polarized. About four times as many men as women attend masculine courses, and about ten times as many women as men attend feminine ones. A slightly higher percentage of women than men attends neutral courses.

3. The degree of polarization is high and is similar in the two federations. In both federations a larger percentage of women takes professional courses and a larger percentage of men goes into academic education.

The analysis of professional courses according to seniority groups presents a similar picture of sexual polarization.

Let us now look at higher nonacademic education, which is usually reserved for those in the higher echelons of education, such as medical nurses and assistants, handicrafts and art teachers, and technicians (Table 38).

Table 37
Professional Courses (nonacademic, less than a year), by Sex and Generation
(in percentages)

Sex and Generation Professional Courses		Second Generation		Kibbutz-Bred		First Generation		Total	
		M	F	M	F	M	F	M	F
No Courses	K.A.	83.1	82	60	55	53	51	61.4	57.8
	I.	87.6	84.3	67.5	54.8	66.5	62.6	72.9	67.3
"Masculine" Courses	K.A.	15	4	33	7.9	37	8.6	31.2	7.6
	I.	10.6	2.3	26.8	5.9	26.2	6.5	21.5	5.5
"Feminine" Courses	K.A.	0.6	11	3	33.4	4.8	35	3.5	30.2
	I.	0.7	10.2	1.6	31.5	3.4	25.3	2.4	22.0
Neutral Courses	K.A.	1.1	2.7	3.6	3.6	4.8	5.1	3.8	4.4
	I.	1.2	3.1	3.9	7.7	3.7	5.6	3.5	5.1
Total	K.A.	100	100	100	100	100	100	100	100
	I.	100	100	100	100	100	100	100	100

1. As we can see, most kindergarten and primary-school teachers are women. We can assume that most of the 3 per cent of the male population trained for early educational work are in primary schools. More than four times as many women as men are in this category. The combined category includes curricula for kindergarten and primary-school teachers; both programs take three years. The courses are separate, but the diploma is rated at the same level in Israel and also in the kibbutz. The few men who do teach never teach kindergarten. There were some two or three cases in the past of men who were trained as kindergarten teachers, but they did not remain on the job.

2. Until 1967, the kibbutz teachers' colleges trained high-school teachers (it is only recently that they became academic). The teachers' colleges now give a B.A. after one additional year of university. These colleges contain slightly more men than women—which upholds the generalization that the higher the level of edu-

Table 38
Higher Nonacademic Education, by Sex and Generation (in percentages)

Higher Nonacademic Education		Second Generation		Kibbutz-Bred		First Generation		Total	
		M	F	M	F	M	F	M	F
No Education	K.A.	91.1	76.0	88.6	81.6	87.0	75.8	88.1	76.4
	I.	95.4	82.9	95.2	88.7	90.5	79.2	92.3	80.9
Kindergarten and Primary School Teachers	K.A.	1.7	13.4	3.2	10.2	3.6	13.7	3.1	13.4
	I.	1.2	9.1	1.9	7.5	2.4	13.0	2.0	11.6
High-School Teachers	K.A.	1.2	1.4	3.4	1.5	3.0	1.5	2.7	1.5
	I.	0.3	0.3	0.2	0.5	0.6	0.4	0.5	0.4
Youth-Aliyah Teachers	K.A.	0.3	0.4	1.3	0.6	1.6	1.2	1.3	1.0
	I.	0.3	0.7	0.9	0.5	1.5	0.7	1.0	0.7
Nurses and Medical Assistants	K.A.	0.1	5.8	0.1	4.6	0.3	4.2	0.3	4.5
	I.	0.1	4.0	0	2.0	0.2	3.7	0.2	3.5
Handicraft and Art Teachers	K.A.	0.8	1.3	0.8	0.6	0.5	1.1	0.6	1.1
	I.	0.3	1.0	0.2	0.2	0.5	0.8	0.4	0.8
Technicians	K.A.	3.0	0.2	1.7	0.2	2.4	0.4	2.4	0.3
	I.	1.8	0.6	1.4	0.2	2.4	0.3	2.1	0.4
Other (Theater, Film, Dance)	K.A.	1.9	1.4	0.9	0.6	1.6	2.1	1.6	1.8
	I.	0.7	1.4	0.3	0.5	1.8	1.9	1.4	1.8
Total	K.A.	100	100	100	100	100	100	100	100
	I.	100	100	100	100	100	100	100	100

cation, the more men there are in it. We also find this to be true among Youth Aliyah teachers, whose training resembles that of high-school teachers, but is of somewhat shorter duration.

3. Most medical nurses, medical assistants, and handicraft and art teachers are women, although the difference between the sexes is much smaller in these fields than in some others.

Table 39
Academic Education, by Sex and Generation (in percentages)

Academic Education		First Generation		Kibbutz-Bred		Second Generation		Total	
		M	F	M	F	M	F	M	F
None	K.A.	90.3	95.0	97.4	99	96.9	98.8	92.6	95.9
	I.	89.0	93.1	95.1	98.3	95.8	97.8	91.5	94.7
Humanities	K.A.	4.2	3.0	1.0	0.4	0.5	0.7	3.0	2.4
	I.	5.1	3.9	2.8	0.8	1.4	1.4	3.8	3.5
Law, Military	K.A.	3.3	1.0	1.0	0.4	1.4	0.1	2.5	0.8
	I.	0.7	0.1	0	0	0.1	0	0.5	0.1
Sciences, Engineering	K.A.	1.5	0.5	0.6	0	1.0	0.1	1.3	0.4
	I.	2.8	1.5	1.2	0	1.3	0.5	2.3	1.3
Agriculture	K.A.	0.1	0	0	0	0	0	0.1	0
	I.	1.3	0.4	0.6	0	1.2	0	1.2	0.3
Medicine	K.A.	0.3	0.3	0	0	0	0	0.2	0.2
	I.	0.6	0.4	0	0	0	0	0.3	0.3
Art, Literature	K.A.	0.3	0.2	0	0	0	0	0.18	0.2
	I.	0.2	0	0	0	0	0	0.1	0
Total	K.A.	100	100	100	100	100	100	100	100
	I.	100	100	100	100	100	100	100	100

4. Most technicians are men, and about six times as many men as women receive a technical education. There is only a slightly higher percentage of women than of men in art education, theater, film, and dance.

In higher nonacademic education, then, most women are trained as kindergarten and elementary-school teachers, medical nurses, and medical assistants. Most men are trained as high-school teachers, Youth Aliyah teachers, and technicians.

Let us now look at academic education. About 7-8 per cent of

Table 39 (Continued)

Male Education: Law and Military, Science and Engineering	K.A.	4.9	1.5	1.6	0.4	2.4	0.2	3.9	1.2
	I.	4.8	2.0	1.8	0	2.6	0.5	4.0	1.7
Female Education: Humanities, Social Sciences, Art	K.A.	4.5	3.2	1.0	0.4	0.5	0.7	3.2	2.6
	I.	5.3	3.9	2.8	0.8	1.4	1.4	3.9	3.4
Medicine	K.A.	0.3	0.3	0	0	0	0	0.2	0.2
	I.	0.6	0.4	0	0	0	0	0.3	0.3
Total	K.A.	9.7	5.0	2.6	0.8	2.9	0.9	7.3	4.0
	I.	10.7	6.3	4.6	0.8	4.0	1.9	8.2	5.4

kibbutz men and 4-5 per cent of kibbutz women receive a substantial college education. Their distribution in fields of studies are classified in Table 39.

In only three spheres are there significant differences between the sexes. There are more men than women in law and military science, sciences and engineering, and agriculture. No significant differences exist in the humanities, social sciences, medicine, art, and literature. If we pool the predominantly male categories and call them male education, and designate humanities, social sciences, and art as female categories, and set aside medicine as neutral education, we once again find polarization. Almost three times as many men as women get a male education; in female education, the men have only a slight advantage. The generation columns show that this advantage for men lies in the first generation and that in the second generation there is a slight advantage for women. The numbers are very small, but since we are dealing with a total population the differences they represent are real enough.

SUMMARY

We began by asking whether education is a dependent or independent variable. We have seen that as an independent variable, it tries to disregard sex differences and to take an egalitarian course through the twelve years of kibbutz education. The egalitarian effect, however, is counteracted by daily experience in the parents' home and by adult division of labor. Western youth culture has gradually penetrated the relatively austere, task-oriented atmosphere of the Children's Society, further eroding egalitarian socialization.

Data on ability and achievement in kibbutz high schools show conspicuously superior performance on the part of the boys. We accept Dar's explanation—the anticipation of future occupational roles—only in part. We argue that high-school studies are vocationally at least as irrelevant for boys as they are for girls. We turned to an analysis of the educational level of the kibbutz population, and found that women receive, in average number of years, as much education as men, but that there are qualitative differences. A larger percentage of men completes high school, and benefits from academic study rather than nonacademic higher education. Also, it is men who predominate in certain areas of study at the college level.

There is considerable continuity between educations and careers. More than 6 per cent of the women take male professional courses, compared to about 25 per cent of the men; about 1.5 per cent of the women receive male academic education, compared to 4 per cent of the men. This corresponds with the actual sexual division of labor (see Tables 6, 7, and 8).

This development of sexual dissimilarity is rather puzzling. Because of the egalitarian socialization of the kibbutz movement and its attitude toward women, its members do not consider either sex superior. Complete sexual equality in the Children's Society, a single standard for premarital sexual activity, a broad equity in sexual conduct, all point to a strong stimulation of sociosexual similarity. Nevertheless we found that a gap begins to appear by age fourteen between the school performances of boys and girls in that boys score and are rated higher than girls in almost every aspect of academic ability and achievement.

How can such egalitarian socialization support sex-typed education and divergent careers? We have already noted the possible impact of the adult division of labor by sex, of familism, and of Western youth culture. Perhaps these are causes. Yet some of these factors have quite contradictory effects—for instance, the new youth culture and familism—and it is odd but provocative that there should be a rather sudden change in behavior and a reversal of basic socialization at the beginning of these young peoples' reproductive lives. Moreover, as we shall see in our discussion of family life, young women not only appear to enjoy maternity and other activities associated with conventional female roles, but they insist on their right to undertake these roles despite the practical and ideological objection of men and older women. Can these women have been brainwashed into female careers and devoted maternity? By whom? Formal socialization, ideology, economic management, and political leadership are all against this. It is true that the choice of jobs for women is somewhat more limited than it is for men, and girls are occasionally cajoled into taking women's jobs by appeals made to their sense of responsibility to the kibbutz. If there are not enough women to care for the children, a girl might be asked to give up, at least temporarily, an alternative career. (Needless to say, such forces also act on men all the time.) But as we shall see in Chapter 10, most girls are satisfied with their jobs and want further professional training in them. So it seems that few women are, or have to be, coerced into taking women's jobs.

Our data about education and careers confirm what the psychological studies have always told us—that women are more interested than men in interpersonal transactions and in activities involving small numbers of people, and that men prefer impersonal and very broad activities, which rarely involve small children. In proposing that kibbutz education may reflect something other or more than sexist rigidity, we do not argue that the pattern is desirable or undesirable. Rather, we suggest only that it may belie a relatively straightforward expression in this community in particular of what individual men and women do with their enthusiasms and skills in general.

At the beginning of this chapter, we discussed the crucial role played by education in radical and reformist societies. The data from the kibbutz underscore the difficulty of effecting sex-related changes through education. Our findings and our few extrapolations are pertinent chiefly to relatively small rural communities and may be irrelevant to big-city mobile populations. Yet the generally recognized and widely lamented fact that patterns similar to those of the kibbutz also occur in large, heterogeneous societies leaves open the following possibility: Except where there are legally binding quotas such as those being imposed in some careers in the U.S. and Canada, most men and women choose to work in ways that reflect sexual specializations of a phylogenetic origin.

David Hamburg (1963) has made the important point that the best question to ask in assessing the behavior of animals, including the human one, is not whether something is natural or learned but, rather, what is naturally *easy* for an animal to learn. For example, children find it easy to learn to talk; they want to talk, and their sensorimotor systems prepare them to do so. However, learning the catechism or the table of chemical elements is less central to our conduct as a species; this requires more formidable supports and rewards than learning to talk does. A refinement of "What is easy to learn?" is "What does the creature *want* to learn?" Have we identified, in the relatively experimental and carefully integrated kibbutz system, a truth about what men and women want to learn and, by extension, find easy to learn? We can make no such assertion. But unless we are certain that sex and gender are irrelevant to all experiences except copulation and childbirth, and that our social nature follows no biosocial patterns, the kibbutz may reveal some central behavioral structure of our species.

Chapter 8

The Military Service
of Women in the Kibbutz

The drive to the paramilitary (Nahal) kibbutz takes us to the top of the Golan Heights, close by dozens of crushed trucks, cannons, collapsed Syrian fortresses; beside the road are numbered entrances to shelters dug all along it. The settlement is ringed with barbed wire. In front of each hut are three wooden barricades, each perhaps fifteen inches thick, with earth and concrete between them. The outsides of most of the barricades are colorfully painted, in the exuberant fashion of building-site billboards turned over to art students. Every man and woman on the settlement carries a weapon. The women's rifles are heavier than the men's.

Many activities are unevenly distributed between the sexes, but war and the use of weapons are among the few that seem universally male. The reason for this may lie deep in our evolutionary past, in man's relatively greater muscular strength, his greater, possibly hormone-regulated aggressiveness, and the related emotional configuration. In extreme situations, of course, women have shared the fighting with men; in Western and non-Western cultures alike there have been women who excelled in war—usually in cases of defense, in which the very survival of the group was at stake. At such times everyone—men, women, even children—has done all he could to resist annihilation. The history of the Zionist colonization and of the state of Israel is one such case. The geopolitics of the emerging Jewish state determined the wide dispersion of isolated communities amid hostile Arabs. From the day it was established, Israel has been surrounded by four Arab states waging war on it; within its borders is a large and potentially bellicose Arab population.

The word *haganah* (defense) has therefore represented one of the most basic elements of the Israeli consciousness. It was the name of the illegal Jewish army before the state of Israel was created. It was and still is especially important to the kibbutz movement. Today almost half the kibbutzim lie within five miles of the 1967 borders. Many others lie amid Arab populations in the Negev and the Judean mountains.

THE PAST

In the early days of the kibbutz movement, the Jewish population of Palestine was protected largely by civil defense units, and each settlement had to take care of itself in the face of an almost full-time emergency. The mobilization of women was an absolute necessity. Women all over the country wanted to share equally with men the responsibility and burden of defense, and the women of the kibbutz took the lead. In 1920 Sarah Tchizik and Dvora Drachler fell in the battle of Tel Chai, but this was an exceptional case—the illegal Hashomer organization rarely allowed women to share in defense, according to one authority, because they didn't want their Arab opponents to consider them unmanly (Slutsky 1972).

In the thirties, the newly established Haganah accepted a few women and trained them to use the revolver and the shotgun, mainly for personal defense. Women were used to transport arms, on the assumption that the British police would not search their dresses for hidden weapons. But women demanded that they be allowed to belong to fighting units. Under the pressure of growing numbers of women who belonged to kibbutzim and moshavim and who almost universally joined the Haganah, the male commanders of the Haganah slowly gave way. The struggle for equality with men culminated after 1936, with the outburst of an Arab guerrilla war against the Jewish settlements that lasted more than three years. Geula Shertok, from the kibbutz Givat Brenner, declared, "I don't want and I shall avoid having anyone endanger his life because of me; nobody will trod down my love of my country and nobody will close my way to that part of the soil for which other people will cast their fate for life and death" (Slutsky 1972). Under this pressure, the kibbutz Ein Harod decided to include women in all the tasks of protective defense, as opposed to offensive actions. In 1937 the Haganah organized the first training course for women commanders, in Kibbutz Gvat. This course was called *coursa* with benevolent irony—"a" is of course the feminine suffix, but *coursa* also means "armchair." Yet the first commando groups of the Haganah included a woman commander.

Each new problem that the Haganah faced provoked further discussion about the right of women to be included. With the outbreak of World War II, the question of women's volunteering for the British army was debated vehemently in the Haganah. People feared that the framework of a foreign army would be unsuitable for Jewish women volunteers. But the women prevailed, and many served in units of the British army.

In 1941 a special commando unit of the Haganah was established, the Palmach (abbreviation of *plugot mahatz,* literally, "commando battalions"). This unit contained many members of kibbutzim and moshavim, some of them women. Later, organized groups of the Israel Youth Movements (*garinim*) joined the Palmach—including all the girls. Since the Palmach undertook special commando tasks that required strenuous physical activity, women were given jobs suited to their physical abilities. But in addition to being secretaries, medical orderlies, and provisioners, they shared battle as privates and officers. Among the 1,200 Palmachi soldiers who fell during the organization's eight years of existence were nineteen women (Gilad and Meged 1954). The most famous of them was Bracha Fold, who died in 1946 in the defense of Tel Aviv.

Women, in fact, took part in one of the most daring projects of the Haganah and Palmach during World War II. Among the parachutists sent to organize Jewish self-defense and revolt in Nazi-occupied countries were two female officers of the kibbutz: Haviva Reick was sent to Slovakia and Hana Szenes to Hungary. Both were captured by the Nazis and executed, and entered the pantheon of the national heroes of Israel.

In 1943 Haganah headquarters published the following order concerning the military service of women:

a. "*The tasks:* the *chavera* must be included in tasks of fighting in which she can reveal maximum effectiveness according to her ability and physical capability. These tasks are mainly tasks of static defense. In those units where the battle activity is mobile the *chaverot* will be assigned tasks of service in the headquarters.

b. *Training:* experience has proven that *chaverot* reach the best achievements in one-sex training units. In mixed-sex units the competition between men and women has overstrained the *chaverot* and impaired their physical ability. Therefore women privates must be trained in one-sex, all-female groups, and only after this basic training will they be sent to the mixed-sex tactical units. Officers, on the other hand, must be trained in mixed-sex training courses" (Slutsky 1972).

The headquarters of the Haganah included a high female officer, Batsheva Haifin, from Kibbutz Yagur. Later the position "Headquarters Officer for Women Soldiers" became a regular part of the headquarters' organization.

At the start of the War of Liberation, there were some 10,000 female soldiers in the Haganah and 50,000 male soldiers. In the first phase of the war, women shared in both the active and defensive battle activities. They were especially efficient in the defense of the border kibbutzim, such as Nirim, Yad Mordechai, Negba, Mishmar Haemek, and Degania. Many fell in battle; some were taken prisoner. In the second phase of the war, the Haganah and the other illegal military groups united to become the IDF (Israel Defense Forces); the war became more offensive and less defensive, and there were fewer battle tasks for women to perform.

THE WOMEN'S ARMY TODAY

In September 1949, the Knesset approved the Bill of National Security, establishing compulsory military service for both men and women; Israel is the only democratic state with compulsory military service for women. At the age of eighteen, each girl is drafted unless she is married or states that for religious reasons she does not want to serve in the army. The length of service has been twenty months; reserve service is required until the age of thirty-four, except for mothers. A crisp indication of the importance of the contribution of women to the war effort is that in 1974, because of the new military situation, the length of service for women was increased to twenty-four months.

The IDF has a special army for women, called Chen (abbreviation of *Cheil Nashim,* literally "women's army"), but the abbreviation itself means "grace" in Hebrew. The commander of the Chen, a woman with the rank of lieutenant colonel, is part of IDF headquarters. The Chen's most important task is giving basic training to all women recruits except the girls of the Nahal. Chen also has responsibility for the general care and surveillance of all the women in the army. Chen has a special camp for the basic training of girls. All the officers of the staff are women, including the base commander, who has the rank of colonel. Interestingly, all the service tasks (kitchen, provisions, guards, etc.) are carried out by male soldiers. Basic training for women includes marching drill, use of weapons, gymnastics, crawling, etc. Live ammunition is used in training. The day lasts from 5:00 A.M. until 9:00 P.M. Most girls find it very difficult to adjust to this strenuous life, especially during the first month of the three-month training. The reaction of at least some girls expresses itself in a mildly sarcastic poster in the training base: the girls drew a picture of a miserable little girl with the initials of the IDF in Hebrew as follows:

Ts	richot	(By explanation, the initials of IDF in Hebrew
H	ayinu	are Ts for tsava (army), H for haganah (defense),
L	hithaten	L for Leisrael (for Israel).

But the girls wrote Ts for *Tsrichot* (we should have), H for *Hayinu* (gotten), L for *Lhithaten* (married). Obviously they imply that if they had married before the age of eighteen they would have avoided the strenuous training (Cohen, 1972:55).

The official statements of the Chen reveal a great deal not only about training but about women in the armed forces:

"Although you cannot see any women soldiers in combat service, you might meet them near the male soldiers before they go out to fight and when they return."

"A very important contribution of the woman soldier to the Army—besides her task in the Army—is her very femininity that makes everything more delicate, softer than usual in the Army, which is always alert to fight. The woman soldier inspires the Army with a cultural atmosphere and helps to create social cohesion."

"Perhaps the most difficult thing for the new woman recruit to the Army is the fear of losing her identity. The uniform, the limitation on coiffure and on the use of cosmetics and jewelry might be perceived as threatening her peculiar identity. But after some days have passed, the woman soldier recovers her identity with the help of the mirror. A light touch of the comb, a delicate line with the eyebrow pencil and an additional touch of lipstick and the woman soldier is herself again, equal to all the other women but nevertheless different from them. And the Army encourages her to be herself" (Cohen 1972).

The girls' uniform consists of a tight shirt or jacket and a miniskirt. According to the commanders of the training base, there is far-reaching consideration of every problem that might arise in the camp. In the lectures given to recruits in the training base before they are given their assignments, emphasis is placed on the positive effects of their femininity in their future jobs.

The very circumstances of our meeting with the commanding officer of the Chen training camp suggest the atmosphere of the unit. The commander sat at the middle of a short table that formed the crossbar of a T; we sat at a long table with a captain and a non-commissioned officer. The table held three plates of excellent cheese pastries, three plates of fruit, and two vases of fresh flowers. On the walls hung photos of the camp and its recruits, and on the desk were photos of the commander's children. We were served coffee by her secretary. The meeting was not brusquely military; although the commander and her staff gave the impression of having mastered their military and administrative jobs, they also showed that they operate in a rather homelike atmosphere, with time and concern for social niceties. This can hardly be said of male IDF units, which are famous for their Spartan air.

After basic training, the women are distributed among the various units of the army. Most become clerks and typists, and work both in unit offices and in the field. Secretaries of regiment commanders accompany their commanders everywhere. Women also are often used for running telephone centers, teleprinters, and wireless communications and for work in equipment laboratories. They also perform very important cultural and welfare tasks in the army: they listen to soldiers' welfare problems, visit the soldiers' homes, and try to help the soldiers' families. As cultural officers, they provide recreation for the boys and teach in the special schools for soldiers who have not had elementary education. Women are also part of the military police. In the air force, they are active in pilot training—working in control towers of military airports and with electronic equipment. By far the most glamorous of all female tasks in the army is the folding of parachutes. That is the one task for which only volunteers are accepted. The work is hard, the responsibility heavy. In the big work hall of the parachute folders, large signs remind the women: "Remember, their lives are your responsibility." Women perform important tasks on behalf of the army outside military posts: they teach and do social work in development towns and new immigrant villages. They help the Israeli police force, which is usually badly understaffed, and work in hospitals during military and civil emergencies.

By now the combat tasks have completely disappeared. Female soldiers do not carry or use weapons. The only exceptions are the girls of the Nahal—a special unit of the army (see page 304) recruited from graduates of Youth Movements, which maintains the framework of the *garin* to some extent during army service. Since the Nahal combines military training and service with agricultural and settlement activities, boys and girls are sometimes together—most important, in a temporary settlement (*heachzut*), where boys and girls share agricultural and military work; both carry weapons within the camp and share armed night-watch duty.

The Nahal girls' basic training is given not by the Chen but by the Nahal training base, and it is somewhat more strenuous. After duty the girls meet the boys of their *garin,* who are receiving basic training at the same camp. After basic, the whole *garin* goes to a permanent settlement for agricultural training or to a temporary settlement. After about a half year together, the sexes separate, the boys going on to advanced army training, the girls to the kibbutz to which the whole *garin* has been assigned. When on leave, the boys join the girls on that kibbutz. Once the boys are discharged, the whole *garin* reunites in the kibbutz. Especially strong *garinim* are assigned the important task of establishing new settlements and founding new kibbutzim.

But even in the Nahal, the attitude to female military activity is relatively unserious, and the military functions of women are sharply curtailed. We visited one Nahal settlement on the Golan Heights on a day when the women were engaged in target practice.

This seemed to afford considerable amusement to the men, and to some of the women as well. A line of some fifteen women were led by a female officer who sporadically required them to fire their rifles at targets. There was much comment in the camp about the importance of staying as far away as possible from the shooting area. A large truck delivering supplies stopped short, and the male drivers watched the practice, all the while cracking jokes about it.

These women practiced only once a month, although, like the men, they carried their weapons with them wherever they went. The camp commander, a man, told us that women were not expected to use the weapons. If the camp were attacked from the ground, the standing orders were for the women to go immediately to the bunkers; if from the air, for both the men and the women to go to the bunkers. Furthermore, he explained, it was pointless for the women to try to shoot their weapons; they were too heavy for them and of relatively poor quality, being old Czech rifles, regarded as weapons of last resort. The commander agreed that the women's activities with weapons were purely symbolic; they were good for their morale and offered them a sense of participation in the Nahal's most serious function, the military.

KIBBUTZ WOMEN IN THE MILITARY

Military service for women is compulsory, but not all women of eligible age serve. Exemptions are made for the following reasons:

1. Women, like men, may be exempted from military service for poor health. The exemption criteria for women are somewhat more liberal than they are for men.

2. Women who declare that military service violates their religious convictions may be exempted after a hearing by a military committee. Usually only very Orthodox women request exemption, which is granted to some 10-15 per cent of those eligible for service; the number of kibbutz women seeking such exemption is negligible—perhaps about thirteen individuals in all.

3. Girls who marry before the age of eighteen are exempt from regular service, but they may be called up later for reserve duty. All mothers or girls pregnant before the age of eighteen are automatically

exempted. About 6.7 per cent of all the women in Israel are married by the age of nineteen, and only 6 per cent of Jewish mothers in Israel give birth by the age of nineteen (Statistical Abstracts 1973).

4. Certain occupations and courses of study, such as medical nursing and police work, constitute grounds for exemption.

The following table shows women's military service in our two federations:

Table 40
Women's Military Service by Generation and Federation (in percentages)

	Second Generation		Kibbutz-Bred		First Generation		Total	
	I.	K.A.	I.	K.A.	I.	K.A.	I.	K.A.
Not Yet Drafted	2.0	5.1	3.4	1.7	9.5	5.5	7.4	5.1
Served in Army at Some Time	85.5	82.9	55.3	62.9	27.2	21.0	42.7	35.6
Exempt for Health Reasons	2.9	6.4	1.9	3.6	1.1	1.6	1.6	2.6
Exempt for Marital Status	5.7	2.8	12.6	10.8	16.3	15.0	13.6	12.5
Exempt for Conscience and/or Religion	0.1	0	0.2	0	0.2	0	0.2	0
Exempt for Age	2.7	1.6	25.0	16.4	43.8	52.5	32.9	40.3
Exempt for Other Reasons	1.1	1.1	1.5	4.5	1.9	4.4	1.7	3.9
Total	100	100	100	100	100	100	100	100

The differences between generations are striking. The first-generation and kibbutz-bred groups were exempted three to five times as much as the second-generation was. About 85 per cent of the second-generation women were or still are in military service. Only a quarter of the first-generation women were in the IDF; about half of them were past eligible age when the present army was created. The kibbutz-bred generation falls between the first and second generations in extent of army service.

The reasons for exemption also differ by generation. The main reason in the second generation is early marriage; in the other two generations it is age, with early marriage a close second. Health exemptions are more prevalent in the second generation than they are in the first-generation and kibbutz-bred groups. Exemptions on religious grounds and for other reasons are negligible, even for members of the religious kibbutzim (approximately 10-15 per cent of the national population). About 5-7 per cent of the women in the census population have not yet been drafted.

The differences between the federations are also striking. The Ichud women of the second and first generations are less often exempted than the women of the Kibbutz Artzi. The kibbutz-bred of the Ichud are more often exempted than those of the Kibbutz Artzi. However, we have no explanation for this.

We have no comparative data on the military service of kibbutz and non-kibbutz women, but we think it safe to assume that the recruitment level is much higher on the kibbutz than it is in the nation's general population. A special factor here is the high frequency of early marriage among Jews of Eastern origin, who are underrepresented in the kibbutzim—approximately 7 per cent as against a national figure of 45 per cent.

The IDF has not been the only military service performed by women of the kibbutz, as Table 41 shows.

This table shows trends contrary to those in the preceding table. Approximately 40-45 per cent of the first generation and approximately 20-30 per cent of the kibbutz-bred generation were in various illegal military units before the establishment of the IDF, as against only 3-5 per cent of the second generation. The most important such unit was the Haganah, in which approximately 40 per cent of the first-generation women served. The differences in participation between the federations are negligible.

What do kibbutz women do in the army today? Let us first note their ranks in the IDF (Table 42).

The differences between the generations are conspicuous. The second generation reaches higher levels; less than a quarter of them remain privates. Two-thirds are noncommissioned and warrant officers, approximately 7 per cent junior officers, and approximately half of one per cent senior officers. The kibbutz-bred group produces very

Table 41

Military Service of Women Not in IDF, by Generation and Federation (in percentages)

	Second Generation		Kibbutz-Bred		First Generation		Total	
	I.	K.A.	I.	K.A.	I.	K.A.	I.	K.A.
No Service	92.7	97.2	70.1	79.2	59.9	55.3	66.6	64.7
Jewish Brigade and Other British Units	0.3	0.0	0.8	0.2	0.7	0.3	0.6	0.2
Haganah	5.2	2.2	26.5	18.2	36.4	41.0	30.4	32.3
Jewish Brigade and Haganan	0.2	0.0	0.0	0.2	0.3	0.4	0.3	0.3
Palmach	0.9	0.0	2.0	1.7	1.2	1.0	1.2	0.9
Jewish Brigade and Palmach	0.0	0.0	0.0	0.0	0.0	0.0	0.0	0.0
Haganah and Palmach	0.4	0.1	0.3	0.5	0.4	0.8	0.4	0.7
Palmach, Haganah, and Jewish Brigade	0.0	0.0	0.0	0.0	0.0	0.1	0.0	0.1
Other Countries' Armies	0.1	0.5	0.3	0.0	0.5	0.6	0.4	0.5
Other	0.3	0.0	0.0	0.2	0.3	0.4	0.2	0.3
Total	100	100	100	100	100	100	100	100

Table 42

Women's Military Rank, by Generation and Federation (in percentages)

	Second Generation		Kibbutz-Bred		First Generation		Total	
	I.	K.A.	I.	K.A.	I.	K.A.	I.	K.A.
Private	25.5	19.8	60.6	72.5	64.5	72.7	48.5	50.8
Noncommissioned Officers and Warrant Officers	67.5	71.8	38.4	26.5	31.0	23.9	46.3	44.1
Junior Officers	6.5	8.2	1.0	0.7	3.7	3.3	4.6	5.0
Senior Officers	0.5	0.2	0	0.2	0.9	0.1	0.6	0.2
Total	100	100	100	100	100	100	100	100

few officers; the first generation produces more, including a comparatively high percentage of senior officers. The very high-ranking women attained military status in the Haganah and continued in the IDF. There are almost no differences between the federations except that the Ichud has a much higher percentage of senior officers than the Kibbutz Artzi has, principally because the Ichud Federation is older.

Table 43 shows the units in which kibbutz women serve.

There are obvious differences among the generations. Second-generation women spread out over a great variety of military units; the kibbutz-bred and first generations are heavily concentrated in the Nahal—perhaps because most people from the first and kibbutz-bred generations who were in the army came to it from Youth Movement *garinim*. But the distribution of the women among units reveals little about what it is they actually do. We divided army jobs in all units into male and female job categories. In the male category we included all those with battle assignments, all officers, and all who work with heavy equipment. In the female category we included clerks, typists, secretaries, provision officers, welfare and cultural workers, the communications staff, those with technical desk activities in the air force, and all those outside the army, such as social workers in development towns and teaching. Table 44 presents the data on these jobs.

In all military units except two, the overwhelming majority of women do female jobs. The two exceptions involve Kibbutz Artzi women, two-thirds of whom have male jobs in the Nahal and in the District Defense. This is probably because more Kibbutz Artzi women than Ichud women have been directed to take officers' courses in these two units—and we have classified all officers as holding male jobs. Of course, not all women with male jobs in the Nahal and the District Defense are officers; they also work in communications, driving, medical tasks, etc. If we pool all male and female jobs, we have the picture presented in Table 45.

We can see that approximately 12 per cent of all the women in the army hold male jobs, and 88 per cent hold female jobs. In the second generation, the women of the Kibbutz Artzi are more polarized; in the kibbutz-bred and first generations, the Ichud is more polarized. This may simply reflect what we have already found in work and political activity, where the same pattern exists.

Table 43
Women's Military Service in Various Units, by Generation and Federation (in percentages)

	Second Generation		Kibbutz-Bred		First Generation		Total	
	I.	K.A.	I.	K.A.	I.	K.A.	I.	K.A.
Not in Army	14.5	17.1	44.75	37.1	72.8	79.0	57.3	64.4
Infantry	10.44	9.9	4.14	2.6	1.75	1.1	3.34	2.6
Paratroopers	4.35	3.5	0.87	1.6	0.31	0.3	1.11	1.0
Tank Corps	6.25	5.9	2.94	0.8	0.68	0.4	1.89	1.3
Artillery	1.67	0.8	1.2	0.2	0.21	0.1	0.6	0.1
Air Force	10.44	9.3	2.07	3.2	1.93	0.8	2.7	2.5
Nahal	19.87	16.3	24.32	38.8	14.92	10.1	16.9	14.0
Navy	1.12	1.1	0.54	0.2	0.1	0.1	1.33	0.2
Cultural Units (teachers, entertainment groups)	4.35	5.4	1.41	2.0	0.62	0.6	1.33	1.6
District Defense (organization of local defense of settlements)	0.89	2.9	4.14	4.4	1.95	4.5	2.0	4.3
Intelligence	1.89	1.9	0.54	0.3	0.21	0.3	0.6	0.5
Communications	5.80	5.0	3.16	1.7	0.82	0.8	1.9	1.6
Ordnance	2.34	1.8	1.42	0.8	0.31	0.2	0.8	0.3
Engineering	1.56	1.8	0	1.1	0.1	0.1	0.33	0.3
Gadna (paramilitary units of high-school students)	3.46	3.7	2.07	0.3	0.51	0.4	1.22	1.0
Provisions	1.67	1.0	0.54	0.3	0.31	0.3	0.6	0.4
Other	9.4	12.7	5.89	4.7	2.47	2.0	4.67	4.0
Total	100	100	100	100	100	100	100	100

Table 44
Women's Jobs Within Military Units (in percentages)

	Ichud		Kibbutz Artzi	
	Female Jobs	Male Jobs	Female Jobs	Male Jobs
Infantry	84.2	15.8	66.4	33.6
Paratroopers	91.7	8.3	96.6	3.4
Tank Corps	95.5	4.5	98.9	1.1
Artillery	91.7	8.3	100	0
Air Force	99.2	0.8	99.4	0.6
Nahal	83.7	16.3	30.4	69.6
Navy	100	0	100	0
Cultural Units (teachers, entertainment groups)	100	0	100	0
District Defense (organization of the local defense of settlements)	79.8	20.2	34.9	65.1
Intelligence	95.7	4.3	100	0
Communications	100	0	100	0
Ordnance	92.9	7.1	97.1	2.9
Engineering	100	0	93.9	6.1
Gadna (paramilitary units of high-school students)	100	0	100	0
Provisions	100	0	100	0
Other	100	0	100	0

Some of our most important information on kibbutz women in military service is not quantitative. For instance, at the Chen basic-training camps, our informants told us that about ten years earlier the kibbutz girls had been the backbone of the women's army. Their superior fitness, their experience in collective life, and their relatively

Table 45
Women's Military Jobs by Generation and Federation (in percentages)

	Second Generation		Kibbutz-Bred		First Generation		Total	
	I.	K.A.	I.	K.A.	I.	K.A.	I.	K.A.
Women's Jobs	84.0	90.5	92.3	77.0	93.0	79.0	89.4	85.1
Men's Jobs	16.0	9.5	7.7	23.0	7.0	21.0	10.6	14.9
Total	100	100	100	100	100	100	100	100

higher education made them the best trainees. They were, in fact, the most assertive yet most cooperative people in the camp. They volunteered for courses to become commissioned and noncommissioned officers; most women commanders came from kibbutzim. They volunteered for the most tedious jobs. But the training officers claimed that recently there had been a decline in the superiority of kibbutz girls. Though they were still better equipped than other recruits were for camp life, they now volunteered in fewer numbers, were more individualistic, and cared more about personal satisfaction in their future army jobs. This information confirms our findings about work, political activity, and education. In the chapter on the family (Chapter 9) we shall consider what may have caused these changes.

In our interviews with women officers of the kibbutz, we were told that in the early sixties, kibbutz women were trained in a separate platoon on the training base. This system was later changed, but the level of expectation toward kibbutz women remained very high. It was generally expected that they would adjust better physically and psychologically to army life than city women would. The collective life of the army was new and demanding for those from the city, but to kibbutz women it seemed to be something of a game. Our interviewees said that these days women from the kibbutz try to evade responsibilities because they feel that the training they are being given is "not serious." As one interviewee said, "All of us knew that we would never use weapons and take part in combat. Therefore we couldn't take it upon ourselves to train the girls in using weapons, field training, camouflage, because we knew that after training they would sit down behind a desk and type letters."

One reason for declining military ambition among women of

the kibbutz was that officers on the training base were constantly together only with other women. Recalled one ex-officer, "It was awful. We called it a *katchkiada* (flock of chattering ducks). The atmosphere was terrible, and we knew that if we went anywhere else, we wouldn't land among girls only."

Our interviewees could not explain why these attitudes were especially characteristic of kibbutz women. They argued that the choice to attend officers' courses is completely individual and unconnected with being a kibbutznik.

Whatever a woman thinks about the seriousness of her activities at the Chen training camp, her functions are very serious once she leaves the camp for her posting. She may, of course, perform tasks that are vital to military activity; at the very least, she will free a man to engage in combat when necessary. This enhanced sense of importance after training is evidently felt by most women in the Chen.

Several of our informants noted that women of the kibbutz, more than other women, have in recent years suffered personal problems arising from sexual relations, pregnancy, and abortion. These problems assumed such troubling proportions that the Chen headquarters asked the Department of Hygienic Education of the Sick Fund of the Histadrut to organize a course on sexual behavior for female officers. The woman responsible for women's affairs in the social affairs committee of one of the federations told us that according to the commander of the Chen, the number of kibbutz women who experience such difficulties is disproportionately high. However, the officers and former officers we interviewed saw no difference between kibbutz and nonkibbutz women in this respect; perhaps, they offered, it is just that troubled kibbutz women are more apt than other women to talk to their commanders about their personal problems.

Whatever differences may or may not exist between kibbutz women and nonkibbutz women, our interviewees all agreed that as both a source of personal satisfaction and a factor in achieving status, military service is much less significant for kibbutz girls than it is for boys.

A man's military career and his rank at the time he is discharged affects his status in the kibbutz, but this is not so for a woman (Shepher 1971). The interviewees also said that what a woman did in the army had scarcely any effect on her choice of work in the kibbutz—unless she had a special talent or inclination before entering the army, which influenced her choice of army job and her post-military one in turn.

For example, highest prestige in the Israeli military is enjoyed by fighter pilots in the air force. The selection for this corps is ruthless; admission to the training program is difficult, and even up to the morning of the ceremony of awarding wings, candidates may be dropped. So great is the pilots' prestige that families of nonkibbutz fliers somehow manage to provide them with small cars during their military service, and fighter pilots from the kibbutz are given cars paid for with kibbutz funds. In view of the extremely high cost of even the most modest cars under Israeli taxation, this is an indication of the kibbutz commitment to military excellence.

WAR AND SEXUAL DIVISION OF LABOR

The kibbutz has always faced security problems, but war is more than just another security problem. Israel has undergone four major wars since 1948. War in Israel means almost total recruitment of working men: a small standing army must be supplemented by all its reserves to face armies many times larger than itself.

We have no data on how the first three wars affected sexual division of labor in the kibbutz. From the personal experience of Shepher, as well as from many memoirs, we can say that women took upon themselves a very great number of male tasks, especially during the War of Liberation. Even in the Sinai Campaign and the Six Day War, both of which were of very short duration, women in the kibbutz undertook to perform many unfamiliar tasks to keep the economy running.

The fourth war was fought during the period of our research, which we had to interrupt when Shepher was drafted into the reserves for seven weeks, as indeed were many of our interviewees. But during and immediately after the war, we were able to investigate exactly what had happened to sexual division of labor while the conflict was going on. Approximately 45 per cent of the kibbutz men were in the army; most of the men still at home were either too young or too old to fight. We hypothesized that this war would change the division of labor as women left their traditional work and moved to production branches, which were now almost depleted of manpower.

We succeeded in collecting numerical data from six kibbutzim scattered around the country and in making detailed observations in one kibbutz.[1] The details were thoroughly unexpected (Table 46).

In only two kibbutzim did the percentage of women doing men's work increase during the war. In Kibbutz A it rose from 31.5 to 40 per cent, in Kibbutz E from 23 to 28 per cent. In two other kibbutzim it did not rise at all, and in Kibbutzim B and F it fell—this, despite a marked decrease of men workers everywhere (in Kibbutz B, for instance, manpower decreased from 73 to 39 per cent, a reduction of almost half the male force). There were other effects as well: men stopped doing women's work, and women doing women's work increased in four of the six kibbutzim—in Kibbutz B from 80 to 97 per cent.

After the war, the return of men workers to their former jobs was very slow, but on the kibbutzim women returned to their former jobs quite quickly. In Kibbutz A, for example, where the increase of women doing men's work had been highest (8.5 per cent), the percentage dropped immediately after the war—not to where it had been but to *below* the prewar level. Only in Kibbutz C was there even a slight increase after the war.

Our category of neutral work includes higher education, art, illness, and army service. During the war, more than half the kibbutz men came under this category, but the percentage of kibbutz women dropped, mainly because institutions of higher learning closed and women students had to go home. After the war, women of some kibbutzim returned quickly, as in Kibbutzim A, D, and E. Men still constituted a high percentage in the neutral category after the war, as a large part of the reserve army was not discharged.

On February 7, 1974, the Kibbutz Artzi summoned a special convention to deal with the problem of rigidity in the division of labor, and published their conclusions. Dr. Menahem Rosner, head of the Center for Social Research on the Kibbutz, reported a quick survey done after the war in the kibbutzim of the Kibbutz Artzi which revealed data very similar to those presented here (e.g., very few women went over to production branches during the war, a somewhat

Table 46
Sexual Division of Labor in Six Kibbutzim Before, During, and After the 1973 War (in percentages)

	Men's Work						Women's Work						Neutral Work					
	Before War		During War		After War		Before War		During War		After War		Before War		During War		After War	
	M	F	M	F	M	F	M	F	M	F	M	F	M	F	M	F	M	F
Kibbutz A	50.0	31.5	44.7	40	69.5	26.7	17.1	44.5	4.3	44.5	5.4	52.6	32.9	24.0	51.0	15.5	25.1	20.7
Kibbutz B	73.0	2.8	39.0	2.3	49	2.0	10.0	80.0	4.0	97.0	4.0	88.0	17.0	17.0	57.0	0.3	47.0	10.0
Kibbutz C	71.0	22.0	41.0	22.0	42.6	25.0	11.0	65.0	8.6	72.0	8.2	68.0	18.0	13.0	50.4	6.0	49.2	8.0
Kibbutz D	76.0	28.0	44.0	30.0	69.0	29.0	6.0	48.0	4.0	59.0	5.0	49.0	18.0	24.0	52.0	11.0	26.0	22.0
Kibbutz E	63.0	23.0	43.0	28.0	42.0	21.0	13.0	52.0	6.0	51.0	10.0	55.0	24.0	24.0	51.0	20.0	48.0	24.0
Kibbutz F	60.7	15.5	30.2	15.1	60.1	12.7	11.3	60.7	3.2	63.3	12.5	61.2	28.0	23.8	66.6	21.6	27.4	26.1

higher percentage assumed management jobs, such as the post of kibbutz secretary, but not the posts of general manager and treasurer). Dr. Rosner offered four possible explanations of these surprising facts:

1. The emergency period was too brief to have any lasting effect on the division of labor.

2. It was impossible to lessen the work involved in child rearing, with the result that no women were free to go into production branches.

3. The exceptional burden placed on mothers by their husbands' absence kept them from adjusting to production work.

4. Sexual polarization of work is so deep that women, especially younger ones, are no longer prepared to work in production (Palgi and Rosner 1974).

On balance, we consider Rosner's fourth point the decisive one, since the three other points can be seen to have had ambiguous effects. Our observations in Ofer confirm this. On Yom Kippur, almost all the young men were taken to the army; the next day, men between the ages of thirty-five and fifty were recruited as well. Fortunately, three young men who had just returned from abroad were not called up. In addition, two weeks before the war twenty young unmarried women arrived, part of a *garin* that was to join the kibbutz later. The kibbutz adolescents, instead of attending school, worked all day. The agricultural branches were largely depleted of men workers, but because the factory's product was necessary to the army, the regular factory workers stayed at their jobs.

Ofer, as we have already mentioned, is part of the region that was struck by the Syrian Frog missiles. Although the kibbutz itself was not bombed, the children had been taken to bunkers where they remained through the night and part of the next day, and this demanded a small increase in educational personnel. There was much less to do in the laundry and kitchen, because now half the male population was absent. Yet none of the women went to work in the production branches. Since most of Ofer's production branches were located some eight miles away from the kibbutz, mothers of young children were reluctant to leave them during this uncertain period. But it is significant that none of the twenty-five childless women of the *garin* left the kibbutz to work in the fields, either. Even in the industrial plant, located at the camp, three adolescent girls went to work, but not a single adult woman. The surplus women worked in the children's houses, the dining room, the kitchen, and the communal store, which, by usual standards, were now all overstaffed. Apart from twenty-four-hour telephone duty, which was shared by three women, all the managerial posts remained in the hands of a few men at the outset. The general manager, away in the army, was replaced by an older man, who had held the post previously. The secretary, also in the army, was replaced by the treasurer, an older man, who assumed both jobs. Not until the end of December did the situation change, when the work assigner, a young man, was called up by the army for six weeks and his post taken by a woman. From the end of October on, workers were urgently needed in the citrus grove for the season's main harvest. High-school children of both sexes put in long workdays, but no young adult women joined them. Even after the October 23 cease-fire, when there was no longer any danger of missiles, the number of workers in the children's houses remained the same.

Our impression—and the whole world's as well—is that the situation was very grave. There was constant worry and fear, and in the first days of the war, some signs of disorientation. The main reason for the unchanging division of labor was that no one had even considered sending grown women to the fields. Another reason was that at the outset, the members of the kibbutz, like most Israelis, thought the war would end quickly. By the third week, when it was obvious that the war would be a relatively long one, it was clearly untenable, especially in the grapefruit-picking season, to maintain that a redistribution of tasks was unnecessary.

As we write now in 1974, the war goes on. While there are agreements of disengagement with Egypt and Syria, the war against terrorists is a daily problem throughout Israel. Under the new system of terror, in just two months, almost fifty women and children were murdered in Kiryat Shemona, Ma'alot, Shamir, and Nahariya. This puts a terrible burden on the kibbutzim, which must provide their own night and day watch; although most of the men have been discharged from the army, many cannot work because of watch duty. Ofer has at least thirty young women who know how to handle weapons—some certainly better than many of the old men who have never been in the army—but no women share the armed night or day watch.

SUMMARY

Fighting, war, and the use of weapons are considered almost exclusively male activities in societies all over the world. We know that beneath the male near-monopoly on violence and warfare may lie physiological processes (Hutt 1972 a, b; Hamburg 1975), and possibly emotional and psychological ones as well (Maccoby and Macklin 1973; Tiger 1969, 1971; van den Berghe 1973). Nevertheless, women in Israel, especially women in the kibbutz, took active part in the Haganah and Palmach, parachuted into Nazi-occupied countries during World War II, and fought alongside men in the War of Liberation. Today, though, the sexual division of labor is even more polarized in military life than it is in work, political activity, and education. Kibbutz women fulfill their duty in the army to a greater extent than the rest of the Israeli population, but they completely accept the feminine approach of the women's army. The commander of a Chen training base told us, "We never disregard the fact that the girls here are going to be married and become mothers. We don't want to impair their feminine personality in any way."

Kibbutz women now ascribe no special importance to their army careers, and their army status does not influence their subsequent civil status. Even war no longer changes the sexual division of labor. After the massacres of women and children in Kiryat Shemona, Ma'alot, Shamir, and Nahariya, a motion was introduced in Ofer's General Assembly to accept into the kibbutz's guard younger women just discharged from the Nahal; it was unanimously rejected.

Despite the history of its people, it is apparently easy for some people committed to peace to accuse Israelis of abandoning the rules of humanity in their skillful creation of military power. As Irving Louis Horowitz has remarked, it is strange that Israelis' commitment to their own survival has been equated with imperialistic and destructive insensitivity to human ideals (1974). It is also important to understand Israel's process of survival. When a young man on guard duty enters a General Assembly meeting of Kibbutz Ofer, a machine gun on his shoulder and shells in his hand, to say something to a friend or spouse or colleague, no one looks up—except perhaps to ask why he is not at his post. Two months earlier, uncomfortably nearby, Israeli children were killed by an enemy attack.

For their own reasons, which are the rock-bottom ones of flesh and blood and bone, Israelis must protect themselves by elaborate military exercise, and they have become accustomed to the military reality; thus they accept the fact that late Friday afternoons the roads of Israel are lined with hitchhikers bearing machine guns on shoulder and cartridges in hand, hoping to spend Shabbat with their parents, spouses, lovers, or friends, or just to find a place to be alone. We have tried in this account of kibbutz life to stress the movement's strong commitment to social justice and human equity. While there can be no plain and simple answer to such questions as "Why do you want to survive?" or "Why do you own guns?" it is our view that the shifting, bewildering calculi of international alliance and hegemony should not and do not corrode the human meaning of the kibbutz enterprise. Quite rightly, the stomachs of serious idealists turn at the thought of guns; yet if social reformation must include self-protection, the entire enterprise should not be accused of lacking scruples or compassion. Just as citizens of Cleveland or Lyon or Budapest expect armed persons to protect them against terrors both known and unknown, so must the Israelis all protect themselves.

Chapter 9

The Kibbutz Family and Utopia

We are being walked around Ofra by its general manager, a big, genial man, who is telling us about the new drainage systems and the new housing under construction. The sun is scorching. As we pass the children's area of the kibbutz, a little girl darts from a house as suddenly as a minnow, to meet her father. He leans down to hug her. "My only private property," he says as they embrace. In a moment she is back with her peers, and we with our economic assessment.

In 1954 a young Harvard anthropologist named Melford E. Spiro, in an article in *The American Anthropologist* that was to make him famous in the profession, questioned the universality of the family in human societies. In 1951 he had done a year of field work in a kibbutz he called "Kiryat Yedidim," where he found that "the family as that term is defined in *Social Structure* does not exist in the kibbutz either in its nuclear, polygamous, or extended forms . . . there is no marriage in the kibbutz, if by marriage is meant a relationship between adults of opposite sex, characterized by sexual and economic activity."

Spiro had accepted Murdock's definition of marriage and the family in *Social Structure;* but in the kibbutz he found a lack of economic cooperation between family members and a system in which children were housed separately, and he declared that marriage and the family do not exist there. Spiro's article, which has been reprinted many times, is celebrated for its description of a family-like unit that is almost functionless.

In a reprint of Spiro's article in a widely accepted reader on the family, we find an "Addendum" dated 1958: "Starting with Murdock's . . . definitions of marriage and family, I concluded that marriage and the family do not exist in the kibbutz, since no single group or relationship satisfies the conditions stipulated in the definitions. If I were writing this essay today, I would wish to explore alternative interpretations as well—interpretations which, despite Murdock's definitions, would affirm the existence of marriage and the family in the kibbutz." Spiro concludes that marriage and family do exist in the kibbutz, and that Murdock's definition is too narrow.

In fact, Spiro was not as wrong as he supposed. Marriage and family in the early kibbutz were so limited in function that an outsider could easily have received the impression that they barely existed. As we noted in Chapter 3, marriage and the family were seen solely as ways of legitimizing permanent sexual cohabitation and procreation, and this was largely the view in the "Kiryat Yedidim" of the early 1950's; in those days the kibbutz family could still be described as a prototype of the "modern" functionless family. By now, the family's functions have increased. But many textbooks continue to feature the Spiro article as a demonstration of the tendency of modern socialistic societies to dispense with the family, or at least to transfer most of its functions to wider social units; for instance, the kibbutz family is linked to the Russian experiment in curtailing the family's range of discretion over resources, time, education, leisure, and so on.

We have seen that the most thoroughgoing change the kibbutz has undergone since its early days is in the importance of the family. We described this social change in our introductory chapter; now we must document it. Unfortunately, early kibbutz literature almost completely ignores such aspects of family life as love, courtship, and mate selection. We do know that the early kibbutzniks ideologically rejected the traditional Jewish patriarchal family on the grounds that membership in it was not voluntary, and substituted for it the commune. Many of the kibbutz's founders had immigrated to Palestine after breaking with their families and traditional way of life. In the *kvutza,* they met others who had gone through the same crisis and held the same values and ideas. They were all together in a foreign country with strange customs, a difficult climate, and hostile neighbors, including many Jews hostile to their radical purposes. How they found welcome and warmth in the surrogate families of the small, communal *kvutzot* is a recurrent theme in the writings of the earliest theoreticians of the *kvutza,* such as Tzvi Schatz and Joseph Bussell (Wurm 1960). A somewhat different presentation of the same theme appears in the famous collective memoir about Kehiliatenu, the first work battalion of the Hashomer Hatsair (Kehiliatenu 1922).

The family everywhere is firmly bound to sex and procreation. The founders of the *kvutza* were young; in addition to longing for an intimate primary group based on similar concerns, ideas, and values, they longed for sexual partners. This created a difficult problem in that the sex ratio was so unbalanced. Moreover, the founders wondered what place sexual relationships should have in a tight solidary group where all people were to be intimate friends and one's first commitment was to be to the group. Could intimate friendship spill over into sexuality? Should sex too be communal?

We have no way of knowing if the idea of communal sexuality was raised in the early kibbutzim. Our informants in Tsvi and Tsvia denied that such a suggestion was ever made. According to one of the founders of Tsvia, "There was never the idea that since we belonged to the commune, we had to share 'the fruits of love' with everyone. There were different types of people, and maybe some of them thought of the possibility. For instance, in one of the first kibbutzim, in the Valley of Israel, there was a man who lived with two women. You have to take into account the spirit of the years after World War I. There was permissiveness in the air, something like that of the hippies today. You also have to understand that we didn't live in an organized community, and we were often lonely. Yet our social life was very intense. We yearned to pour out our souls to someone. Finding a woman to make love to wasn't the only problem. Some of us were looking for mothers, and some of the girls were looking for older men to be their fathers."

A woman of the same kibbutz told the story of an exceptional case of an unwanted pregnancy:

"One time a girl became pregnant, and the boy didn't want to acknowledge their relationship and left the kibbutz. After the girl had given birth to a daughter, one of the members of the kibbutz went as her husband to the hospital to take her home. The little girl was registered under her mother's name and has been living in the kibbutz ever since. We understood 'free love' as the freedom to choose your lover not according to what your mother and father want for you but according to your own feelings. This didn't mean promiscuity. Just the opposite, in fact. Once you chose your partner, that was it. Oh, there were a few boys and girls who were promiscuous, but the reaction of the kibbutz was very hostile and they were made to leave as soon as possible."

One of the woman founders of Tsvi told us:

"We didn't have promiscuity. Sexual relationships didn't depend on the marriage ceremony, but certainly they depended on deep feelings. In the Youth Movement, we had been educated to seek freedom from traditional chains. But we had been socialized in 'good Jewish homes,' so despite all the talk about free love and an occasional light touch, whenever things started to get serious, we girls resisted. Boys and girls lived together in tents and never went to bed together."

"I remember heated discussions, especially among the girls, about free love, but it was only talk," agreed another member. "Talking was the outlet for tension. This was three years before the first family was created in the kibbutz."

Another influence was the harsh life in the early period. People worked very long hours, on most days from sunrise to sunset. The standard of living was low, the food and clothing very simple. Under such circumstances, preoccupation with eroticism and love was unlikely. A song from the Third Aliyah renders the situation simply enough.

> I paved the road all through the day,
> My brain boiled in my skull.
> And in the evening, what a pity,
> I had no strength to go for a walk.

To "go for a walk" usually meant to stroll with a girlfriend or boyfriend outside the camp—almost the only chance for privacy. Even in these situations young people found their way to each other. The problem was the scarcity of girls. Our informants cited cases of two or three boys falling in love with the same girl. When she finally chose among them, the losers had to suffer the situation or leave the kibbutz, which some of them did; there were even cases of suicide.

Despite the austere life, girls paid attention to their appearance. Cleanliness took the place of cosmetics, and orderliness substituted for sophisticated clothing. Our informants could recall only a few exceptions, girls who preferred cultivating their appearance to heavy labor in the fields. These girls met with sharp informal criticism and usually left the kibbutz. The ideal image of a kibbutz girl consisted of a sunburned face, calloused hands, simple attire, a clean and orderly appearance, and warm sociability. The ideal love relationship was not based on sexuality, even though the ultimate need for it was acknowledged. The emphasis was on intimate friendship and ideological and personal empathy.

It took a long time for people to decide who would be their partners for life, for permanence was expected. Once the decision had been made, all the couple had to do was ask for a separate room or tent; there was no ceremony. The community acknowledged the creation of the new family simply by noting that the spouses lived in the same room. The couple did not appear together as a unit in any of the formal or informal gatherings of the kibbutz, such as the Assembly, dining room, and work assignments; they dealt individually with all situations. For a long time, especially in the Hashomer Hatsair, wives were called by their maiden names, and in the Kibbutz Artzi, wedding rings were not in use until the early sixties.

Even the family room was not a private sanctum. Stern economic conditions prevented the building of new apartments or even tents for the growing number of couples. For emergencies, the institution of the "primus" was developed wherein a single boy or girl lodged in the room or tent of a married couple. This intrusion on the couple's only place of privacy created an almost unbearable situation. To engage in any sexual activity, the couple had to be able to determine their primus's absence from home, and this they could not always do accurately.

Not even such circumstances as those deterred people from entering family life. With the birth of children, the family gradually achieved wider legitimacy. This became easier as new groups joined the kibbutzim. Nevertheless, until the War of Liberation, the family as an institution remained modest and inconspicuous. After the war, the family became more visible and began to acquire broader functions, especially in consumption and education.

FAMILY LIFE IN OFER

Family life springs from courtship. When a boy on leave from the army brings his girlfriend home, it is taken for granted that the girl will spend the night in his room (his roommate, if also on leave, must find other lodgings; this is considered a peer's duty).

Girls usually engage in courtship much earlier than boys and go through its preliminary phases within their own kibbutzim. At fifteen or sixteen, they are often going out with boys four or five years older than they who are in the kibbutz as part of a *garin,* and by the time they are sixteen or seventeen they may visit their boyfriends in their rooms.

In the kibbutz it is generally assumed that a deep emotional relationship is a precondition of sexual intercourse. When a boy and girl live together, the liaison is considered "serious." Although young people are never formally interfered with, those who change partners too frequently are criticized by public opinion, which here, as elsewhere, takes the form of gossip. Public opinion may be equally harsh about "Don Juans" and female *parparit* (butterflies), but it is somewhat more tolerant of the boys. A boy's community does not usually witness the early phases of his courtship or know the girl, whereas a girl's courtship takes place within her own kibbutz. For their part, parents play absolutely no role in mate selection. The few who try to are severely sanctioned.

When an affair looks to be serious, people begin asking, "Nu, when are we going to drink?"—meaning, of course, drink at the wedding. When a generally recognized *zug* (couple) shows affection in public, the only acceptable outcome is marriage. There is no formal engagement. The wedding date is set after consultation with the housing committee as to when the couple will receive an apartment, with the *ekonomith* as to when the festive wedding meal can be arranged, and with the couple's parents. "We are in no hurry," the young people say, and many couples live together for a long time before the actual wedding takes place.

In some kibbutzim of the Kibbutz Artzi, the time when couples live together before the wedding functions as a sort of "trial marriage." It is rare for couples who enter a trial marriage to separate (Rosner, personal communication).

The wedding ceremony is a grand affair, with all the members of the kibbutz taking part. In Ofer in the last decade, the average number of guests invited from outside the commune has been 300. The bride acquires a white wedding dress, a veil, the right shoes. Before the wedding day she visits a hairdresser and beautician. The boy's preparations are more moderate. All he has to do is go to the rabbi to arrange for the ceremony, and buy wedding rings. The main burden falls on the kitchen, which must prepare a meal for 500 to 600 people, and on the culture committee which must prepare the *messiba,* the entertainment program for the festive evening. The parents of the couple occupy themselves sending out invitations, and usually the mothers get new dresses for the event.

On the day of the wedding, the kitchen is like a beehive. One group prepares food, sweets, and drink, another tables, chairs, and benches for the guests. The clubhouse is turned into a reception room. Children run around directing the guests to their proper places. At sunset, the rabbi arrives and goes to the parents' room to determine if everything has been duly made ready for the ceremony. The *chupa* —the traditional ritual canopy for the wedding—usually stands in an open place. The religious ceremony itself is brief; since most of the principals are not religious, the content and traditional nuances are not taken very seriously. Cameras click and smiles flourish, and after the ceremony the great meal begins.

The religious ceremony is a duty to the state: the new couple is officially accepted by the kibbutz in the *messiba.* The *messiba* has two aspects, one serious and one gay. In the serious part, a text taken mostly from the *Song of Songs* is both recited and sung, and the secretary of the kibbutz hands the couple a document written on parchment, imitating the religious *ketuba*—essentially an agreement to pay the wife a certain sum in the event of divorce (on the kibbutz this is, of course, purely symbolic). The gay part consists of light entertainment and the recital of humorous events from the couple's life and love story, spiced with songs and dances. After the *messiba,* there is dancing to an orchestra until well past midnight.

The new apartment the young couple occupies is usually better furnished and equipped than the oldtimers'. The couple may go on a honeymoon at once, or, if they wish to travel abroad, postpone it. For about a year they spend all their time together and show signs of affection in public. Soon enough, however, they become another of the kibbutz's prosaic families.

Many people, especially women, are preoccupied with which young woman will be next in line for the new *kita* in the babies' house. Pregnant women are the objects of everyone's care and attention.

When the young woman goes to the hospital for delivery, there is a mood of apprehension in the kibbutz. When at last the telephone message comes from the hospital, everyone hurries to congratulate the new father, and occasionally the grandparents, and when the mother returns with the baby, there is a reception for the new parents in the clubhouse.

Family life is an important consideration in the kibbutz. Spouses are supposed to eat with their partners in the dining room, sit with them in the General Assembly, when films are shown, and at other cultural events, and in general to know where they are. They are supposed to go on annual vacations together and do their night-watch duty together.

The family home is the home of the couple only. The children join their parents in the afternoon, and for five o'clock tea or coffee (even adolescents who spend very little time at their parents' apartment usually appear to have tea and cake with the family). There are multigeneration families in Ofer that sometimes organize gatherings of the entire extended family. Birthday parties and wedding anniversaries, to which friends are invited, are celebrated by the family.

Family apartments in Ofer are quite large and elaborate, entailing considerable maintenance. Thursday evening is the usual time for cleaning, and no committee meetings are held then; the wives are busy washing floors, cleaning carpets, doing the kitchenette and bathroom. Husbands help somewhat reluctantly, perhaps because the wives have made it clear that they do not think much of their cleaning ability. The men usually do the "hard" work, such as taking out garbage, beating carpets, and fixing electrical outlets and garden pipes. Part of the Thursday ceremony is baking. Since most of the sons and daughters in the army come home for leave on the weekend, cakes must be ready by Friday.

Shabbat and holidays are the occasions for serious family life. Although these days the husband or wife may work part-time, most people get up later than usual and sometimes have breakfast at home rather than in the dining room. Children come home in the morning to spend almost all day with their parents, eating lunch with them in the dining room. Saturday afternoon is for sleep or rest; young children rest with their parents.

Crises of family life are viewed by the kibbutz with ambivalence.

Family life is considered private business, but when separation or divorce occurs, the kibbutz's sympathy is usually given to the partner considered wronged. If the family cannot work out its quarrel, the spouses may seek assistance from the social affairs committee. Sometimes a family crisis stays on the committee's agenda for more than a year as efforts to conciliate and arbitrate continue. The arbitration is usually carried out by one or two specially delegated members who are on good terms with the spouses.

In cases of divorce, the spouses usually agree on who will remain in the apartment and who will leave; it is usually the woman who keeps the apartment. Widows and widowers can continue living in their apartments even if the quarters were not intended for single people. "Broken" families are usually considered complete families for most purposes.

In the kibbutz, then, the nuclear family is the most important social unit to both the individual and the social structure (Shepher 1969a, 1969b), but there is very intense interaction between agnatic and lateral kin, and between consanguines and affines. In Ofer, for instance, the limited development of "extended families" can now be seen. Three of them are represented in the genealogical charts, pages 215-217.

Family A has twenty-one members of four generations, between the ages of three and eighty-three, eleven of whom are adolescent or adult women. Family B has fourteen members of four generations, between the ages of three and seventy-eight, five of whom are adolescent or adult women. Family C has fifteen members of three generations, between the ages of one and sixty-five, five of whom are adolescent or adult women.

The general interaction is equally intense in the three families, but only in Family A do we see a female line which is reflected in work. The head of the system is the matron of seventy-eight. She is still a very active woman, working thirty hours a week and serving as kibbutz postmistress. She is also very family-minded, the custodian of twenty-one birthdays, eight wedding dates, and such events as births, circumcisions, and bar mitzvahs. In her family of twenty-one there is, on the average, one such event each month, and when it occurs, the old woman organizes "her girls" to prepare the festive get-together for the whole family in the old barracks where the great-

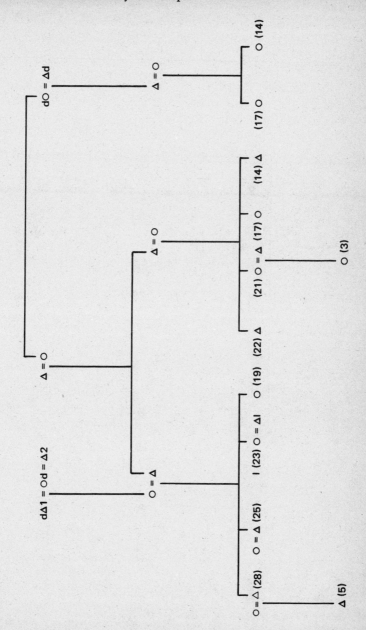

Family A

Family B

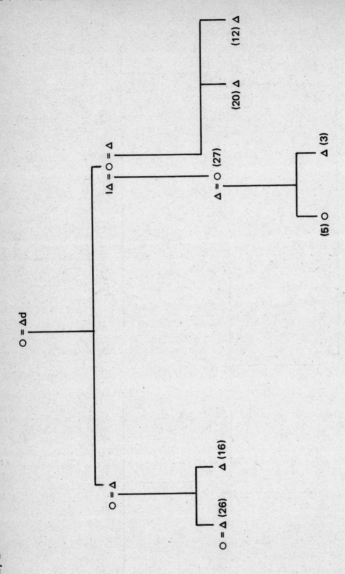

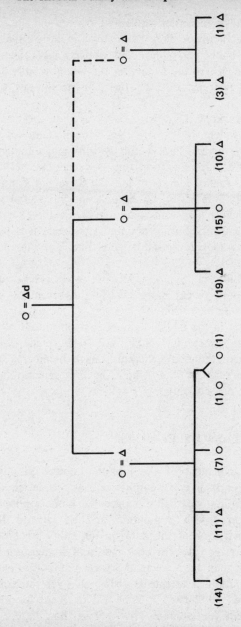

Family C

d = deceased
l = left the kibbutz
--- = adoption
number in parentheses = age of third and fourth generation
∧ = twins

grandparents live. She is a master cook and baker, and stimulates all the women in the family to help her deliver materials from the kitchen, peel, cook, bake, set tables, and prepare gifts. She does much of the work herself. All the women in the family readily accept her authority, which is transmitted by the daughters-in-law to the granddaughters.

The collective work of the "girls of A," as they are called in the kibbutz with benevolent joking, is always very pleasurable, creating as it does an atmosphere of large-family warmth and commitment.

In Family A, the four-generation line is patrilineal, in Family B matrilineal, yet no family hierarchy has developed in Family B. The matron of Family B is a very good cook and baker, but she is less effective in organizing her family's four girls. To the extent that there is any hierarchical relationship among the women, it is usually along the grandmother-daughter-granddaughter line. The same is true in Family C.

An intensive study of a larger kibbutz with several quasi-extended families would reveal more clearly the extent to which female hierarchy is characteristic of the large, multigenerational family as a social form in the kibbutz, rather than the result of some idiosyncratic factor. Distinctions would have to be made between older kibbutzim, where the first generation have members' status, and newer kibbutzim such as Ofer, where the first generation have the status of resident parents only.

THE CONSOLIDATION OF FAMILISM

The main concrete indicators of the kibbutz family's vitality are nuptiality, fertility, and divorce. To emphasize that certain tendencies are special to the kibbutz, we shall compare the kibbutz population to both Israel's rural Jewish population and its general Jewish population. Let us first look at the data on nuptiality (Table 47).

We see that marriage rates for both men and women are much higher in the kibbutz than they are in the rural population and the general Jewish population. The rate is rising all over the country, and during the decade 1962-1971 it grew 1.8 per cent for kibbutz men and 1.3 per cent for women. This is less than in the rural

Table 47
Marriage Rates* 1962–71 in Kibbutzim, the Rural Jewish Population, and the General Jewish Population

Year	Kibbutzim		Rural Jewish Population		General Jewish Population	
	Men	Women	Men	Women	Men	Women
1962	10.8	9.9	7.4	7.0	7.3	7.3
1963	10.3	9.8	7.0	6.5	7.6	7.6
1964	11.6	11.2	7.3	7.0	7.8	7.8
1965	10.7	10.1	7.5	6.9	8.0	8.0
1966	11.1	10.8	7.5	6.9	8.0	8.0
1967	11.9	10.8	7.7	6.9	7.7	7.7
1968	13.1	12.0	8.4	8.1	8.6	8.6
1969	12.7	11.5	8.8	7.7	9.3	9.3
1970	13.0	11.9	9.0	8.1	9.5	9.5
1971	12.7	11.2	9.8	8.6	9.9	9.9

*Source: Statistical Abstracts of Israel, 1963–1973
    Rate: 1 marriage/1000 population

population (2.4 per cent and 1.6 per cent respectively) and general Jewish population (2.6 per cent). Actually, these figures are somewhat misleading, because marriages are registered according to people's addresses at the time of their wedding. Since many kibbutzniks marry outsiders, the kibbutz marriage rates are higher than the statistics suggest. A better measure is birth rates (Table 48).

In absolute numbers and in rate of growth, the kibbutz has the highest score. In 1972, the rate was 27.2 in the kibbutz, but only 23.4 in the general Jewish population and 26.6 in the rural population. The birth-rate increase is even greater. During the decade, the kibbutz rate grew by 6.1 per mil, the rate of the general Jewish population by only 1.5 per mil, and the rural populations decreased by 1.8 per mil. *In fact, it was during this decade that the kibbutz became the most fertile part of the Jewish population.* 1962 the general rural population had a birth rate of 28.4 per mil and the kibbutz

Table 48

Gross Birth Rates* 1962–72 in Kibbutzim, the Rural Jewish Population, and the General Jewish Population

Year	Kibbutzim	Rural Jewish Population	General Jewish Population
1962	21.1	28.4	21.9
1963	20.9	26.2	22.0
1964	22.2	26.6	22.4
1965	23.5	26.9	22.6
1966	23.0	24.2	22.4
1967	25.2	23.7	21.5
1968	27.0	24.7	22.8
1969	28.0	24.6	23.4
1970	28.2	25.0	24.2
1971	29.8	25.5	25.2
1972	27.2	26.6	23.4

*Source: Statistical Abstracts of Israel, 1963–1973
Rate: 1 birth/1000 population

population 21.1 per mil; ten years later, the picture was reversed. Since almost 85 per cent of the Jewish rural population belong to kibbutzim and moshavim, increased fertility more than counterbalances decreased fertility in the moshav (an interesting fact in itself, insofar as the moshav has a family-centered social pattern).

Divorce rates may also indicate the vitality of the family. Until the last decade, the kibbutz had a higher divorce rate than the general Jewish population; it usually equaled the rate of Tel Aviv, which was the highest in Israel. In 1954, for instance, the divorce rate of kibbutz husbands was 1.55 per cent, of kibbutz wives 1.91 per cent, and of the general Jewish population 1.43 per cent Table 49 shows divorce rates in this decade.

We see that today the kibbutz divorce rate is lower than that of the general Jewish population but somewhat higher than that of the rural population. During the decade, the divorce rate of kibbutz

Table 49
Divorce Rates* 1962–71 in Kibbutzim, the Rural Jewish Population, and the
General Jewish Population

Year	Kibbutzim		Rural Jewish Population		General Jewish Population	
	Men	Women	Men	Women	Men	Women
1962	1.0	1.1	0.6	0.6	1.0	1.0
1963	1.0	1.1	0.6	0.6	1.0	1.0
1964	0.8	1.0	0.6	0.5	1.0	1.0
1965	0.7	0.7	0.5	0.5	1.0	1.0
1966	0.7	0.9	0.5	0.5	0.9	0.9
1967	0.8	0.9	0.5	0.5	0.9	0.9
1968	0.8	0.9	0.6	0.5	0.9	0.9
1969	0.8	0.9	0.5	0.5	0.9	0.9
1970	0.8	0.8	0.5	0.5	0.9	0.9
1971	0.8	0.9	0.6	0.5	0.9	0.9

*Source: Statistical Abstracts of Israel, 1963–1973
   Rate: 1 divorce/1000 population

husbands fell 0.2 per cent, and of kibbutz wives 0.3 per cent; in the
general Jewish population, the decrease was 0.1 per cent; in the rural
population, the rate of husbands did not fall, and that of wives decreased by 0.1 per cent.

Gross rates of marriage, birth, and divorce may be influenced
by age, mortality, and sex ratio. Unfortunately they are the best
indicators we have; no gross or net reproduction rates and net rates
of marriage and divorce are available for the kibbutz population.
But we do have a rough indication that in the past decade the kibbutz
family has become a stable and fertile unit.

To get a general picture of our two federations, Tables 50a and
50b show data on marital status and age for these populations.

A very large percentage of the kibbutz population is or has
been married—in the Ichud, more than 91 per cent of the women,
in the Kibbutz Artzi more than 93 per cent. The respective figures

Table 50A

Population of the Ichud Federation by Sex, Marital Status, and Age (in percentages)

Age / Marital Status	Men			Women		
	Single	Married	Divorced and Widowed	Single	Married	Divorced and Widowed
50 +	6.87	29.89	70.35	10.86	25.16	70.64
40 +	5.47	17.70	11.63	1.94	18.16	13.75
30 +	6.35	22.55	12.21	6.00	20.16	7.62
20 +	81.31	29.86	5.81	81.20	36.52	7.99
Total	100.0 (18.06)	100.0 (79.65)	100.0 (2.29)	100.0 (8.78)	100.0 (83.57)	100.0 (7.65)

Note: The percentages in parentheses indicate relative proportions of marital statuses for both sexes.

Table 50B

Population of the Kibbutz Artzi Federation by Sex, Marital Status, and Age (in percentages)

Age / Marital Status	Men			Women		
Sex	Single	Married	Divorced and Widowed	Single	Married	Divorced and Widowed
50 +	6.3	30.59	62.69	13.31	26.13	63.68
40 +	6.1	20.95	15.42	2.57	19.95	16.41
30 +	8.3	23.37	13.43	6.01	22.34	12.25
20 +	79.3	25.09	8.46	78.11	31.58	7.66
Total	100.0 (10.95)	100.0 (86.33)	100.0 (2.72)	100.0 (6.50)	100.0 (87.12)	100.0 (6.38)

Note: The percentages in parentheses indicate relative proportions of marital statuses for both sexes.

for men are 82 per cent and 89 per cent. Most of the divorced and widowed in both federations are in the highest age group. About 80 per cent of all the singles in both federations and both sexes are under thirty. As the average marriage age for both sexes is between twenty and thirty, we can assume that many of the singles in this age category will marry. The estimated percentages of people above thirty who have not married are 3.37 per cent of Ichud men and 2.26 per cent of Kibbutz Artzi men, 1.65 per cent of Ichud women, and 1.42 per cent of Kibbutz Artzi women.

Kibbutz life is therefore essentially made up of married couples. In fact, single people have become such a problem in recent years that the kibbutz tries to arrange situations in which they can find partners—through work assignments in the kibbutz or a year's leave for work in the city, where the supply of prospective mates is greater, or a two-year assignment of activity outside the kibbutz—say in the federations' administration, for example. If all these efforts fail, a single person may be sent to the interkibbutz marriage bureau, whose staff of social workers and family counselors try to make a connection between singles who seem suitable for each other. Several times a year the department organizes weekends, vacations, and trips both in Israel and abroad for its clientele—all financed by the kibbutzim and the various federations. Often the department succeeds; old bachelors marry divorcees and widows, sometimes having to change their residences. As a result of these efforts, the estimated 1.5 to 3.3 per cent of singles is now dwindling, and many are spared a future of loneliness that would have been all the bleaker in the extremely family-centered kibbutz.

What about the children of these marriages? Tables 51a and 51b describe our two federations according to sex, number of children, and marital status.

The single most significant fact in these tables is that approximately half of all married kibbutzniks have three or more children. The overall average is about 2.8. Approximately 80 per cent of the married people and 75 per cent of the divorced and widowed have at least two children. Only about 15 per cent have one child, and very few have none at all.

An extremely small number of unmarried men and women in both federations was registered as having children—in both federa-

Table 51A

Population of the Kibbutz Artzi Federation by Sex, Number of Children, and Marital Status (in percentages)

Sex	Male				Female			
Marital Status \ Number of children	None	1	2	3+	None	1	2	3+
Single	98.27	1.24	0.38	0.01	96.78	2.79	0.43	—
Married	4.64	15.77	29.17	50.42	2.71	15.44	29.51	52.35
Divorced or Widowed	8.96	20.40	36.32	34.32	4.16	22.98	38.95	33.91
Total	15.01	14.31	26.21	44.47	8.91	15.09	28.22	47.78

Table 51B

Population of the Ichud Federation by Sex, Marital Status, and Number of Children (horizontal percentages)

Sex	Male					Female				
Marital Status \ Number of children	None	1	2	3+	Total	None	1	2	3+	Total
Single	96.31	3.25	0.37	0.07	100.0	96.27	2.76	0.65	0.32	100.0
Married	6.43	15.26	28.92	49.39	100.0	3.98	15.49	29.30	51.23	100.0
Divorced or Widowed	13.37	21.51	34.30	30.82	100.0	6.32	22.68	33.83	37.17	100.0
Total	22.82	13.23	23.89	40.06	100.0	12.26	14.92	27.13	45.69	100.0

tions, approximately 0.034 per cent of the total adult population. Most of these people are in high age brackets, and some of them have unusual histories. We have already described one in our discussion of the founding generation. Another is a young woman who had been so disappointed by a love affair that she decided never to marry. She was, however, unwilling to forego the experience of motherhood and asked a man outside the kibbutz to impregnate her. She reared the child in the kibbutz. We were unable to follow up on each case history, but we do know that all the children involved were raised in the kibbutz without discrimination. The number of such children in the two federations is about 200.

Another trait of the kibbutz is that the existence of children does not in itself seem to prevent divorce. In the Ichud Federation, 50 per cent of the category "divorced or widowed men" are divorced, as are 34 per cent of "divorced or widowed women." Even if we assume that everyone in the "no child" category is divorced rather than widowed, it still turns out that most divorced people are parents. Collective education and child care clearly relieve parents to a great extent of the fear that divorce may seriously jeopardize their children's development.

WOMEN'S PART IN THE DEVELOPMENT OF FAMILISM

The emphasis on the family as the basic social unit in kibbutz life has been called familism. We use the term in a relative sense; what the kibbutzim practice is far from the true familism of the traditional Chinese, for example. But seen in the light of the early kibbutz ideology about the family, the term is justified today. Children's housing and the "hour of love" (sheat haahava)—the morning half-hour when mothers take their children out of the children's houses to play or walk with them—are two important indications that it has been women who have principally generated the rise of familism.

Public opinion about housing was investigated twice in the Ichud Federation, first by Talmon (1958) and then by Shepher (1967). Table 52 presents their data on support for and rejection of familistic housing.

By 1955 the majority of the women in the kibbutz supported

Table 52
Changes in Attitudes toward the Children's Housing System, 1955–65, in the
Ichud Federation (in percentages)

	1955		1965	
	Men	Women	Men	Women
Support Collective System	49.0	37.0	44.8	24.8
Support Familistic System	40.0	51.0	46.9	68.0
No Opinion	11.0	12.0	8.3	7.2
Total	100.0	100.0	100.0	100.0

familistic housing; only 40 per cent of the men agreed. A decade later, the gap between men and women had widened; in 1965, more than two-thirds of the women—but only 47 per cent of the men—supported familistic housing. If we categorize the kibbutzim as conservative and liberal, the gap between the sexes is the same. In the conservative kibbutzim, women's support of familistic housing grew from 39 per cent to 59.6, men's from 23 per cent to only 37. In the liberal kibbutzim, women's support grew from 66 per cent to 75, men's from 53 per cent to 53.6.

More important, women sparked and sustained the process of change in every kibbutz where familism had been introduced. The women started with informal discussions, brought the question to the agenda of the education committee, where they usually constitute the majority, then created pressure to bring the problem before the General Assembly (which is a legitimate form of preliminary lobbying) for a positive vote; where they had to, they resorted to propaganda, and even threats within their families. Most of the men who were leaders in the process were husbands of the most forceful women advocating change.

In the long and fervent discussions that took place, it was often said that the familistic system would put an added burden on women. The usual answer was, "We don't mind, we're ready to do anything to have our children with us during the night." Indeed, the work load of women is much heavier in familistic kibbutzim. Children who have slept at home must be brought to the children's houses by their mothers, since their fathers usually start work early in the fields. The mothers, of course, also work, but first they must awaken their children, wash and dress them, and take them to the children's houses. The sexual division of domestic labor is more polarized in familistic than in collectivistic kibbutzim. Owing to the need for separate rooms for the children, the family has a larger, better-equipped apartment; the women therefore have more work to do, but the men participate no more than they do in the collectivistic system (Shepher 1967). It is clear that women's desire for familism is not dampened by the added work it creates.

The other manifestation of women's role in stimulating familism is the recent phenomenon of the "hour of love." This custom was started by young kibbutz women some time after 1964. Like most of the other social changes in the kibbutz, it has undergone the interesting transformation from deviation to innovation to legitimacy. At first, some women who were not working due to convalescence, vacation, or flexible work schedule went to the children's houses and, with or without the nurse's approval, took out their children. Later, the women working inside the kibbutz contrived work schedules that enabled them to spend at least half an hour a day with their children. This innovation created problems: children whose mothers did not come to pick them up felt frustrated; the nurses themselves needed time to take out their own children, which they could do only if all their charges were tended by their mothers. So the practice was legitimized by the education committee, which made it compulsory and gave it the name "hour of love."

In some kibbutzim this familistic intrusion in collective education imposed severe problems on the women who worked outside the kibbutz, such as teachers in district schools. In Ofer, one young high-school teacher declared she would continue her work in the district high school, six miles from the kibbutz, only if she were driven home and back every morning for the "hour of love" with her two-and-a-half-year-old daughter. As there was no way to arrange this, she took a job within the kibbutz. This admittedly was an exceptional case, but the "hour of love" did create many difficulties in all four kibbutzim we investigated, despite some grandmothers or husbands who worked at home, making the situation easier. In fact, the new practice has discouraged young women from pursuing further education and work outside the kibbutz (Shepher 1967).

At this point, we must briefly discuss the theories of Bruno

Bettelheim. In *Children of the Dream* (1969), based on seven weeks of research in 1964, Bettelheim devotes a short chapter to kibbutz women. Perhaps because of his particular view of psychoanalysis, in which the roots of behavior are held to be unconscious, repressed, and otherwise concealed, Bettelheim hypothesizes that communal education has its source in kibbutz woman's deep anxiety about her inadequacy as a mother. This inadequacy, he says, has its source in her rejection of the ghetto culture's strong maternal image and social patterns. Therefore, when she wanted there to be equality of the sexes, she was "acting on her anxiety."

This theory is not securely based on evidence; Bettelheim himself declares that "some of what I deduce here as the inner source of women's fears about their own mothering ability is speculation." Our evidence contradicts almost everything Bettelheim claimed in his book. We believe that the gradual polarization of sex roles, which according to our data was in full force by 1964, does not indicate that sexual equality was a reaction to a deep anxiety. On the contrary, we believe that it was positive ideology that men and women wanted to put into practice. They gradually abandoned hope of being able to do so fully because sexual division of labor became indispensable for everyday life (since it was never suggested that men could care for small children). If they had been deeply anxious, as Bettelheim claimed they were, then presumably the kibbutz would have tenaciously maintained an egalitarian division of labor, and women would not have entered conventionally female work at first with acquiesence and finally with devotion and enthusiasm.

According to our data, Bettelheim's theory that communal education is rooted in this same anxiety is false. Let us assume for the sake of discussion that his proposition is true—that first-generation kibbutz women created communal education because they felt that they were inadequate mothers. What about the second generation of kibbutz women? Why should they be more familistic, more "feminine," than their mothers? Where would *their* anxiety come from? Not only did the mothers return to traditional female roles, the daughters found the social norms of communal education—already diluted by the mothers' compromises—insufficiently "feminine" and familistic. Bettelheim might always have argued that the second-generation women rebelled against their mothers, enthusiastically embracing femininity and familism. But both the polarized sexual division of labor and familism were initiated and carried out by the first generation; their daughters' role was to consolidate them. Talmon's data (1956), collected eight years before Bettelheim did his research, already reflected a highly polarized division of labor and a strong spirit of familism. Ten years later, Shepher (1967) found that the second generation was slightly more familistic than the first. And now our recent research shows that mothers and daughters together returned to both the sexual division of labor and familism, which Bettelheim claimed the mothers had originally wanted to reject.

True, the "hour of love" seems bizarre to many kibbutz members, but the mothers of the first generation never tried to dismantle it. Male managers loudly protest the loss of work hours and the interference with the basic principles of communal education. But the female "establishment" of the education committees of the kibbutzim and federations maintain the practice despite its ideological inappropriateness.

DOMESTIC DIVISION OF LABOR AND AUTHORITY

Today the typical kibbutz apartment consists of one and a half rooms, a small kitchenette, and a balcony. In the twenty to twenty-five kibbutzim where children sleep in their parents' apartments, there is usually an additional room. The apartment is not large—about forty square meters, or 430 square feet—but still it must be cleaned, the beds must be made, the dishes must be washed (every kibbutz family consumes at least one meal a day at home—the afternoon tea or coffee—and occasionally a family decides to have a dinner or a Saturday morning breakfast at home). The apartment often needs minor electrical or plumbing repairs. Laundry is taken care of by communal institutions, but still it must be delivered and picked up. And the small garden around each apartment—usually a lawn with flowers but in some cases with one or two fruit trees as well—must be tended. How is this work divided between husband and wife?

One way to ascertain how people divide work is to ask them, but one cannot be sure that they are telling the whole truth. Participant observation is a much more reliable method, but difficult and time-consuming. We used both methods. We asked our interviewees, "In your family, who usually performs the following tasks?" Table 53 summarizes the answers in our four kibbutzim.

Despite differences among the four kibbutzim, there are some regularities in the division of labor. The first four tasks—repairs, gardening, taking and picking up laundry—are usually performed by men. Tasks connected with food and cleaning the apartment are usually performed by women. The transferring and handling of money are done by both sexes; when a kibbutznik needs money, he must go to the secretariat and ask for cash.

Many activities are performed jointly. When we compare the total percentages of all thirteen activities, we find that only 20 per cent of the respondents claim that there are certain tasks that are done by men only. The remaining female respondents attributed more tasks to themselves than their husbands attributed to them. Two activities are uniformly reported as being carried out by women—cleaning the kitchenette and cleaning the lavatory.

Participant observation verifies most of the data in this table, and also indicates that some work reported as being done jointly is actually subject to sexual division of labor. The usual criterion of the division of household labor in the kibbutz is physical ability: "heavy work" is done by the men, as are technical tasks such as working with electricity and plumbing; activities connected with the interior of the apartment are done mostly by the women. But in the weekly cleaning of the apartment, an inner division of labor can be discerned. For instance, the husband may remove garbage, clean rugs and carpets, move furniture, and even wash the floor (or, failing that, bring water for the wife to wash the floor with). Cleaning, dusting, polishing, vacuuming, and always and especially cleaning the kitchenette and cleaning the lavatory are the wife's job. A similar division of labor operates in gardening, with the heavy work of digging, hoeing, and mowing usually being one by the man, and the weeding, planting, and picking of flowers by the woman.

There are many individual exceptions to this general pattern. In some families, all tasks are done by the woman, usually because the husband works long and unusual hours. This situation is ridiculed in kibbutz gossip; people call the husband an *effendi*, Arabic for a feudal landlord who gives orders but does nothing himself. In some

Table 53
Reported Division of Domestic Labor in Four Kibbutzim (in percentages)

Kibbutz	Ofer						Ofra						Tsvi						Tsvia					
Interviewee	Man			Woman			Man			Woman			Man			Woman			Man			Woman		
Who Performs Activity	M	W	M+W	M	W	M+W	M	W	M+W	M	W	M+W	M	W	M+W	M	W	M+W	M	W	M+W	M	W	M+W
Repairs	44	12	44	62	15	23	75	0	25	76	2	22	52	12	36	44	16	40	67	0	33	74	5	21
Gardening	38	12	50	46	17	37	57	6	37	55	16	29	37	25	38	40	16	44	27	20	53	37	16	47
Taking Laundry	33	14	53	26	36	38	44	6	50	51	10	39	52	12	36	40	13	47	33	13	54	20	15	65
Bringing Laundry	24	30	46	16	35	49	46	17	37	44	20	36	46	13	41	20	33	47	20	33	47	20	30	50
Taking Food Products	14	53	33	8	76	16	9	50	41	9	53	38	0	76	24	7	67	26	6	67	27	5	85	10
Preparing 5 o'clock Tea	4	53	43	2	56	42	6	45	49	4	54	42	4	52	44	4	47	49	0	67	33	0	58	42
Washing Dishes	7	21	72	8	40	52	11	25	64	10	36	54	4	17	79	4	36	60	6	47	47	10	40	50
Cleaning Apartment	2	38	60	0	52	48	4	51	45	3	64	33	0	39	61	0	44	56	6	47	47	10	40	50
Washing Floor	18	48	36	10	53	37	6	35	55	4	46	50	21	21	58	16	40	44	13	27	60	11	28	61
Cleaning Kitchenette	7	79	14	2	84	14	6	61	33	4	70	26	0	64	36	0	92	8	0	73	27	0	95	5
Cleaning Lavatory	3	86	11	2	86	12	2	72	26	2	76	22	4	84	12	4	92	4	0	67	33	0	80	20
Transferring Money	26	34	40	31	22	47	23	19	58	26	22	52	12	54	34	16	28	56	40	6	54	21	21	58
Handling Money	36	16	48	20	16	64	6	12	82	6	10	84	13	26	61	12	28	60	40	0	60	10	10	80
Performed Together	20	38	42	18	45	37	22	32	46	22	37	41	19	38	43	31	20	49	20	35	45	43	18	39

families, almost everything is done by the husband, usually because
the wife is sick. Sanctions against this situation are much milder
than against the first; this suggests the compensatory effects of the
social norms.

We venture to state that the wife usually does at least twice as
much household work as the husband, some eight hours a week to
his three to four. If we take into account that most men work one
hour more than the women do each day, we see that the total working
hours are in balance; thus, kibbutz women have an advantage over
working women in many other societies, who may carry two heavy
burdens without relief in either.

Household division of labor is a favorite subject of small talk,
especially among men. On Thursday afternoon, a man says to his
friends, "I have to hurry. If I'm not home by five o'clock, I'll catch
it from my wife." When asked just what he contributes to housework,
a typical man's answer is, "I do what I can, but her standards for
cleaning are too high. I'd do more, but what I do isn't good enough
for her. She says that if I did it, she'd just have to do it again." Such
apparent rationalizations are usually accepted by the wife with good-
hearted irony. In fact, it seems that the husband's physical presence
during cleaning is more important to the wife than is his actual participation. Wives expect to be praised by their husbands for their
household abilities, and rarely complain about their laziness.

The division of authority within the family is much more egalitarian than the division of work. Most of the interviewees claimed
that decisions are made jointly. Observation verifies this; husband and
wife discuss every important activity and decide together what to do
with their free time, how to spend money, whether or not to have
another child, what to study, which jobs to take, what political cause
to embrace. It is considered legitimate to postpone deciding whether
to accept an important political nomination until after one has talked
it over with one's spouse, for such tasks usually mean transferring
most of one's household work to one's spouse. The only sphere of
decision-making in which the wife's authority is usually unchallenged
is household cleanliness and order and aesthetic matters. And sometimes the mother has the upper hand in regard to the education of
small children.

In the division of work and authority, then, the kibbutz is a picture of "companionship marriage" (Burgess and Locke 1953; Bott 1954)—a picture, however, in which the sexual division of labor is still preserved. Egalitarian ideology seems to be more effective in the microstructure of the family than in the macrostructure of the kibbutz.

MULTIVARIATE ANALYSIS

Thus far in this narrative one might conclude that the basic causes of division of labor are now clear: women cannot achieve high positions in the political system because they are burdened with children and in general preoccupied with family life. This is the classic problem of "women's two roles"—the basic conflict between her family obligations and her professional or political status or both. To verify such an hypothesis, we must reanalyze our data to see whether family roles do indeed stunt a woman's chance of rising on the political ladder. We have already examined the variables of marital status and number of children. (We also looked for correlations with political activity of such background variables of age, education, and military rank.) We maintain that it was innovative not only to examine the effects of these variables (especially number of children) on political activity, but also to see whether family and background variables affect work and sphere of activity, and whether these work variables mediate the effect of the background variables on political activity. We subjected the following variables to a multivariate stepwise regression analysis.[1]

Year of birth
Marital status
Number of children
Education
Military rank
First work
Longest work
Last work
Sphere of activity
Level of activity

We assumed, for we could not be absolutely certain, that the first five variables are comparatively independent. The first twelve years of education are an independent variable, but higher education may be an outcome of work or even of political activity; since the basic education is undoubtedly an independent variable, we included education in this category. We further assumed that work and sphere of activity are variables affecting political status. Work is the province of everyone in the kibbutz, but political activity is not. We concluded that the level of activity that indicates political status would be the dependent variable.

This arrangement of the variables is not arbitrary. It is deeply rooted in the usual ways of achieving status in the kibbutz. Marital status, number of children, education, and military rank all influence what work a person will do, in what sphere he will be active, and the level of political activity he will reach. Certainly, such variables as intelligence and sociability are equally important, but for the purposes of this study it was impossible to acquire such data.

A primary analysis of our data led us to exclude two variables from the first five. The zero-order correlations of marital status and military rank were so small that we concluded they have no independent impact on our main variables. Marital status, of course, has an impact on number of children, but this variable is so evident as to be virtually useless to us. Since, as we saw in Chapter 5, there is a very high correlation among the three work variables, to simplify our analysis we used only one, last work.

As we explained in Chapter 4, we do not have data on sphere of activity or on level of activity for the Kibbutz Artzi Federation. Therefore the complete multivariate analysis can be presented only for the Ichud. Since we have seen repeatedly that the differences between the two federations are very small, we can be confident that the analysis of the Ichud data fairly represents the Kibbutz Artzi as well.

The multivariate analysis is presented in the following two figures —path analysis—and one table. The figures describe direct and indirect correlations among the variables for Ichud men and women. They show direct influence, and indirect influence through other intervening variables. Table 54 gives figures on the kind of influence that four variables have on the level of activity, the total influence being represented by the zero-order correlation between the variable and level of activity. Then there is the direct influence that the variable has

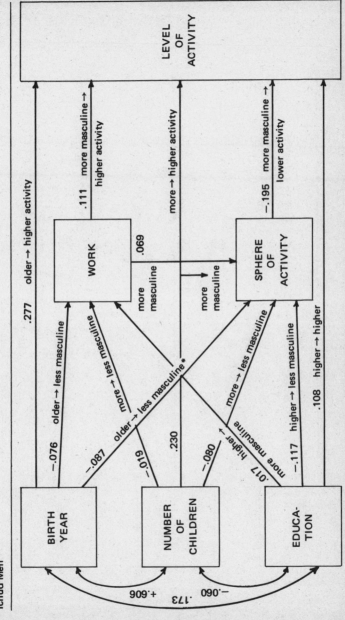

*Summarized figure based on an analysis of ten variables. Four variables were excluded from the presentation of the relationships: however they were included in the calculation of the relative influences.

Figure 5*
Ichud Men

Figure 6*
Ichud Women

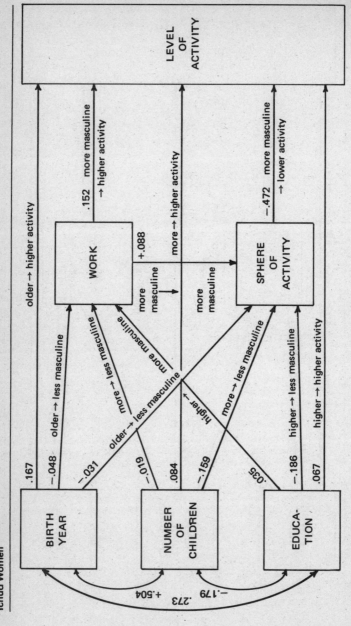

Table 54
Direct and Indirect Influences of Independent Variables on Level of Activity

Sex	Type of Influence	Variables			
		Year of Birth	Number of Children	Education	Work
Men	Total*	+.287	+.348	+.106	+.104
	Direct**	+.277	+.230	+.108	+.111
	Indirect***	+.010	+.118	−.002	−.007
Women	Total	+.177	+.202	+.101	+.11!
	Direct	+.167	+.084	+.067	+.152
	Indirect	+.010	+.118	+.034	−.041

  *zero order correlation with level of activity
 **weighted direct influence on level of activity
***weighted indirect influence on level of activity through other independent
   variables

on the level of activity. Last, there is the indirect influence that the variable has through other variables on the level of activity.

The *direction* of the correlations is identical in men and women. For instance, we find the unsurprising correlation that the older one is, the higher the level of activity one is likely to reach. The differences between the sexes lie in the *intensity* of the correlation, and in the fact that for men the three basic variables have a much stronger direct influence on the dependent variable than they do for women. What this means is that in the case of women more than of men, the way to higher political activity is through work and excellence in spheres of activity, especially female ones. In the case of men, education especially affects level of activity directly.

Let us now compare the influence of the three basic variables on the dependent variable.

1. *Year of Birth*

  a. The older one is, the less masculine the work one does. This correlation is not very strong, and it is easily understood: few women, and they are usually young, do men's work; and men, as they grow older, are transferred to less physically demanding service work, which is defined as female.

b. The older one is, the less masculine the sphere of activity in which one is involved. The correlation is very weak, and also easily understood: few women, and they are usually young, enter masculine spheres of activity.

c. The older one is, the greater one's chances of rising to a high level of activity. The correlation is stronger for men than it is for women. For both sexes, the influence of age is direct.

2. *Number of Children*

a. If we follow the path analysis through work, we find a very few low negative correlations between number of children and type of work. That is, a woman who has more children than other women is only a little less likely to enter masculine work than they. A masculine job correlates positively with higher activity, but number of children has almost no impact on this path of advancement.

b. Number of children has a strong negative correlation with masculine sphere of activity. There is an even stronger negative correlation between masculine sphere of activity and high level of activity: women with many children have less chance of entering a masculine sphere of activity than women with few children, but a greater chance of reaching a high level of activity. According to the data, *having a large number of children not only does not impair a woman's chances of reaching a high level of activity, it increases them somewhat.*

c. The more children men and women have, the higher their level of activity; the influence is mainly direct in the case of men, but almost completely indirect in the case of women. This means that having many children does not keep a woman from reaching high status nor, on the other hand, does it make her reach a high level of activity. *This negates the hypothesis we considered earlier.*

3. *Education*

a. Education correlates negatively with number of children for both sexes; this correlation is much stronger for women than for men.

b. Education has only a slight impact on type of work, but the more education a woman receives, the greater her chance of doing masculine work and of reaching a high level of activity.

c. Education correlates negatively with male sphere of activity for women, and through sphere of activity with level of activity. This means that for women, the usual path to a high level of activity is a higher education leading to activities in the female sphere, leading in turn to a high level of activity. For example, a young woman with a high academic education becomes a teacher or manager of a high school, and through this is elected chairman of the education committee and a member, perhaps even secretary, of the secretariat.

d. Education has a direct positive correlation with level of activity for both sexes. On women the impact of education is not strong; for men, however, education opens doors to a high level of activity.

In these correlations we see that a woman has two main paths to a high level of activity—the feminine sphere of activity, and masculine work. We cannot ignore the impact of number of children on a woman's level of education; we see once again that the kibbutz can relieve a woman of the burden of child rearing, but not of the burdens of pregnancy, birth, and nursing. Men have the same main channels to a higher political activity as women do, but the correlations with the kind of work and sphere of activity are weaker.

All of this sounds very complicated, and some of it is, but an analysis of the facts leads to two basic conclusions. First, the kibbutz did not change the way of nature; childbirth does have some impact on a woman's work and political career. Second, having a large number of children does *not* prevent the woman of the kibbutz from rising to a high political position; in fact, the opposite seems to be the case. All the correlations among variables are the same for men as they are for women; the differences are not in kind but in intensity.

If the kibbutz has relieved women of the burden of maternity and given them paths to high positions, why do so few of them reach such positions? Our path analysis measures only correlations, not frequencies; it is true that women are severely underrepresented in the higher political echelons. Does this mean that in order to bring many women to high political activity and high status it is not enough to remove the barriers of housewifery and motherhood? Or does it mean that even when women have the opportunity to move into political activity, they favor other activities?

(One widely publicized explanation for such a situation in the U.S. was advanced by Matina Horner [1972], who argued that because of, *inter alia,* their fear of occupational success resulting from cultural values and their socialization, women were likely to fail much more frequently than men. However, a recent replication of Horner's test [which was, in any event, nonbehavioral in nature] by Adeline Levine and Janice Crumrine [1975] demolishes Horner's argument; in the replication, 700 men and women exhibited similar fear of success. Horner had tested ninety women only; the "fear of success" may exist, but Horner's argument does not prove it.)

Our own findings touch the very core of the scientific problem presented to us by the kibbutz. Students of the origin of the family (e.g., Washburn and Lancaster 1968) have hypothesized that it is probably related to the sexual division of labor. Pleistocene hunters lived in a socioeconomic organization with a sexually polarized division of labor and high mutual dependence. Kibbutz members, like more than 99 per cent of the human species today, are not hunters and gatherers; nevertheless, they still stubbornly divide work, political activity, and education between the sexes. And they still mate, establish families, and have children. Is sexual division of labor, in the widest sense, then, a precondition of a successful mating system? In the widest sense, sexual division of labor means not only that certain tasks are usually done by men and certain others by women, but also that in a given population, the majority of men and women will not, over a period of time, be very responsive to ideologies or to technical and social changes that could blur that sexual polarization. During the six decades of the kibbutz's existence, two parallel processes have taken place: sexual division of labor has changed from an egalitarian to a polarized state, and familism has developed. We are therefore compelled to ask if the division of labor has polarized *because of* the increased importance of the family. The kibbutz family is "modern" rather than "extended" in that it is highly dependent on the nuclear core of the married couple, and may require for its stability the relative permanence of sexual attraction or at least of elaborate emotional reciprocity.

We reported in Chapter 6 that dominant women are not very attractive to dominant men, at least according to the imperfect measure of known extramarital sexual relations. In her recent article based on a small number of cases, Abernethy (1974) gathers primatological, ethnographic, and psychiatric data suggesting that male dominance facilitates human male-female copulatory behavior, whereas female dominance inhibits it. A different explanation could be that after polarization began, both men and women became more inclined to marry and have children.

Neither hypothesis is easily proved or disproved; demographic, economic, and security factors may also have influenced the rise of familism, and it may be futile to seek deeper meanings in the historical process we have described. Nonetheless, the decisive contribution of Darwin's biological science was the discovery of the real link between sexual selection, natural selection, and the consistent behavior of the species. At the outset of this report, we indicated that we did not assume that on a priori grounds humans were exempt from the laws of nature, and we remain struck by the consistency of the pattern of sexual division of labor under a wide variety of contexts. Obviously our implication is that the stubborn development of family and political life in the kibbutz reveals once again a broad propensity in the human potential—one described and evaluated by commentators as varied as Popes and radical feminists. In the final chapter, we will discuss this critical issue more fully. We want to turn now to what men and women of the kibbutz think about, what they set out to do, have in fact done, and do today about the sexual politic.

Chapter 10

Dreams and Reality

A former army officer: "When we were girls, we admired the women of the kibbutz—their work clothes, their sun-darkened skin, the usefulness of their lives. They were our ideal. Now they admire us. They admire our Tel Aviv chic."

A member of the secretariat explaining the fact that the clothing allowance in the kibbutz is higher for women than for men: "Women not only need dresses, they need new dresses."

In previous chapters we reported more what people do than what they say, think, or feel. The behavior we studied is relatively easy to observe and record. But it is also important to know the attitudes of kibbutz members, and these are not so easy to learn. The few who read our study in manuscript cast no doubt on our results and showed no surprise. The characteristic reaction to our description of kibbutz women was: "I knew the situation was bad, but not that bad." This suggests that there is no great gap between our perception of the kibbutz and that of the subjects whose attitudes we sought to understand.

We wanted to know how the men and women of the kibbutz feel about sex differences in the division of labor, political activity, and domestic life. Do they continue to maintain their ideological commitment to sexual equality? And how do they face the discrepancy between ideology and facts? Do kibbutz women suffer because of the sex-typed division of labor, feeling trapped in the prison of the kitchen and the children's corner (Gavron 1968), or are they satisfied with their work? Are they content with their political activity or do they want more involvement and higher rank? How do they feel about the growing familism? Are there unhappy members in the male-dominated kibbutz from which general sex-linked equity of social and economic rewards has all but disappeared?

Our description of the history of the kibbutz showed that kibbutz members in general and kibbutz women in particular have long been aware of the discrepancy between ideology and reality in the sexual division of labor. This awareness is itself a very important kibbutz characteristic. The kibbutz is a soul-searching society. This basic value of self-realization serves almost constantly to activate members' social consciences. Though there is sometimes a tendency to put aside values in favor of daily reality, there are always people who take it upon themselves to remind the community of its shortcomings. The community then somewhat reluctantly embraces the issues and tries to mend its ways, if only by reiterating its past rhetorical decisions. Although kibbutz members sometimes react to the discrepancies between ideology and social reality with lip service, bad conscience, or resignation, they do not stop seeking improvement, or even aspiring to perfection. They feel responsible for the conduct of a serious exercise of moral will—an exercise they know is of interest to many people all over the world.

We explained in Chapter 4 that we limited research on attitudes to four kibbutzim because attitudes had been widely investigated twice about eight years before; we wanted only to be certain that basic attitudes had not changed since then. In order not to overburden the reader with data, we will present some relevant material from the two earlier researches in the context of our findings about the four kibbutzim. We believe that the consistency between these studies will be clear. We will briefly survey the findings of Rosner (1969) and Shepher (1967) without providing tabulated data, which in any case the reader can find in the original publications. We will then present some of the data we collected in our four kibbutzim. As to the congruence between the data about facts in our four kibbutzim and the data about the whole population, one of the authors mockingly remarked, "The total population seems to be a very representative sample of the four kibbutzim."

Rosner (1969) published a very thorough study of changes in the kibbutzniks' perception of the equality of women in the kibbutz. He compared the general attitude of the kibbutz toward sex differences to attitudes found through similar studies in France and Germany.

He found that the basic kibbutz attitude is extremely egalitarian: kibbutzniks think that most human characteristics are not sex-typed. (In contrast, the French and Germans consider less than one-half to one-third of human characteristics non-sex-typed).

In 1965-1966, Rosner asked his interviewees about the suitability of various work branches for both sexes. His subjects, he found, had distinguished among groups of work branches. One group consisted of jobs in child care and the communal store, needlework, and medical nursing; from 86 to 97 per cent of the interviewees agreed that these jobs are more suitable for women than for men. The second group included plumbing, tractor-driving, electrical work, and truck-driving; from 80 to 94 per cent of the interviewees agreed that these are more suitable for men than for women. Ten other work branches —teaching high-school mathematics, dairy farming, poultry-raising, waiting in the dining room, elementary-school teaching, tree-nursery work, textile work, cooking, kitchen management, fine (intricate) mechanics—were seen by a majority of respondents as being equally suitable for men and women. In all, ten of the eighteen work branches were not sex-typed by most of Rosner's interviewees.

Another important sign of egalitarianism was the response to Rosner's question, "Do we have to continue in the segregation between male and female jobs?" Two-thirds of the interviewees answered no. The most common criterion for male work was physical strength; for female work, those qualities believed necessary for the care of small children, needlework, and medical nursing.

It is important to note that a very large percentage of the interviewees said that most or all political positions, including two of the four most important ones—those of secretary and work coordinator— are equally suitable for both sexes. A very slight majority thought that the chairman of the health committee should be a woman and the chairman of the sports committee a man. Sixty-two to 92 per cent thought that the treasurer, general manager, and chairman of the security committee should all be men.

Rosner also wanted to know whether his interviewees considered the extent of women's political activity in the kibbutz sufficient. Fifty-one and a half per cent answered yes, 44.8 per cent no. This indicates that the kibbutz women must be aware of the discrepancy between the ideology and their own attitudes on one hand and social reality on the other. Rosner's female interviewees blamed not the men but themselves for women's relative lack of political activity. To the question, "Do men object to a woman branch manager?" 63.5 per cent answered no, 29.6 per cent said yes. Most of these women who claimed that men objected to a woman branch manager explained that the men did so out of vanity; only 0.3 per cent of all the interviewees used such arguments as, "It's the nature of things that men like to rule."

Rosner's interviewees were convinced that, despite its shortcomings and imperfections, there is more sexual equality in the kibbutz than in the average Israeli city: 75.5 per cent claimed that the kibbutz shows more equality in division of household work; 54.9 per cent that it shows more equality in politics; 49.4 per cent that it allows more women to participate in positions of general management; and 49.6 per cent that it is relatively egalitarian in division of work. It is interesting that these attitudes faithfully reflect the relative successes and failures of the kibbutz in achieving sexual equality. Rosner concluded that the majority of the women maintained a basically positive attitude toward egalitarianism.

Shepher (1967) was interested mainly in the impact of familism on kibbutz social structure. Because familistic housing was demanded principally by women, he paid attention to sex differences in some of his questions. Rosner had studied a representative sample of the Kibbutz Artzi population, and Shepher was to work in the Ichud Federation; they did not know of each other's research until it was too late to coordinate their questionnaires and obtain comparable data. Nevertheless, Shepher's findings are very similar to Rosner's. He found the basic attitude toward the sexual division of labor egalitarian. About 88 per cent of his interviewees said that domestic division of labor should be equal, that most work and political activity is suitable for both sexes, and that the present situation was not very agreeable in that it deviated from their ideology. His interviewees all claimed that there should be equality in political activity, but only 46 per cent of them said there should be equality in consumption, and only about 20 per cent said it should exist in work. Shepher found the attitude toward formalizing family life highly positive, as reflected by the desire on the part of 76 per cent of the men and 85 per cent of the women for the traditional Jewish wedding ceremony.

The most important data we can draw from this research are about satisfaction. Investigating in detail the system of rewards in work, political activity, and kibbutz life in general, Shepher found that in work 69 per cent of both the men and the women had a positive or very positive sense of rewards. Only 17 per cent of the women and 24 per cent of the men complained about their work (the difference between the sexes is not statistically significant). Seventy-eight per cent of the men and 84 per cent of the women said they were very satisfied with social relations at work. In political activities, 69 per cent of the men and 72 per cent of the women claimed they were satisfied; 19 per cent of the men and 18 per cent of the women complained of dissatisfaction. Of those who were not active politically, only 18 per cent of the women and 21 per cent of the men wished to be more active. In regard to general satisfaction with kibbutz life, 81 per cent of the women and 80 per cent of the men said they were satisfied or very satisfied.

Shepher found no statistically significant differences between men and women in regard to their satisfaction with their work, political activity, and kibbutz life in general. He found that the overwhelming majority of the women were satisfied or very satisfied with all these things. In neither the Kibbutz Artzi nor the Ichud was there any indication of dissatisfaction or rebellion against work and political situations.

That was all in 1965-1966. Now we will give our own findings from 1973. The reader will recall that we investigated a sample in four kibbutzim, one young and one old from each federation. To isolate the factors of ideology and seniority, we tabulated our findings according to those two variables (senior and junior, Ichud and Kibbutz Artzi). As our data here concern this four-kibbutz sample, not census populations, we did subject our findings to statistical tests.

We asked our interviewees whether they considered any kinds of work completely female. The results appear in Table 55.

Approximately 75 per cent of our interviewees felt that such job distinctions exist. More important, there was no significant difference in attitude between the men and women regardless of how one groups the four kibbutzim. This corroborates what Rosner and Shepher found almost a decade earlier. The same distinctions among work branches were also found: small-child care, needlework, and medical nursing

Table 55
Answers to the Question, "Are there kinds of work you consider completely feminine?" (in percentages)

Seniority, Federation, Answers Sex	Senior Kibbutzim		Junior Kibbutzim		Ichud Federation		Kibbutz Artzi Federation	
	M	F	M	F	M	F	M	F
Yes	74.5	73.6	76.7	75.0	78.6	78.1	75.0	69.1
No	23.4	24.5	18.6	18.8	18.0	15.1	21.9	25.0
Don't know	2.1	1.9	4.7	5.2	3.4	2.8	3.1	5.9
Total	100.0	100.0	100.0	100.0	100.0	100.0	100.0	100.0
	χ^2 = n.s.		χ^2 = n.s.		χ^2 = n.s.		χ^2 = n.s.	

were considered female work, and jobs requiring heavy physical labor were considered male. Other tasks were regarded as neutral, even though in reality they are sex-typed.

We asked our interviewees, "Is there any difference in the prestige of female work compared to that of male work?" The results are in the following table:

Table 56
Answers to the Question, "Is there any difference in the prestige of female work compared to male work?" (in percentages)

Seniority, Federation, Answers Sex	Senior Kibbutzim		Junior Kibbutzim		Ichud Federation		Kibbutz Artzi Federation	
	M	F	M	F	M	F	M	F
Yes	42.2	38.8	31.3	53.3	41.3	63.8	29.2	32.9
No	44.5	45.0	50.6	31.1	44.4	24.6	52.3	50.0
There is no sex-typed work	4.4	8.1	7.2	10.0	4.7	4.3	7.7	11.5
Don't know	8.9	8.1	10.9	5.6	9.6	7.3	10.8	8.6
Total	100.0	100.0	100.0	100.0	100.0	100.0	100.0	100.0
	χ^2 = n.s.		χ^2 = 9.85 df = 3 p = 0.02		χ^2 = 6.89 df = 3 p = n.s.		χ^2 = n.s.	

In the junior kibbutzim, more women than men say there is a difference in prestige between female and male work, and more men than women reject the notion. The differences are significant. The same divergence exists in the Ichud kibbutzim, but the extent is not statistically significant. In the senior kibbutzim and in those of the Kibbutz Artzi, there is no attitudinal difference between the sexes: a majority of both men and women rejects the notion of differential esteem. Perhaps the difference between the sexes in the junior and Ichud kibbutzim reflects the reality we found in the census data—that in junior kibbutzim polarization is greater than it is in senior kibbutzim, and that in the Ichud there is a slightly greater polarization than there is in the Kibbutz Artzi. However, we cannot be certain, for our four kibbutzim are not necessarily representative of the two federations.

Most of the people who claimed there was a difference in esteem between male and female work attributed it to production work, which is male and which creates income. They did not go on to explain why the majority of production workers are men.

We asked our interviewees whether they agree or disagree with the following statement: "Men and women are different by nature; as a result of this, they have different occupational roles. Men are suitable for heavy physical work, work with machines, and work in management and organization. Women are suitable for work in education and for work that creates a feeling of home, such as cooking, washing, and nursing the sick." The answers are shown in Table 57.

Most of the people agree at least partially with the statement, and very few reject it outright. The difference between the sexes here is one of emphasis. There are statistically significant differences only in the junior kibbutzim. But this statistical significance is not as great as that in Table 56. Although more women than men reject the statement, more women than men also accept it (the men have an attitude of partial agreement). This reflects the kibbutz dilemma of division of labor: they cannot ignore their daily social reality, but they cannot forget their ideology.

Let us now turn to questions of reward and satisfaction. We asked our interviewees: "Are you satisfied in your present work?" The results are in Table 58.

In none of the four groups is there a statistically significant dif-

Table 57
Answers to the Statement, "Men and women are different by nature" (in percentages)

Seniority, Federation, Answers / Sex	Senior Kibbutzim		Junior Kibbutzim		Ichud Federation		Kibbutz Artzi Federation	
	M	F	M	F	M	F	M	F
Agree	34.2	22.4	20.8	31.5	34.6	35.9	11.8	19.0
Agree Partially	51.2	67.3	66.3	45.6	60.3	51.3	73.5	55.6
Disagree	14.6	10.3	12.9	22.9	5.1	12.9	14.7	25.4
Total	100.0	100.0	100.0	100.0	100.0	100.0	100.0	100.0

$$x^2 = \text{n.s.} \qquad x^2 = 9.14 \qquad x^2 = \text{n.s.} \qquad x^2 = 4.62 \text{ n.s.}$$
$$df = 2$$
$$p = 0.02$$

Table 58
Answers to the Question, "Are you satisfied in your present work?", by Sex, Seniority of Kibbutz, and Federation (in percentages)

Seniority, Federation, Answers / Sex	Senior Kibbutzim		Junior Kibbutzim		Ichud Federation		Kibbutz Artzi Federation	
	M	F	M	F	M	F	M	F
Yes	70	76	51.1	56.2	72.5	79.3	73.8	64.8
No	7.5	7.4	27.3	24.0	1.4	6.1	11.5	9.8
To Some Extent	22.5	16.6	21.6	19.8	26.1	14.6	14.8	25.4
Total	100.0	100.0	100.0	100.0	100.0	100.0	100.0	100.0

$$x^2 = \text{n.s.} \qquad x^2 = \text{n.s.} \qquad x^2 = \text{n.s.} \qquad x^2 = \text{n.s.}$$

ference between the sexes. The majority give a positive answer, a minority a negative or partially positive one. The lowest level of satisfaction is in the junior kibbutzim; there, 51 per cent of the men and 56 per cent of the women profess satisfaction in their work; in the senior kibbutzim, the corresponding figures are 70 and 76 per cent. Interestingly, in both groups more women than men give a positive answer, though this may be the result of a chance error. In any case, a considerable majority of the women claim satisfaction in work.

We could not content ourselves with these results because of the possibility that the social expectation of satisfaction in work could distort our findings. We therefore asked another question: "Would you like to change your work?" The following table includes the results:

Table 59
Answers to the Question, "Would you like to change your place of work?"
(in percentages)

Seniority, Federation, Answers Sex	Senior Kibbutzim		Junior Kibbutzim		Ichud Federation		Kibbutz Artzi Federation	
	M	F	M	F	M	F	M	F
Yes	37.8	28.0	21.2	33.3	25.9	26.3	27.5	36.8
No	46.7	56.0	58.74	41.9	53.4	51.3	55.1	42.6
Perhaps; Don't Know	15.5	16.0	20.16	24.8	20.7	22.4	17.4	20.6
Total	100.0	100.0	100.0	100.0	100.0	100.0	100.0	100.0

$$\chi^2 = \text{n.s.} \qquad \chi^2 = \text{n.s.} \qquad \chi^2 = \text{n.s.} \qquad \chi^2 = \text{n.s.}$$

There is no significant difference between men and women in any of the subgroups. In the younger kibbutzim, and those of the Kibbutz Artzi, more women than men wanted to change their work. In the Ichud kibbutzim, there was no difference between the sexes, and in the older kibbutzim, more men than women wanted to change their work. All those differences may result from a sampling error. Moreover, in all the subgroups, the majority of both sexes do not want to change their work. The percentage that wants to change work is smaller than the percentage that claims work satisfaction (except for men in the junior kibbutzim); even if we assume that not wanting to change work is the better indicator of satisfaction than actually expressing dissatisfaction, the majority of women do not protest the present situation.

Wishing to discover the plans and desires of those who said they wanted to change their work, we asked them two questions: "Where would you like to work?" and "Assuming that there are no limitations on choice of work, what work would you choose?" In all four kibbutzim, we found only three women who wanted to work in agriculture—one in the orchards, one in the tree nursery, and one "with plants and animals." The women's desires lay in other directions— teaching, photography, folklore research, child care, clerical work in the industrial plant, music composition, art, physiotherapy, cosmetics. That most of these jobs are within the existing sexual division of labor implies that most kibbutz women are not hostile to that division and in fact are satisfied with their work.

Let us return to political activity. We asked our interviewees, "Do you think the women in your kibbutz have full opportunity for political activity?" The answers were:

Table 60
Answers to the Question, "Do you think the women in your kibbutz have full opportunity for political activity?" (in percentages)

Seniority, Federation, Answers, Sex	Senior Kibbutzim		Junior Kibbutzim		Ichud Federation		Kibbutz Artzi Federation	
	M	F	M	F	M	F	M	F
Yes	81.3	80.7	85.8	81.8	79.8	77.4	95.6	86.1
No	16.7	14.0	6.6	12.2	13.1	16.7	4.4	8.3
Don't Know	2.0	5.3	7.6	6.0	7.1	5.9	0	5.6
Total	100.0	100.0	100.0	100.0	100.0	100.0	100.0	100.0

$\chi^2 =$ n.s. $\chi^2 =$ n.s. $\chi^2 =$ n.s. $\chi^2 =$ n.s.

A very great majority of both women and men answered yes. The lowest percentage is 77.4, for Ichud women. There was no significant difference between men and women. Knowing the social reality, we asked, "In your opinion, why are there few women in the following tasks—secretariat, treasurer, general manager, work organizer?" and gave nine possible answers, permitting our interviewees to choose as many as they wished. Table 61 gives the answers.

These reasons appear most frequently: women are not elected because they do not want to be elected; they do not have the time because of housework and children. The frequencies in the four

Table 61

Answers to the Question, "Why, in your opinion, are there few women in the following tasks—secretariat, treasurer, general manager, work organizer?"

Seniority, Federation, Answers, Sex	Senior Kibbutzim		Junior Kibbutzim		Ichud Federation		Kibbutz Artzi Federation	
	M	F	M	F	M	F	M	F
They do not want to be elected and therefore are not.	25.0	17.3	11.0	18.5	12.5	17.1	19.6	20.0
They want to be elected but are not.	3.4	4.1	9.9	12.3	10.7	5.7	2.9	13.9
They do not want to be elected.	25.0	21.4	15.5	15.4	19.0	20.7	17.6	19.8
They are elected but do not take the job.	1.1	0	0	2.5	0	0.1	0	3.5
They are not suitable.	6.8	4.1	9.3	6.8	10.7	0.6	4.9	6.1
Men prevent them from entering the jobs.	3.4	3.0	7.2	4.9	5.9	0.6	6.8	3.5
Public opinion is against electing women to these jobs.	7.9	15.3	9.9	14.8	10.7	17.8	7.8	12.2
They do not have time because of housework and children.	17.0	17.3	19.8	13.0	22.6	17.8	10.7	6.1
Other reasons.	11.3	16.3	17.1	11.7	7.7	8.5	29.4	20.0
Total	100.0	100.0	100.0	100.0	100.0	100.0	100.0	100.0

χ^2 = n.s. χ^2 = 15.3 n.s. χ^2 = n.s. χ^2 = 15.49 n.s.

groups are slightly different, but there is no significant difference in the answers of men and women. The reason "The men prevent them from entering the job" was chosen by very few men or women (the highest percentage is 7.2, by men in the junior kibbutzim). And comparatively few answered that "Public opinion is against electing women to these jobs."

Men and women agreed that the main reasons for women's underrepresentation in the highest political jobs is their unwillingness to assume those jobs and their encumbrance by housework and child care. Very few claimed that women are unsuited to those tasks or that men seek to prevent their election. We saw in Chapter 9 having a large number of children clearly does not prevent women from reaching high political positions. We suggested that though housework exists, it is not so burdensome as to prohibit political activity.

Finally, we asked, "Do you think the women are satisfied with their situation in the kibbutz?" Here are the results:

Table 62
Answers to the Question, "Do you think the women are satisfied with their situation in the kibbutz?" (in percentages)

Seniority, Federation, Answers	Senior Kibbutzim		Junior Kibbutzim		Ichud Federation		Kibbutz Artzi Federation	
Sex	M	F	M	F	M	F	M	F
Yes	36.1	47.8	33.3	36.0	24.3	30.7	40.5	60.4
No	63.9	47.8	50.6	49.3	61.4	56.0	52.4	39.6
Don't Know	0	4.4	16.1	10.7	14.3	13.3	7.1	0
Total	100.0	100.0	100.0	100.0	100.0	100.0	100.0	100.0
	χ^2 = n.s.		χ^2 = n.s.		χ^2 = n.s.		χ^2 = n.s.	

There are no statistically significant differences between the sexes, but there are differences between the groups. In the senior kibbutzim, the women are evenly divided on whether women are satisfied, but a majority of the men think they are not. In the young kibbutzim, about half the men and women think women are not satisfied; one-third think they are. In the Kibbutz Artzi kibbutzim, a majority of men think they are not. In the Ichud kibbutzim, a majority of both sexes think women are not satisfied.

When we asked our interviewees why they thought women were dissatisfied with their situation in the kibbutz, they gave two reasons. One was that the general attitude toward consumption and education work is less positive than that toward production work, which generates income. The other reason was the lower level of professionalism of female work.

How can we explain these data, which contradict three independent research projects by showing that the majority of women are satisfied with their work and political activity? When people are asked whether or not they are satisfied, the majority say they are, but when they are asked whether women are satisfied, the majority say no. Rosner, in a personal communication, has drawn our attention to the interesting fact that in four consecutive researches of his and of Antonovski (1970), whenever people were asked about their attitudes, the picture they presented was much more positive than when they were asked to judge an existing situation. The general impression that women are not satisfied with their lives in the kibbutz is widespread in the kibbutz movement. There is evidence, to date undocumented, that when a family leaves the kibbutz, it is usually the wife who has initiated the move.

If some kibbutz women are dissatisfied, perhaps it is not because they do not do the same work or reach the same political levels as men do, nor because they cannot fully realize the egalitarian kibbutz ideology. Rather, to judge from what pressures they have exerted to affect their lives, the reason may be that the extent of familism is inadequate to them. They are dissatisfied because they do not have their children around them enough and cannot devote enough attention to their families—as the development of the "hour of love" indicates. Pressure to expand familistic housing continues to be exerted in the Ichud Federation. During 1974, the number of familistic Ichud kibbutzim rose from twenty to twenty-five, and pressure from still more kibbutzim to change the system has caused the federation to lower the financial requirements for introducing family housing. A proposal has been prepared by its secretariat but has not yet been approved by the central committee. In the Kibbutz Meuchad Federation, the higher political institutions have been compelled to put the question on their agendas. In the Kibbutz Artzi, the question is widely debated, especially in the young kibbutzim, in spite of the federation's strongly negative attitude toward it. The intensity of the familistic tendency is unequal in the three federations, as is shown by still unpublished research by Rosner about the second generation in the kibbutz (Table 63).

The family's functions in consumption continue to increase; the comprehensive budget has become almost universal in the Ichud, and more and more kibbutzim in the other federations introduce it with or without the federations' approval.[1]

We have seen that if kibbutz women are dissatisfied with the

Table 63
(After Rosner)
Attitude Toward Familistic Housing of the Children by Sex, Generation, and Federations

Federation	All Interviewees				Kibbutz Artzi				Kibbutz Meuchad				Ichud			
	First Generation		Second Generation		First Generation		Second Generation		First Generation		Second Generation		First Generation		Second Generation	
	M	F	M	F	M	F	M	F	M	F	M	F	M	F	M	F
Absolutely Positive	10	21	13	29	1	2	5	11	10	26	17	38	21	40	22	47
No Clear Attitude	14	12	33	23	20	6	31	27	17	22	36	23	21	18	33	16
Absolutely Negative	34	26	19	14	24	51	30	24	14	28	15	8	6	18	7	6
Average*	3.6	3.2	3.2	2.7	4.3	4.0	3.7	3.4	3.5	3.0	3.1	2.4	2.9	2.5	2.7	2.0
Total	100	100	100	100	100	100	100	100	100	100	100	100	100	100	100	100
N	196	200	446	449	82	81	188	191	51	51	115	113	63	68	143	145

*Lickert Scale—the higher the average, the more negative the attitude

actual division of labor and with the frequency and level of their participation in politics, they can strive for greater equity.

But even a war does not motivate them to move into male work. Their desire to change their work is not directed toward male tasks or toward greater political activity.

Let us now investigate attitudes toward the division of domestic tasks. We asked our interviewees about work in and around their homes, intending to elicit norms and attitudes. "In your opinion," we asked, "who should perform the following activities?" The husband, the wife, or both? We were especially interested in the percentage who chose the egalitarian norm of joint activity. The following table shows the results in the four kibbutzim:

Table 64
Support for Egalitarian Division of Labor between the Sexes (in percentages)
(Question 45)

Kibbutzim, Sex, and Difference between Sexes / Spheres of Work	Ofer			Ofra			Tsvi			Tsvia		
	M	F	M-F	M	F	M-F	M	F	M-F	M	F	M-F
Household repairs	7	28	−21	34	38	−4	42	54	−12	41	15	26
Garden work	66	55	11	37	73	−36	64	79	−15	70	63	7
Taking laundry	70	50	20	39	48	−9	48	69	−21	75	57	18
Bringing laundry	84	45	39	53	48	5	50	60	−10	75	57	18
Bringing food home	60	41	19	42	39	3	48	50	−2	58	52	6
Preparing 5 o'clock tea	60	43	17	68	76	−8	70	60	10	52	47	5
Washing dishes	77	67	10	76	79	−3	76	95	−19	83	68	15
Cleaning apartment	60	84	−24	69	77	−8	76	87	−11	75	73	2
Washing floor	40	52	−12	70	67	3	79	87	−8	75	84	−9
Cleaning kitchen	20	28	−8	57	44	13	50	62	−12	62	31	31
Cleaning bathroom	20	27	−7	61	46	15	52	54	−2	72	38	34
Taking cash	90	78	12	90	81	9	75	78	−3	72	84	−12
Storing cash	80	70	10	88	91	−3	69	77	−8	90	89	1

$r_s = 0.679$ $r_s = 0.704$ $r_s = 0.797$ $r_s = 0.812$

$p = 0.02$ $p = 0.01$ $p = 0.01$ $p = 0.001$

The most impressive fact reflected in this table is that a large percentage chose the egalitarian pattern. The tasks for which the percentages are small are those in which the actual division of labor is not egalitarian, such as household repairs (usually done by men) and cleaning the kitchenette and lavatory (usually done by women). But even for such tasks, the percentage of people in all the kibbutzim choosing the egalitarian pattern was not low. For instance, in Tsvi and Ofra, a considerably high percentage of both women and men chose the egalitarian pattern in all three activities.

While men's and women's attitudes toward certain tasks differ somewhat, they are in substantial general agreement in all the kibbutzim. A Spearman Rank Order Correlation Test resulted in highly significant similarities. This means that husbands and wives are usually in accord about the sexual division of domestic labor. If we compare the attitudes to the facts, we again see that the differences are not very great. In most of the kibbutzim, attitudes are usually more egalitarian than is reported behavior; this shows that kibbutzniks are aware of the discrepancy between the ideological blueprint and their daily reality.

We asked two questions about the division of authority in decisions about domestic and community life. Table 65 gives the results.

The percentages supporting egalitarian division of authority are even higher than are those supporting egalitarian division of work. The percentages are somewhat lower in the items "choosing a job for yourself" and "choosing a job for your spouse." Here kibbutz ideology favors individual decision-making. Men and women agree to a very great extent on the desired authority pattern. The Spearman Rank Order Correlation Coefficients are very high. The discrepancy between attitudes and reality is smaller here than it is in the case of work. What we have here is a microcosmic reflection of what we observed in the kibbutz as a whole: sexual division of labor is much more polarized in work than it is in the division of authority. Within the family, the attitudes toward both division of labor and division of authority are rather egalitarian, but the latter are more so: similarly, the actual division of labor is more polarized sexually than is the division of authority. Moreover, the discrepancy between attitudes and facts concerning work is wider here than it is between attitudes and facts concerning authority.

Table 65
Support of Egalitarian Division of Authority between the Sexes (in percentages)
(Question 46)

Kibbutzim, Sex and Difference between Sexes / Spheres of Authority	Ofer			Ofra			Tsvi			Tsvia		
	M	F	M-F	M	F	M-F	M	F	M-F	M	F	M-F
How to spend time	92	97	-5	100	100	0	86	100	-14	90	100	-10
How to spend money	92	95	-3	89	94	-5	91	100	-9	80	100	-20
Having another child	100	100	0	91	93	-2	82	100	-18	88	93	-5
Decision on studies	60	71	-11	77	77	0	63	60	3	86	88	-2
Public activity	50	62	-12	85	71	14	54	65	-11	86	81	5
Spouse's public activity	55	60	-5	81	66	15	54	66	-12	81	87	-6
Spouse's studies	44	68	-24	79	76	3	59	71	-12	80	81	-1
Choosing a job	22	40	-18	36	30	6	28	36	-8	41	70	-29
Choosing a job for spouse	11	43	-32	37	35	2	28	27	1	50	68	-18
Political task	22	33	-11	38	27	11	28	52	-24	44	68	-24
Spouse's political task	22	36	-14	39	31	8	33	50	-17	44	68	-24
	$r_s = 0.898$	$p = 0.0001$		$r_s = 0.883$	$p = 0.0001$		$r_s = 0.908$	$p = 0.000$		$r_s = 0.7307$	$p = 0.02$	

If our data are accurate and our explanation valid, we can conclude that insofar as women are dissatisfied in the kibbutz, it is not principally because of polarized sexual division of labor and politics and an oppressive familism, as it so clearly is elsewhere. Rather, it is because familism does not yet provide women with as much "feminine" activity and family life as they desire. Furthermore, there are interesting differences between men's and women's grievances: men often make more strenuous criticism than women do about the socioeconomic status of women. This underscores the old problem of relating wish to deed, ideology to reality, personal ambition to existing situations. We often found either a negative or barely supportive correlation between attitudes and behavior; this should suggest the general importance of critically questioning studies of social reality which depend on attitude data. While the effects of opinion and consciousness should by no means be considered trivial, they apparently are not decisive, and they mask or ignore important personal and social processes.

Chapter 11

Conclusions

With three of the four women assistants on our project, we are taking lunch at a Druse restaurant atop Mount Carmel, near the University of Haifa. About our findings, one woman says, "Why is it all so surprising? What did you expect the women to do?"

We have maintained that the study of the kibbutz is promising ground for understanding sex differences everywhere and their impact on the division of labor. In 1956 two pioneering students of the problems of working women, Alva Myrdal and Viola Klein, pointed out that the basic social adjustment necessary to support wives and mothers who want careers centered on "collective houses in which such services as cooked meals, laundry, day nurseries, etc. can be obtained at a reasonable price by the families living in them." These things are built into the kibbutz system. The kibbutz, with its deep ideological commitment to the equality of all human beings and, of course, equality of the sexes, also offers women the independence prerequisite to equality. All in all, the kibbutz is perhaps the most likely place for the development of equality of the sexes.

Like most students of the issue, we do not settle for solely legal interpretation of equality; we distinguish between formal and actual equality of the sexes. Sexual equality does not exist in most societies mainly because men and women consistently do different work and therefore have unequal status. This difference in occupational prestige is itself puzzling. Is low status attached to women's work? Or does the work have low status because women do it? Do cooking, sewing, and child care by definition have relatively lower prestige or do they have low prestige because women do them? The evidence suggests that the second answer is true; we have witnessed the gradual decline in prestige of certain occupations when they become feminized, such as elementary-school teaching and clerical work (Sullerot 1971).

If, however, factual equality of the sexes depends on occupational roles, it can be achieved only if differential work prestige disappears or if men and women do the same work. The first condition is hardly achievable; in a complex society, there will always be some jobs that are differentially rated, along with the skills, talents, and education needed to perform them. It seems to us, therefore, that sexual equality cannot exist until work allocation and consequently work status do not have gender as a criterion.

Here we must point out a recurrent if obvious theme in feminist writings (e.g., Janeway 1971; Barrett *et al.* 1974; Rosaldo and Lamphere 1974)—that women are not only women but persons. It is argued that even the use of the words "men" and "women" gives rise to sexist bias. Anthropologist Constance R. Sutton introduced a motion at the 72nd Annual Meeting of the American Anthropological Association under which the AAA would "urge anthropologists to become aware in their writing and teaching that their wide use of the word 'man' as generic for the species is conceptually confusing (since 'man' is also the term for the male) and that it be replaced by more comprehensive terms such as 'people' and 'human beings,' which would include both sexes." The motion was passed by voice vote (AAA Annual Report 1973, April 1974).

How can women prove that they are not only women but human beings? One way is by taking jobs usually done by men. Cooking a meal, caring for a child, sewing a dress, are considered women's work; managing a corporation, teaching at a university, and presiding at a political convention are "human" work, although it is not obvious why it is more genuinely "human" to manage a corporation than to rear a child. Interestingly, "humanness" in much feminist writing frequently is not used to characterize the work of a truck driver, an agricultural wage worker, or a sewer cleaner. If "humanness" implies high prestige work, a great majority of both men and women are evidently doomed to "unhuman" careers. But if we disregard this bias and accept the idea that division of labor should occur without any regard to sex differences, the case of the kibbutz becomes significant.

In Chapters 5 through 9, we presented extensive data on kibbutz women that allow the following conclusions:

1. Early in kibbutz history, more than half the women worked for a considerable time in production. Then came a long, gradual process of sexual polarization of work. Today the sexual division of labor has reached about 80 per cent of maximum.

2. Sexual division of labor is more polarized in the second and kibbutz-bred generations than it is in the first generation, and more polarized in younger kibbutzim than in older ones.

3. Despite complete formal equality in political rights, women are less active in the General Assembly than men are, as measured both by their presence in the Assembly and by the incidence of their participation. Women are somewhat overrepresented in committees dealing with social, educational, and cultural problems; they are seriously underrepresented in committees dealing with economy, work, general policy-making, and security.

4. The higher the authority of an office or committee, the lower the percentage of women in it. At the highest level of the kibbutz, women make up only 14 per cent of the personnel.

5. Women seem to have special problems sustaining all-female work groups; they usually prefer mixed-sex groups or male leadership.

6. Men and women receive nearly the same number of years of education; in fact, women have a slight edge. Advanced schooling, however, differs in kind for each sex. Women are overrepresented in higher nonacademic education leading to such jobs as elementary-school teaching, kindergarten teaching, and medical nursing. Men are overrepresented in higher academic education leading to such jobs as agriculture, engineering, economics, and management.

7. From the ninth grade on, women consistently fall below men in scholarly achievement. This discrepancy between the sexes seems to be wider here than in comparable modern societies.

8. Although women, like men, are drafted into the army, the overwhelming majority of kibbutz girls (like other Israeli girls) do secretarial and service jobs there; few do characteristically male work or occupy command positions. The conception of the women's army as essentially a substitute unit, also providing back-up aid and encouragement for the fighting men, is completely accepted by the kibbutz girls. There has, however, been a steady expansion of the range of noncombat tasks for women.

9. Even the long, demanding Yom Kippur War did not substan-

tially change the division of labor in the kibbutzim, even though almost half the men were called up by the army for a long period.

10. The family has risen from its initial shadowy existence to become the basic unit of kibbutz social structure. It now fulfills important functions in consumption and education, and there are demands for further expanding its function. Increased familization is indicated by high and growing rates of birth and marriage, and by a decreasing divorce rate. The status of singles, especially of women, is becoming more and more problematic, to the extent that the family, the kibbutz, and even the federations now try to help them marry.

11. The main instigators of familization are women, whose attitude toward familism is more positive than men's.

12. Attitudes toward equality have always been more egalitarian than actual behavior has. This discrepancy causes recurrent soul-searching within the kibbutzim and federations.

POSSIBLE EXPLANATIONS

Before we try to explain our findings, we wish to examine some of the possible interpretations of our data.

1. *The argument of insufficient revolution* would hold that despite the ideological commitment of the kibbutzim, the kibbutz revolution has not been a total one. At first, more than half the women worked in production. And yet very few men shared cooking and washing, and none sewing and child care. When more children were born, service work increased and women had to leave their work in production to attend to those tasks, which men still did relatively rarely.

To this argument we reply that in the beginning, there were so few service tasks that only a handful of people were needed to do them. And as for production, everyone who could help there was badly needed because of the extreme difficulties of economic survival. The low technological level of the early kibbutzim made physical strength an important attribute; it was unreasonable to transfer men from jobs of hard labor to the kitchen and replace them with women. Still, ideology had an impact on the division of labor, and the kibbutz deviated widely from the traditional sex typing of work in the culture of the founders' origin. It is true, however, that basic ideas of who was more suitable for which work resisted ideology more stubbornly than did other operating assumptions.

Why were the early kibbutzniks not as radical about sexual division of labor as about private property, religion, competition, urban life styles, etc.? Perhaps we should even ask why the early kibbutzniks could not afford to be as radical about it. Is there any society where men are as widely and consistently involved as women in cooking, sewing, washing, and child care? The answer being no, we can argue that the kibbutz did more to avoid sexual division of labor than did any other society.

But as physical strength has become progressively less relevant in most work, why shouldn't men and women be interchangeable now? The answer is that women have no personal or social inclination to yield certain service tasks to men, and men are reluctant to yield certain production tasks to women. Even when technological development obviates one of the basic reasons for sexual division of labor, the division remains. The theory of insufficient revolution leaves us with more tough questions than satisfying answers.

2. *The socialization argument* would explain our findings by pointing out that since the founders of the kibbutz were socialized in a culture where sexual division of labor was polarized, they would have internalized the values and norms behind polarization, and therefore would not have been able to carry out their revolutionary aims or to socialize the second generation successfully.

There are several problems with this argument. First, if the results of primary socialization are unalterable, why don't we witness the same failure in other aspects of kibbutz life? If we accept that the founders came from the *shtetl* as described by Zborowski and Herzog (1969), we must wonder what happened to the norms of individualistic, achievement-oriented, competitive behavior central to that society. Instead of these, the kibbutz stressed cooperation, mutual help, and economic rewards independent of social role and work performance. Despite some small compromises, the system of equal economic rewards is intact and flourishing today. Why didn't basic socialization remain unalterable here? The same question must be raised about the *shtetl's* plutocracy and piety, lastingly replaced on the kibbutz by direct democracy and a secular or even antireligious ethos.

There is also an important methodological problem in the socialization argument. Even the most radical feminists agree that male dominance is universal in contemporary and historically known societies (Millett 1970); they argue that men and women everywhere are socialized to internalize "male-dominated values and norms." But if basic socialization has an unalterable impact on values, norms, and attitudes, then we can never change the sexual division of labor. Furthermore, we can never find sound scientific evidence that sexual differences and sexual division of labor reflect cultural values and norms. To prove that sexual differences, including sexual division of labor, are either biologically or culturally determined, we would, for example, have to take a hundred male and a hundred female babies, socialize them without male-dominated values, and see whether this results in sex differences and in sexual division of labor. (We think it would, but we can never prove it, any more than feminists can prove the opposite.) If basic socialization is truly unalterable, there would be no acceptable socializers for our 200 babies; anyone we chose would be contaminated by his own basic socialization. And we could not simply leave our 200 babies without socialization and return to see whether they had developed a sex-typed or a non-sex-typed society, since it has often been proved (Davis 1940, 1947, 1949) that babies without socialization do not develop into human beings.

So the socialization argument too leaves us with more questions than answers. Of course, we do not argue that socialization has no impact on personality; what we are arguing is that there are differences in various spheres of life in regard to the extent to which resocialization is possible. We are also aware, as was rejected in the first half of our century, that socialization does not work on a *tabula rasa*. There is at birth a basic diagram, a set of biologically determined dispositions, which has been called a "biogrammar" (Tiger and Fox 1971). Culture (i.e., socialization) in its plasticity may go against those dispositions, but not for long and not for many people, without causing serious difficulties for both the individual and society. For instance, Shepher (1971) has proved that kibbutz children educated in a peer group are not attracted to one another sexually and do not marry one another, even though such unions are not only sanctioned but encouraged by public opinion. This biologically determined disposition against incest is more important than are socialization and public opinion. The same phenomenon has been found by Wolf (1966, 1968, 1970).

3. *The male conspiracy argument* states that to maintain their supremacy, men conspire against women. By forming a coalition, they block the entry of women into prestigious occupations and the higher echelons of the political system (which has, of course, often been the case). The most effective way to do this is to dominate socialization by inducing women to not only accept inferior status themselves but to compound and perpetuate the problem by raising their young to accept the same inequities. We agree that this is indeed a partial explanation—that the bonds men form are unhelpful to the careers and ambitions of women (Tiger 1969, 1975b). But as we have seen, this part of the male conspiracy argument does not apply, since the kibbutz established itself in the aggressive search for sexual equity.

In the beginning, there were more men than women in the kibbutz; if they had wished to, they could have acted as a group against the women. We have no evidence that they ever did so. Perhaps certain men considered certain women unacceptable for certain political positions—just as they considered certain other men unacceptable. It may also be true that a majority opinion of many men and women kept some women from certain positions. But we are confident in stating that such majorities did not originate in any male conspiracy. In fact, our study in Ofer showed that the opposite was true.

In Ofer, there is constant pressure, mostly from men, for women to assume greater political responsibilities, due to a shortage of suitable men and a relative abundance of talented women. A woman of fifty, with a brilliant intellect, a talent for organization, and excellent leadership qualities, was asked several times to assume the tasks of secretary, treasurer, or work coordinator. If she had agreed, she would have been elected in the General Assembly unanimously. She always refused the offers. During and after the Yom Kippur War, the kibbutz offered the difficult task of the work coordinator to a woman, an offer that had been made every year to one woman or another. Under the pressure of the war, three women accepted, but each one resigned after a short while, claiming family responsibilities. Recently a young man was elected to the position. He is much less talented than any of the three women, and the managers (all of them men) of agricultural and industrial branches sadly recall the good old days when the work coordinators were women.

After the last national convention of the Ichud Federation, Kibbutz Ofer had to elect new members to the federation's council. The secretariat nominated two men and two women. When these nominations were presented to the Assembly, both women asked not to be elected, because membership in the council would require them to be away from the kibbutz for one or two days a month. One of the women is a young elementary-school teacher with a six-year-old daughter; the other is a kindergarten teacher with four grown children and two grandchildren.

Even the most belligerent fighters for sexual equality in the kibbutz (most but not all of whom are women) do not argue that men block women's way. They usually point to the unwillingness of women to assume political responsibility. Wherever a woman shows a talent and inclination to accept responsibility, the way is open for her. Activating women in work and political activity is more a task of Ofer's men than of its women. All in all, this hardly amounts to a male conspiracy against the women.

4. *The retreat argument* supplements the argument of insufficient revolution and goes like this: when women realized they had lost all hope of staying in production because no men would assume responsibility for child care and other service tasks, they retreated into the service branches and presently lost all desire to escape from them; since they were doing for the community what a housewife would do for her own family—cooking, washing, babysitting, etc.—they began to enjoy their self-imposed seclusion within the family (this would explain their enthusiastic support of such social changes as familistic housing and the "hour of love").

Although this argument points up some well-established facts, it interprets them questionably and colors them with the word "retreat." It may be true that kibbutz women assumed responsibility for education and consumption and then gradually identified with those social roles. In the national council of the Kibbutz Artzi in 1966, the most important leader of the federation's women, Yona Golan, stated that the federation should not send women back to the fields and bring men to the kindergarten; rather, that is should see that women's work enjoyed the same prestige as men's and not be considered any less of a contribution to the community's well-being. Golan thus challenged a male-centered, feminist attitude that sees humane, important, and prestigious work as male. Economic expansion, which centers on production, still lingers as a goal in much of the kibbutz movement, but more and more investment and manpower are being given to education and consumption.

One can consider such rediscovery of women's roles a retreat only if one thinks that the abolition of sexual division of labor necessarily constitutes progress. Progress is by definition positive, retreat negative. Without using these value judgments, one must ask whether the return of women to women's roles has had a negative impact on the kibbutz, which some say it has. At a recent convention of the Kibbutz Artzi, several speakers condemned the "hour of love" as an indulgence that interfered with the children's education schedule and the mothers' work schedule. It is relevant to note that most of the complaints came from men—a fact not very compatible with the argument that men conspire to push women back into traditional housewifery.

5. *The external influence argument* claims that the kibbutz did its best to carry out the "androgynous" revolution, but could not sustain it against the influence of the sexist norms of the society around it. There are many facts to contradict this. Israeli society in its early years was similar to kibbutz society as far as the sexual division of labor was concerned. Women did men's work; such institutions as the Working Women's Council (Moetzot Mapoalot) and the Organization of Working Mothers (Irgun Imahot Ovdot) participated more than a little in the labor force, at least until the establishment of the state in 1948, when formal legal protections for all citizens were established.

The kibbutz has always stood in flagrant opposition to the Israeli system of private property. Capitalistic individualism and competition did not influence the kibbutz system, but neither did sexual division of labor, in which urban Israel somewhat resembled the kibbutz system. The kibbutz is an open society rather than a "total institution" (Goldenberg and Wekerle 1972), and its openness is not selective. The kibbutz could not and does not open its gates to influences on sexual division of labor and close them to influences on capitalistic individualism. In the late 1950's, thousands of kibbutz members received millions of German marks in reparation payments. This most seductive external influence could have resulted in the desertion of the kibbutz by thousands of members who preferred to keep the funds rather than turn them over to the kibbutz treasury. The number of people who did desert was surprisingly small—in Ofer, one family in seventy. If external influence is so strong, why should it hold sway only in the sexual division of labor and not in economic and political patterns?

The five arguments we have presented all have some point to them, yet none can sufficiently explain why, despite structural advantages and ideological fervor, the kibbutz has not lived up to its goal of abolishing sexual division of labor. True, the kibbutz has ensured complete formal equality between the sexes and enabled women to fulfill themselves in work, polity, and education. But the kibbutz has reached greater sexual polarization in work than has the surrounding society (so that alleged external influence should now work in the opposite direction). Only 34 per cent of Israeli women are in the labor force, and they constitute only 24.5 per cent of the total working population (Statistical Abstracts of Israel 1973). This percentage is higher than that of Spain, the Netherlands, Norway, Luxembourg, and Portugal, but lower than that of all the rest of Europe and the U.S.A. (Sullerot 1971). And within Israel, the percentage of women who work in agricultural and industrial production, clerical positions, and management is still much lower in the kibbutzim.

The kibbutz has been conspicuously successful with other aspects of its ideology. It maintains its communal economic and social organization, its direct democracy, its system of collective education. It remains rural and secular. We do not mean to suggest that in all these institutions the kibbutz has succeeded in maintaining an original and flawless integrity; there have certainly been compromises and dilutions. But nowhere have the institutions changed to the point where their core has been impaired. Why then is it principally in the sexual division of labor that failure has been so pervasive and overwhelming?

BROADER ANSWERS

It should be clear that we regard any formal sociological explanation for what we have described as partial and, by itself, inadequate. Some sociologically describable variables, such as sex, age, social class, and ethnic origin, determine behavior more than others do. But there is no way to gauge their respective influences. One of the aims of biology is the assessment of what is central to an animal's survival and success; as in other sciences, such assessment requires the data and techniques of other disciplines. When biologists cannot explain why something happens, they can examine the physiology of the event. If the ways of studying the physiology are too crude, they can turn to the chemistry and physics of the organ involved; if that fails, molecular biology may have a role to play. The history of science is littered not only with mistakes and with hypotheses mercifully abandoned, but with once-sturdy disciplinary boundaries that can no longer keep one fact isolated from others.

Perhaps the first social thinker to insist on the interplay of disciplines was the fearless Karl Marx, who turned his integration of the several social sciences into an immensely powerful theory. He strove to assimilate in his work what was known in every science. It is not common[1] knowledge that he wrote to Darwin, offering to dedicate *Das Kapital* to him, for he saw a connection between his own synthetic economics and Darwin's effort to organize knowledge of living things—a connection recalled by Engels at Marx's graveside. And Marx's synthetic system—whatever its inadequacies then and now—did provide a way to organize not only socioeconomic but also symbolic and cultural phenomena. He and Engels also sought to relate their work to the evolutionary anthropology and biology of their time (e.g., Trigger 1969; Joravsky 1971; Tiger 1973; Morin 1973; Fox 1973; Freeman 1966; Heyer 1975; Tiger 1975a).

But as many have recently noted, the social sciences in both Marxist and capitalist traditions have been systematically isolated from the biological sciences, for reasons we have already mentioned. The result is that in a study such as this, one must argue as if for the first time that on purely scientific grounds, organisms of different sexes and ages respond differently to social stimuli, and that such stimuli may not be the exclusive determinants of the social action of these organisms. Among the primates and other animals, this is well-established. To be sure, it is also becoming clear that social stimuli play a greater role in animal societies than was once thought. Though there are limits to their flexibility, complex animals show individual differences and are very sensitive to changes in population and social structure. The controversies over the respective relevance of species-specific genetic factors and local environmental factors often appear to turn on the metaphorical question of whether the cup is half full or half empty.

We cannot forget the relevance of genetic transmission of behavioral characteristics. A chicken does not behave like a turtle or a cobra; a rhesus does not behave like an orangutan; a collie like a Newfoundland. These animals not only do not look alike, they do not behave alike, and these differences between them are anything but random. So it is with humans. If we can assume that human behavioral nature is totally plastic, we are assuming in effect that cross-cultural similarities result either from cultural diffusion or from coincidence. While coincidence and diffusion are certainly partial explanations of cultural universals, they are by themselves inadequate —first, because in this theory human organisms are held to contribute nothing to human life, and second, because some cultural universals exist under such different circumstances that it is highly unlikely that they will have sprung up independently in very diverse communities. It is simply very improbable that they result from spontaneous invention or development, and thus attention must be focused on the common human factors, not only on the variable environmental ones. One useful method of approaching human biosocial nature without constructing a rigid strait jacket that rules out variation and option has been adapted from the study of human language. All human languages have, in Chomsky's phrase, a "universal grammar" (1966, 1968). Languages, and even dialects, vary considerably and reflect different cultural patterns. But all human language is as marked by a system as is human metabolism; individuals differ in metabolism, and some groups vary slightly from others, but there is a system—and in the production of language there is also a species-wide pattern. The only surprising thing about this is that John Locke's *tabula rasa* notion had been successful for so long that it was deemed a breakthrough when it was shown that we, like other animals, show species-wide unity in our communication.

In an effort to develop what may be a behavioral baseline from which cultural variation developed—a biogrammar—Tiger and Fox (1971) united the concept of universal grammar with Count's concept (1973) of a biogram, the basic form of an animal's social life. Count's argument maintains that it is improbable that any animal's behavior is random. The more complex the animal, of course, the more extensive the opportunities for variety in social responses, and the fewer the range of responses that could be considered "genetically programmed behavioral propensities" (Tiger and Fox 1966).

In discussing biogrammar, we have restricted ourselves to *Homo sapiens,* thereby avoiding both homologous and analogous comparisons with other animals. The use of such comparisons has been shown in both ethology and biology (e.g., Tinbergen 1963; Lorenz 1974; Blurton-Jones 1972; Eisenberg 1966), but some people have preferred to interpret them as demeaning to humans and vaguely threatening to human freedom (e.g., Gluckman 1972; Cook 1974; Gould 1974) or incorrect on methodological grounds (e.g., Callan 1971; Larsen 1974). We limit the scope of our remarks here because we feel that our case is strong enough supported by exclusively human documentation. We can assuage protectors of *Homo sapiens* by focusing on that particular ape alone.

We have already cited evidence that sex differences in political and economic activity are universal, that the care of young children is virtually everywhere a female monopoly, and that some widely argued explanations for this universality are weak, improbable, or partial. Our data show that although some 10 to 15 per cent of the women in the kibbutz express dissatisfaction with their sociosexual roles, the overwhelming majority not only accept their situations but have sought them. They have acted against the principles of their socialization and ideology, against the wishes of the men of their communities, against the economic interest of the kibbutzim, in order to be able to devote more time and energy to private maternal activities rather than to economic and political public ones. Obviously these women have minds of their own; despite obstacles, they are trying to accomplish what women elsewhere have been periodically urged to reject by critics of traditional female roles. Our biogrammatical assertion is that the behavior of these mothers is ethologically probable: they are seeking an association with their own offspring, which reflects a species-wide attraction between mothers and their young. Usually women have no choice but to have close contact with their children; in the kibbutz, the opposite is true. So, what kibbutz women *choose* to do may be significantly related to what other women elsewhere routinely do under similar circumstances, if also apparently more constraining ones. A single case cannot define a species, but given the experimental style of kibbutz society, the result is certainly revealing.

We shall now comment briefly on what may be the species-specific mother-child connection. It has customarily been assumed that the thrust of ethological and biological explanations of behavior is genetic. However, the most interesting recent discussions of the mother-infant dyad have stressed behavioral contributions to the child's maturation. Affection, verbal stimuli, and touch are finally as important for the health of a growing child as food, shelter, and warmth; foundlings given the "necessities" may sicken or die without truly human contact. As the kibbutz shows, this contact need not be with the mother: any responsible person will do; it is perhaps from the mother's point of view that the substitution is least adequate.

Abraham Maslow (1973: 229) noted that most utopias have been created by men. The records available to us suggest that the men who dominated the public life of the kibbutz also strongly influenced basic child-care policy. Had women been more fully and assertively involved, the severance of the link between mother and child as a matter of theory and then of practice might have been less extreme. Today kibbutz mothers may be responding not only to their need to be close to their children but also to their children's ability to elicit these feelings from them. Tinbergen (1974) argued that autism in children may result from their not receiving the necessary stimuli they try to elicit through their behavioral repertoire; denied basic "behavioral nutrition," they manifest this drastic form of withdrawal. Just as protein deficiency in the early months of life will retard myelinization and development of the brain and thus affect intelligence and other functions (Montague 1973), so may behavioral deprivation induce autism.

This is indeed a turnabout—biologists arguing that social deprivation is the cause of physiological deficiencies, including, in extreme cases, death. The ethological argument, then, is not that the genetic process is omnipotent but that *biologically necessary social interactions are basic to both emotional and physical health.* It is significant that the first Nobel prize for work in ethology, awarded in 1973 jointly to Karl Von Frisch, Konrad Lorenz, and Niko Tinbergen, came under the official category of Medicine and Physiology; the statement accompanying the awards said that ethological study of behavior is directly relevant to individual and community health (see also Marler and Griffin 1973).

Since mother-child interaction is necessary for the child's health (Bowlby 1969, 1974), both mothers and children in the kibbutz may be reacting to a strenuous violation of the biogrammar governing their relationship. Blurton-Jones (1972) suggested that studies of the milk of human mothers, the sucking rates of babies, and the time between their feedings indicate that "Man shows features in both mother and baby which are typical of those mammals in which the young feeds almost continuously." Clearly the biogrammatical rules, if such rules exist, need not be followed precisely; the kibbutz example suggests that one can drastically alter the ways of being a mother under the stimulus of ideology and still produce children who are able to live competently in and outside their communities. (That kibbutz-bred people function well in Israeli politics, education, and the military is disputed weakly, without direct evidence, by Goldenberg and Wekerle 1972.) But under changed economic conditions where there is less insecurity about ideological experimentation, the women and perhaps the children began a return to a pattern more typical of our species—and perhaps more appropriate to a mammal with our evolutionary history and need for extensive socialization.

To some, the idea of women seeking intimate association with their children may seem vaguely obsolete and generally inhibiting of broader human development. But one must remember that from the time kibbutz women become fecund, they are routinely provided with contraceptives; if they have children, it is because they have chosen to. Moreover, the intimacy of the kibbutz ensures that adolescent girls have ample contact with nearby children, so that the process of mothering becomes relatively familiar to them. (Many Euro-American women, because of the residential and age-graded pattern of their lives, lack this useful preparatory experience with children.) It is not surprising that inexperienced mothers externalize their uncertainties and ambivalences and blame men, patriarchy, their communities, or some other part of their social world. Their accusations are in part well-founded, since they have not been given realistic instruction, either formal or informal, in child rearing. And unless women stop having any or as many children—which low birth rates during the early seventies suggest that some may have decided to do—their decreasingly maternal-linked education, socialization, and expectations will make greater the hazard that their sociosexual life will be out of joint with what they know and want.

In a demonstration of the interplay of community and physical processes, Raphael (1973) suggested that such a routine physiological matter as successful breast-feeding may sometimes depend on a supportive and informative social network. Her argument requires more empirical testing, but if, as we know, physical illness and even death can be caused by social events such as "black magic" or voodoo, then the far less dramatic problem of inability to breast-feed may demonstrate the importance of social life for mothering (see also Abernethy 1973; Wade 1974). It is also possible that the emphasis that women in the kibbutz place on motherhood is in part occasioned by their reaction to or rebellion against their own mothers, who cultivated a nonmaternal life style. Friedan (1963) made a similar suggestion in proposing that the home-centeredness of American women of her generation was a pendulum response to their mothers' bluestocking coolness to maternity. This is perhaps a plausible explanation for American women, but for kibbutz women it is less useful, because the law of parsimony is violated and an unnecessary element is introduced into the argument. It is perhaps clearer and simpler to say that these women have made their own decisions. How can their commitment to motherhood be merely their way of rebelling against their mothers? Where would they have learned this style of maternal devotion, since their mothers, aunts, and friends did not adopt it before them? Why not leave home (in this case, the kibbutz) like countless rebels? The strategy of their "rebellion" happens to be the general one of the human female. Can they be so pummeled by resentment that they decide to spend twelve to twenty years in close contact with three or four young children? It is far more likely, and more respectful of their dignity, to say that these women know their own minds and act accordingly.

This explanation admittedly does not allow for the feminist grievance that women are forced at every important step of their lives to conduct themselves according to the norms of men. Their argument assumes that men are the center of all things, and that women, lacking any autonomy, must forego thoughtful and independent choices. Our data suggest that the women in the kibbutz do not act in so craven a way; that they are not only independent of the men in the kibbutz but willing and able to act in important ways frowned on and unsuccessfully opposed by the men. It is precisely such male-centered arguments as those of Mitchell, Firestone, and Millett which provide a basis for accepting men's standards as the most important ones, and which directly or indirectly corrode the importance of concerns and enthusiasms which women have and which men may neither accept nor understand.

It is paradoxical to argue that there are no important differences between the sexes but that men alone are both greedy for power and effective in retaining it, and that women are painfully susceptible to the duress of men. Proponents of the feminist critique have usually assumed the truth of the first principle and urged the destruction of the social forms taken by the second. Another tactic, more consonant with empirical data, could be to assess the rights, obligations, and enthusiasms that would follow if indeed there were important differences between the sexes. However, the social scientists who might provide firm ground for reaching such judgments have traditionally ignored these differences. Now, understandably, out of respect for the moral validity of the feminist movement, most have stood down from examining the grounds of social reform unsentimentally. But even the most moral people can be wrong; in this case, if feminist theorists are wrong in their estimate of what women want, not only will they fail to attract broad support, they will induce some followers to devote themselves so firmly to predominantly male patterns of work, politics, reproduction, and values that they will forego an aspect of life they could enjoy along with others. It is an irony that just when countless men and women and even nuns and priests are openly having liberal sexual relations, a new morality urges women to devalue and limit femininity and maternity.

If the predisposition of mothers to be with their offspring is a positive attraction, not a negative retreat, it is because of our mammalian and primate origins and the long, formative hunting-gathering period of our evolutionary past. If Blurton-Jones (1972) is right in maintaining that we are a "carrying" (in the sense that babies are carried, as by chimps, rather than nested, as by eagles or cats) rather than a "caching" species, the enthusiasm of women in the kibbutz and elsewhere for association with their children is further clarified; the same is true of Lee's findings (1970) about Bushman women, who on gathering expeditions in the hot Kalahari desert carry their children on their backs up to the time the children are four years old, despite the fact that there usually are responsible adults around who could spare the women this arduous task. Lee's calculation of the fewer calories expended by the mothers compared to the food values they acquire fails to explain why the mothers take their children with them. The simple reason is that when the children are threatened with their mothers' absence, they start to cry, and apparently this is enough to induce the mothers to take them along. Why kibbutz women—and Bushman women—should choose to be with their children now perhaps makes more sense (see also Hinde 1974:229-45).

In fact, it is generally easier to understand our findings about women and children in the kibbutz than about the marked sexual divisions of work and of economic and political activity. All the explanations we considered have failed to link the basic biological function of gender—reproduction—with the social patterns we found. We discovered that while the kibbutz began to show increased sexual division of labor, its birth rate increased and familism grew. We suggest—we cannot prove it at this stage of our research—that the rate of childbirth and the division of labor are causally related. The division of labor increased when both pronatal attitudes and economic security were creating increasingly suitable conditions for children. Every parent knows how much children cost, in energy and time, as well as in money; even on the kibbutz, a high birth rate deprives adults of resources that would otherwise have been theirs. It can be argued that there are other good reasons for producing more children—to contribute to the security of the state, for example, or to encourage the growth of the kibbutz movement. But these concerns were even more urgent in the early days, when the kibbutzim were smaller, fewer, and more precarious; the kibbutzniks did not determine to have more children then for these reasons alone, and there is no reason to believe they did so later on.

We know that the birth rates not only of other animals but also of humans are affected by social circumstances (Grebenik 1972).

Nevertheless, it appears to be a rule of biogrammar that as part of the broad reproductive process, the sexes tend to create distinctions between themselves, and sometimes in ways that are not directly or indirectly reproductive. In the case of humans, these distinctions may involve work, play, politics, and war. In other words, what have been termed "patriarchal attitudes" may be fundamental reproductive patterns of *Homo sapiens*. We are not certain that this is so; we are seeking something more substantial than attitudes to explain such a sturdy and widespread pattern of human behavior.

It has been suggested from both a feminist viewpoint (e.g., Greer 1971) and an ethological viewpoint (e.g., Tiger 1969) that the sexes segregate in marked and statistically decisive ways. The persistence of the pattern may well have been central to the persistence of our species in the past. Of course, such segregation is not necessarily inevitable or desirable now; it has, however, been part of a successful breeding system that has allowed humans to populate various areas of the world in large numbers. Given the crisis of overpopulation, it may be very undesirable for such segregation to continue if it stimulates or even supports human fecundity. Indeed, one may ask whether the current feminist perturbation, its legal, moral, and economic thrust aside, is a cognitive expression of a hidden biological process—a species reacting to overpopulation. Meanwhile, men and women in the kibbutz have no qualms about bearing children; perhaps that is the reason they divide the sexes and increase their birth rates, acting against the trends of the socially concerned progressive elements of Euro-American society, with which they otherwise often align themselves.

We have been focusing on the prime reproductive period of kibbutz women, because we believe that it is during those years that women make critical choices. But women's reproductive phase occupies an ever-smaller part of their lives as life span itself increases and children are born to them earlier and closer together. The economic and political future of the women now mothering three or four children remains to be seen. Whatever they do, life in the kibbutz will give them more support and assurance than women outside the kibbutz receive. Their children will be taken care of and educated until maturity; they will be given jobs and economic security; and they will probably be among relatives and friends of long standing. Women outside the kibbutz can be confident of nothing of the kind; indeed, recent trends toward increased divorce and desertion of wives and children by husbands, and the courts' increasing reluctance to automatically provide alimony and other security to women who are capable of working, all put added strains on women. In vast numbers, they end up physically and legally with the children they have borne.

The broader question raised by these developments may be related to the question of the origin of the family in the human primate line, which is a vast subject we cannot possibly review here. In the kibbutz system, both men and women work throughout their active years in the general economy of their communities, and all are in effect wage earners. In the rest of Israel, as in most other societies, women have to depend on others (uncles, aunts, sisters, brothers, cousins, husbands, lovers, friends, any person or organization) for at least some economic support in order to raise their young: outside communal settlements such as the kibbutz, this economic transfer takes place chiefly through the kinship system.

One of the functions of the kinship system is to regularize such support despite the sexual or other enthusiasms of the individuals involved. As Tiger and Fox formulated it (1971:71), the chief function of any kinship system is to protect the mother-infant bond from the relative fragility and volatility of the male-female bond. Men's and women's attractions to each other are often enough short-lived; the kinship system persists to ensure economic support to the temporarily dependent woman and her young. This can be effected, as we said, in a variety of ways, by a parent, or another relative, or by the state in the form of welfare, as in the U.S., or in the form of more dignified but essentially similar payments, as in Sweden. In Euro-American societies, and more and more in others as well, the most common pattern of such transfer payments is by a workingman to his wife and children. A high proportion of women work outside the home, as many as half in some communities and age groups, but the predominant source of family income still comes from men.

The broadest question in the study of human kinship systems is also very incompletely answered: Why do men, to the extent that they do, support children and women? Why should an industrial worker in Reims, New York, Kiev, or Toronto give almost all his income to his family, and keep only a very small portion for himself? It can be argued that in return he is given shelter, food, laundry service, sexual access to a woman, etc. But would he not be better off, from his selfish point of view, if he dwelled in a bachelor apartment and used his entire income for his own social, sexual, aesthetic, and other pleasures? If men are so selfish, so intent on exploiting, depriving, and stunting women, why do they not avoid long-term commitments altogether and coolly look to their own sociosexual self-interest? Relatively few men do so. Without for a moment disputing the inequity that persists between men and women in politics and work, we should direct future research to what stimulates men to enter family life, and whether such stimulus is related to the sexual divisions of the kibbutz and other societies.

The present moral argument for extensive reform of the situation of women has existed for a long time in North America, Europe, and elsewhere (e.g., O'Neill 1971; de Beauvoir 1953; Mill and Mill 1970). The reason it is now the object of such urgent public and private attention is related to perturbations in the mating system—one of which, we suggest, is that men are in practice or in prospect fast becoming "liberated" from responsibilities to women and families. Faced with the possibility of living independently without men, women are demanding the jobs and rights that will enable them to support that independence. To put it another way, if men give the impression that they cannot or will not fulfill their part of the reproductive bargain, they must cede their economic perquisites. To kibbutz women, confident of their own and of their men's sexual dignity, and of their own economic security as well, this presents no problems; they are enthusiastically reproductive. Yet while their birth rate rises, their sisters elsewhere are less and less certain about gender and sex, about their commitment to men and men's commitment to them. Some have responded to the rapid moral and social devaluation of maternity by having fewer children—which is understandable, both in the political terms framed by advocates of limiting population and in the context of kinship, mating, and parenthood that has simultaneously brought the species to numerical prosperity and peril.

We have defended the narrower adequacy of our own sociological argument, but at the same time we have underscored the inadequacy of sociological analysis alone by placing it in a comparative biosocial framework. We have also made room for the new questions that such knowledge provokes. As social scientists, we have claimed the kibbutz to be what its founders and citizens as utopians claim it to be—an experiment that affirms possibilities for radical change in social forms and in people's commitments to one another. We have found that the aspect of this experiment involving major changes in women's lives was substantially less successful than all others, and we believe that this fact can be useful in evaluating what may be a deeply rooted pattern of human behavioral nature.

Though such a conclusion will be painfully unpopular just now, we estimate that our data about women in the kibbutz are in accord with the data of others about human and mammalian sex differences. We suggest that the current controversies about sex and gender are rooted in major structural, social changes, and that their abrasive effects can be most effectively mitigated or eliminated if we take the measure of the creature who is always the focus and instrument of what is happening. We have tried, apart from this essentially Fabian stance, to take no judgmental positions on these matters—for, when all is said and done, rhetoric and illusion claim no more influential place in social science than they do in surgery.

Perhaps we did make one judgment—that people's actions are not necessarily the unhappy performances of the duped and confused, and may well reflect what people wholeheartedly want to do. Whether women who do not live on kibbutzim will or should be affected by the lives of women in the kibbutz is not a question we can answer. All we can fairly say is that few other women enjoy the supporting facilities available in the kibbutz, and this should give pause to those who seek to emulate their example. As for those who claim that women who are eager to bear and raise children are tyrannized and obsolete, they can see for themselves how contemporary women in the kibbutz are.

It is very possible that the controversies about sex and gender which we have touched on here are the result of a growing recognition on the part of both men and women that the old sexual certainties are cracking if not crumbling—in which case, the kibbutz is here to provide a challenging (if, to some, discouraging) example of the complexity of developing novel social forms that offer sexual, political, and economic dignity. And of course it cannot be responsibly ignored because in these bedrock matters of birth, love, and child care, nothing less than the tutored heart and the informed imagination will finally do.

Appendix A

Questionnaire of Census

1	no. of punch card
2	no. of federation (1-3)
3-4	no. of kibbutz
5-7	no. of person
8	population qualifier
9-19	last name
20-25	first name
26-32	ID no.
33	sex
34-35	year of birth
36-37	month of birth
38-39	country of birth
40-41	country of emigration
42-43	year of emigration
44	marital status
45-46	age at first marriage
47-52	ID no. of spouse
53-54	age at birth of first child
55-59	age group of children
60-62	age group of children from earlier marriage
63	number of children
64-65	country of birth of father
66-67	country of birth of mother
68-69	year of joining the kibbutz
70-71	year of admission to membership
72	pattern of preparation to kibbutz
73	residence before coming to kibbutz
74	membership in Israeli youth movements
75	membership in youth movements abroad

76   time and age of membership in youth movements
77   tasks in youth movements
78-80   official use

1-7   numbers of identification as in first card
8   service in army between ages 18-23
9   part of army
10-11   unit of army
12   job in army
13   army courses
14   rank in army
15-16   year terminated army service
17-18   month terminated army service
19   service in other armies
20-21   third year of service
22-23   place of third year of service
24   overall education
25   secondary education
26   higher education
26   higher education other than university
27-28   university education
29-34   professional courses
35   district or national courses
36-38   kibbutz movement courses
39   time spent in courses
40-56   work and social activity
57   area of work branch
58   level of work branch
59   time spent in tasks
60   youth leader tasks in kibbutz
61-63   area of tasks—how long it has been performed
64   age when tasks done
65-66   membership in elective bodies
67   membership in movement professional organization, e.g., of painters, writers, photographers
68-69   hobbies
70   driver's license
71-80   knowledge of languages

Appendix B

Questionnaire used in the survey in the four kibbutzim

1. Where have you worked since you joined the kibbutz?
2. Do you have a permanent work place?
3. If you do not have a permanent work place, what is the reason?
4. Is it desirable that everyone have a permanent work place?
5. What does permanency give to the worker?
6. Are you satisfied in your present work?
7. What is the source of satisfaction in your present work?
8. Would you like to change your work?
9. If yes, to what work? Why?
10. Suppose there were no limitations concerning work. What sort of work would you choose? Why?
10a. Do you consider your work your profession?
11. Are there kinds of work you consider completely female?
12. If your answer is yes, give three examples.
13. Are there kinds of work you consider completely male?
14. If your answer is yes, give three examples.
15. Is there any difference in prestige of female work compared to male?
16. If yes, how is the difference expressed?
17. In your opinion, what is the source of the difference?
18. Would you be prepared to give the following work to men:
    a. baby care
    b. care of toddlers
    c. care of kindergarten children
    d. care of all schoolchildren
    e. needlework
    f. cooking
    g. medical nursing
19. Why, in your opinion, is it possible or impossible to give these kinds of work to men?

20. Would you be prepared to give the following work to women:
    a. tractor-driving
    b. work on citrus plantation
    c. work in orchards
    d. mechanical shop work
    e. truck-driving
    f. general managership
    g. secretarial
    h. work coordinating
    i. treasurer's post
    j. dairy
    k. poultry
21. Why, in your opinion, is it possible or impossible to give those kinds of work to women?
22. "Men and women are different by nature; as a result of this, occupational roles they have are different too. Males are suitable for heavy physical work, work with machines, work in management and organization. Women are suitable for work in education, for work which creates a feeling of home, like cooking, washing and nursing the sick." Do you agree with this quotation?
23. Which of the following jobs have you ever had:
    a. secretary
    b. treasurer
    c. general manager
    d. work coordinator
    e. work assigner
    f. purchaser
24. Of which committees have you been chairman?
25. Of which committees have you been a member?
26. Have you ever managed an agricultural branch?
27. If yes, when and for how long?
28. Do you think the women in your kibbutz have full opportunity for political activity?
29. Why, in your opinion, are there so few women in the following tasks —secretary, treasurer, general manager, work coordinator?
30. In your opinion, should there be a proportional representation of women in all the jobs and political activities?
31. Why do you think so?
32. Is there in your opinion the same effectiveness in employing men or women in all the jobs?
33. Do you think that there is some work in which the employment of both sexes is advisable? What are those?

34. If that is advisable, why in your opinion is it not implemented in your kibbutz?
35. Do you think the women are satisfied with their situation in the kibbutz?
36. What has to be done in order to improve the situation?
37. Here is a list of leisure-time patterns. Which of these do you spend alone and which with your spouse?
    a. spending time with children
    b. talking with friends
    c. political activity in the kibbutz
    d. cultural activity in the kibbutz
    e. watching television
    f. clubhouse
    g. listening to music or reading in your room
    h. handiwork
    i. hobbies
    j. rest
    k. studying
    l. other (specify)
38. Please rank the items according to the time you devote to each.
38a. Please rank the items according to the importance you see in them.
39. Is the way you use your leisure time satisfying for you?
40. If not, why?
41. If not, is it possible to change that? How?
42. Who in your family performs the following activity?
    a. repairs
    b. gardening
    c. taking laundry
    d. bringing laundry
    e. taking food products
    f. preparing five o'clock tea
    g. washing dishes
    h. cleaning apartment
    i. washing floor
    j. cleaning kitchenette
    k. cleaning lavatory
    l. transferring money
    m. handling money
43. Who in your family has more authority in making the following decisions?
    a. how to spend time
    b. how to spend money

    c. having another child

    d. decision on studies

    e. public activity

    f. spouse's public activity

    g. spouse's studies

    h. choosing a job

    i. choosing a job for spouse

    j. political task

    k. spouse's political task

44. Who in your family cares for the following:

    a. contact with nurses and education committee

    b. problems of child nurture

    c. social problems of children

    d. social problems of adolescents

    e. play with the children

    f. contact with committee of social affairs

    g. social contact within the kibbutz

    h. maintaining social contact within the kibbutz

    i. contact with extended family within the kibbutz

    j. contact with family outside the kibbutz

    k. contact with secretary or secretariat

    l. contact with work assigner about your own work problems

    m. contact with work assigner about your spouse's work problems

45. In your opinion, who should perform the following activities? (same list as question 42)

46. In your opinion, who should have more authority in the following decisions? (same list as question 43)

47. In your opinion, who should care for the following things? (same list as question 44)

48. Does or did having small children prevent you from leaving the kibbutz for a considerable time?

49. Do you attend the General Assembly?

50. Under what conditions do you attend the General Assembly?

51. Why do you go to the General Assembly?

52. Under what conditions do you not go to the General Assembly?

53. Why don't you go to the General Assembly?

54. Do or don't you agree with the following statements?

    a. Women are usually not interested in economic matters.

    b. Women are usually not interested in political matters.

    c. Women are interested in social matters.

    d. Women are interested in personal problems.

e. Women are interested in questions of consumption.

f. Women are interested in problems of education.

55. Which of the following statements express your opinion?

   a. Men try to influence how their wives vote in the Assembly in matters of economy and organization.

   b. Women try to influence how their husbands vote in social problems, personal problems, and problems of consumption and education.

   c. There is no connection between the vote of the husband and that of the wife.

   d. Usually the family votes similarly.

   e. Usually the husband's opinion has more influence on the wife's than vice versa.

56. Do you think there are subjects in which the wife influences her husband's opinion?

57. If yes, what are they?

58. Do you think there are subjects in which the husband influences his wife's opinion?

59. If yes, what are they?

60. Is there anything you were not asked about and want to add?

Appendix C

A Refined Concept of the Sexual Division of Labor

The concept of sexual division of labor needs certain clarifications. In a standard ethnography one would read such statements as, "Hunting is male work, gathering is female work," or "In culture 'X' mat production is female work, but in society 'Y' it is male work." This presents several problems.

Does "female" work mean that it is done always and exclusively by women or predominantly by women? For instance, in most hunter-gatherer societies, some gathering is always done by some men, but hunting is almost never done by women. The two quotations used as examples above are of different levels and therefore uncomparable. The first uses a *broad* category as unit of division of labor, the second a narrow category. Obviously in statements using a broad categorization, there is *less* chance of finding exclusively male or female work, whereas in a narrow categorization the chances are greater to find one: "mat production" is a specific work, whereas "gathering" is a broad category including different activities. From the point of view of division of labor (not only sexual), the narrower the category, the less significance it has. A narrow task may have been sex-typed because of a random historical event or a ritual tradition.

Using broader categories, one usually finds that sexual division of labor presents statistical rather than absolute differences: that is, certain occupations are *predominantly* but not exclusively male or female. The more division of labor is differentiated, the more frequently broad categories emerge. In modern society, one can find such broad categories as agriculture, industry, management, and housework, none of which is ever done solely by one of the sexes.

The word "predominantly" may mean 51 per cent of the working population, 66.6 per cent, or 75 per cent. Obviously it must be an arbitrary decision of the investigator, where he sets the limit of sex typing. (c.f. Gross (1968) who proposes to use the indices of Duncan and Duncan (1955) and Gibbs (1965) for the same purposes. We think that our indices are more sensitive, but note that the polarization in the United States is less than in the kibbutz according to the Gibbs indices. Moreover, the tendency for male occupations to become male-segregated and resistant to female entry, while female occupations become less segregated, has its parallel in our data.) Moreover, there remains the possibility that a broad category has subdivisions in which exist all-male or all-female work. For instance, in most pastoral societies, animal husbandry is predominantly male work, but milking may be exclusively female work.

Even if we agree that an occupation is predominantly male or female, there remains the question of this fact's social significance. Obviously allocation of males and females to certain occupations is dependent on the proportions of men and women in the population—that is, the sex ratio. In a society with a high sex ratio, such as the United States frontier, most occupations tend to be predominantly male. In societies with a low sex ratio, such as the U.S.S.R. or any society after a major war, most occupations tend to be predominantly female.

Considering all these problems, we tried to find an index that measures the sex typing of work categories that takes into account the sex ratio of the able-bodied adult population. Here the sex ratio proved a very inaccurate measure. Sex ratio is defined in a population as

$$\frac{M}{F} \cdot 100$$

which is an accurate measure for total population, in which extreme values are improbable. But if we want to compare the general sex ratio with the sex ratio of a work category, we face the problem of extreme cases. Let us suppose that in a certain society, the sex ratio in the working population is

$$\frac{M}{F} \, 100$$

The sex ratio of a work category in that society would be

$$\frac{m \cdot 100}{f}$$

If we want to measure the deviation of the specific from the general sex ratio, we would have

$$D = \frac{M}{F} \, 100 \, - \, \frac{m}{f} \, 100$$

What is the range of D? For ease of analysis, we can omit the multiplier 100:

1. $D = \dfrac{M}{F} - \dfrac{m}{f}$ where M and m, F and f ($M + F = 1.0$ and $m + f = 1.0$) are proportions rather than absolute numbers.

  1.1 If $\dfrac{M}{F} = \dfrac{m}{f}$ then $D = o$, and we have absolute "equality," or no sex typing of work.

  1.2 If $m = o$ and $f = 100$ (an all–female work category),

  $D = \dfrac{M}{F}$, which is equal to the sex ratio of the total population.

  1.3 If, however $f = o$ and $m = 100$, (an all–male work category), the value of D is undefined, since $\dfrac{100}{0}$ has no meaning. To correct this, the following alternative has been suggested by one of our colleagues, Dr. B. Kedem (Kimmelfeld), a statistician.

2. $D = \dfrac{M}{M+F} - \dfrac{m}{m+f}$

  which is obviously the difference between the proportion of men in the two populations. Here the range becomes easier, since

  2.1 if $M = m$, then $D = o$

  2.2 if $m = o$ and $f = 100$, then $D = M$ and

  2.3 if $m = 100$ and $f = o$, then $D = M - 1$, so the range of D is

  $$M \leftarrow o \rightarrow M - 1$$

This still is not a very convenient measure. For instance, if $M = 0.5$, D will move from 0.5 to $-\,0.5$ through 0. But if $M = 0.53$, D will vary from 0.53 and $-\,0.47$ through 0. Moreover, if we have to compare two populations with different sex ratios, we have problems. Therefore we suggest the following improvement of the index.

3.

$$D = \dfrac{\dfrac{M}{M+F} - \dfrac{m}{m+f}}{\dfrac{M}{M+F}} \quad \text{if } m \leqq M$$

and

$$D = \dfrac{\dfrac{M}{M+F} - \dfrac{m}{m+f}}{\dfrac{F}{M+F}} \quad \text{if } m \geqq M$$

Obviously, then,

    3.1 if $m = M$, $D = 0$

    3.2 if m 0 and f 100, $D = +1$

    3.3 if $m = 100$ and $f = 0$, $D = -1$

$$\text{since } \frac{M}{M+F} - 1 = \frac{F}{M+F}$$

Now we have a classical index moving $-1 \leftarrow 0 \rightarrow +1$ independent of the sex ratio differences between populations.

Let us examine the following situation.

	Society A	Society B
Proportion of Men in Able-bodied Population	55	45
Proportion of Men in Agriculture	80	76

Which society is more sex-typed in agriculture?

$$D_A = \frac{55-80}{45} = -0.55$$

$$D_B = \frac{45-75}{55} = -0.56$$

Society B is more sex-typed, even though 24 per cent of the working population in agriculture are women, as against only 20 per cent of women in Society A.

Sometimes, however, we have to take into account the size of occupations offered to men and women. Obviously, if there are more work places in male-sex-typed work than in female-sex-typed work, this widens the possibility of females entering male work. To take work supply into account, we must use the usual contingency measurement χ^2 and C, which has a maximum of 0.707 in a four-cell table; then we can measure the deviation from this maximum by calculating a general

$$C_{adj} = \frac{C}{Cmax}$$

which will give us a comparable measurement moving from $0 \rightarrow +1$.

Let us assume that in societies A and B there are only two types of work: agriculture, which is predominantly male, and housework, which is predominantly female. If we hold the work supply constant, we have the two following four-cell contingency tables:

SOCIETY A

	Male Work (Agriculture)	Female Work (Housework)	Total
Men	4800	700	5500
Women	1200	3300	4500
Total	6000	4000	10000

The sex ratio remains 55 per cent male in the general population; the ratio of men in male work (agriculture) remains 80 per cent. The supply of male work is arbitrarily set at 60 per cent.

$$\chi^2 = 3788 \quad C = 0.524 \quad Cadj = 0.741$$

In Society B, the supply situation would be the same.

SOCIETY B

	Male Work (Agriculture)	Female Work (Housework)	Total
Males	4560	40	4600
Females	1440	3960	5400
Total	6000	4000	10000

$$\chi^2 = 5435; \quad C = 0.594 \quad Cadj = 0.840$$

So despite more women working in agriculture, Society B is obviously relatively more sex-typed with 10 per cent (Cadj A = 0.741   Cadj B = 0.840).

If, however, we put the work supply in Society B at 50 per cent = 50 per cent, we have the following contingency table:

SOCIETY B

	Male Work (Agriculture)	Female Work (Housework)	Total
Men	3800	800	4600
Women	1200	4200	5400
Total	5000	5000	10000

Then χ^2 = 3623

$\quad\quad$ C $\quad$ = 0.515

$\quad\quad$ Cadj = 0.73

Now Society B is less sex-typed.

Obviously the contingency tables give a more refined measure than the D index.

Appendix D

Appendix D. Matrix of Correlations
Ichud Men

High Score =	Older	Married	Many	High	High	Masc.	Masc.	Masc.	Masc.	High
	Birtyear	Marstat	Nbchild	Milrank	Educat	Firstwor	Longwork	Lastwork	Actspher	Levelact
Older Birtyear	1.00000	0.00613	-0.60604	0.47712	0.17320	-0.52248	-0.51394	-0.50792	-0.18018	0.28738
Married Marstat	-0.00813	1.00000	0.19865	0.08668	0.00596	0.08590	0.06988	0.06472	0.00333	-0.00409
Many Nbchild	+0.60604	+0.19865	1.00000	-0.09287	-0.05986	0.42912	0.42406	0.40974	0.17562	-0.34822
High Milrank	-0.47712	+0.08668	-0.09287	1.00000	0.20455	-0.17244	-0.18777	-0.19502	-0.04722	-0.05001
High Educat	-0.17320	+0.00596	-0.05986	+0.20455	1.00000	-0.03393	-0.03368	-0.05937	0.09215	-0.10597
Masc. Firstwor	-0.52248	-0.08590	-0.42912	+0.17244	+0.03393	1.00000	+0.79095	+0.71185	0.17206	-0.14913
Masc. Longwork	-0.51394	-0.06988	-0.42406	+0.18777	+0.03368	+0.79095	1.00000	+0.83030	0.19017	-0.12895
Masc. Lastwork	-0.50792	-0.06472	-0.40974	+0.19502	+0.05937	+0.71185	+0.83030	1.00000	0.18743	-0.10400
Masc. Actspher	-0.18018	-0.00333	-0.17562	+0.04722	-0.09215	+0.17206	+0.19017	+0.18743	1.00000	-0.26281
High Levelact	+0.28738	+0.00409	+0.34822	+0.05001	+0.10597	-0.14913	-0.12895	-0.10400	-0.26281	1.00000

Appendix D (Continued) Matrix of Correlations

Ichud Women

High Score =

	Older Birtyear	Married Marstat	Many Nbchild	High Milrank	High Educat	Masc. Firstwor	Masc. Longwork	Masc. Lastwork	Masc. Actspher	High Levelact
Older Birtyear	1.00000	0.20092	-0.50426	0.58786	0.27278	-0.57599	-0.57228	-0.56604	-0.10128	0.17652
Married Marstat	-0.20092	1.00000	0.14478	0.13658	0.02176	0.04327	0.03638	0.03244	0.01608	0.00366
Many Nbchild	+0.50426	+0.14478	1.00000	-0.28183	-0.17857	0.57125	0.56961	0.55278	0.19329	-0.20173
High Milrank	-0.58786	+0.13658	-0.28183	1.00000	0.26221	-0.33277	-0.31872	-0.31049	-0.00182	0.04154
High Educat	-0.27278	+0.02176	-0.17857	+0.26221	1.00000	-0.19478	-0.20087	-0.22448	-0.14083	+0.10134
Masc. Firstwor	-0.57599	-0.04327	-0.57125	-0.33277	-0.19478	1.00000	+0.89773	+0.85287	+0.16500	-0.14267
Masc. Longwork	-0.57228	-0.03638	-0.56961	-0.31872	-0.20087	0.89773	1.00000	+0.91626	+0.17898	-0.15033
Masc. Lastwork	-0.56604	-0.03244	-0.55278	-0.31049	-0.22448	0.85287	0.91626	1.00000	+0.14774	-0.11133
Masc. Actspher	-0.10128	-0.01608	-0.19329	-0.00182	0.14083	0.16500	0.17898	0.14774	1.00000	-0.50822
High Levelact	+0.17652	-0.00366	+0.20173	-0.04154	+0.10134	-0.14267	-0.15033	-0.11133	-0.50822	1.00000

Appendix E

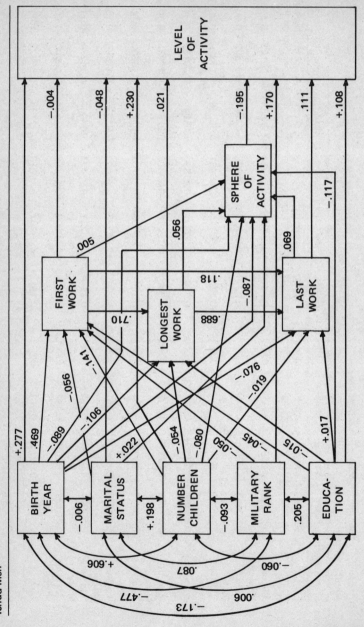

Appendix E (Continued)
Path Analysis
Ichud Women

Notes

Chapter 3

1. Among the useful works for interested readers are Bettelheim 1969; Darin-Drabkin 1962; Douard 1961, Friedman 1967; Ichud Habonim 1971; Kanovsky 1966, Konopnicki 1968, Leon 1969, Liegle 1971a; Liegle 1971b; Meier-Cronemeyer 1969, Neubauer 1965; Pallmann 1966; Rabin 1965; Shapira 1971; Spiro 1956; Spiro 1958; Viteles 1966.

2. There are kibbutz-like collective rural communities outside Israel, mainly in Japan. Not much is known about them except that there are more units than in Israel—almost 500—but most individual units are much smaller than the Israeli ones. Some of those collectives were influenced by Israeli kibbutzim (see Altman 1970).

3. Three types of demographic data can be used as a basis for estimating the kibbutz population:

    a. The data of the 1972 State Census

    b. The data of the Central Auditing Association of the Cooperative Collective Movement (Brit Hapikuach shel Hakooperatsia Hachaklait Haovedet), organized within the Histadrut (General Federation of Labor)

    c. The data of the departments of statistics of the kibbutz federations Unfortunately, none of these data are exact. The State Census data disregard people temporarily out of the kibbutz, and therefore give low numbers. The data of the Central Auditing Association are taken from annual balance sheets, which are not always demographically accurate. The data of the federations are the best, but not comprehensive: until recently, for instance, the religious kibbutzim have not had statistical departments (they now intend to join the Ichud Federation to gather statistical data about their kibbutzim). Our estimate is based on the data of the federations.

4. In a few cases known to the authors of a married person's member-

ship being terminated, the spouse voluntarily left the kibbutz. From hearsay we know of such situations resulting in divorce. We cannot say whether the termination was the cause of the divorce or rather a pretext for it.

5. These requirements vary in controllability. Membership in the kibbutz federation is automatic and indirect, through the kibbutz's affiliation. Membership in the Histadrut is direct and is expressed by accepting Histadrut basic principles and paying membership fees, which include health insurance in the organization's Sick Fund (Kupat-Cholim). Membership in the World Zionist Organization is mainly declarative, though there is a nominal membership fee. Israeli citizenship is automatic for natives and for immigrants who entered the country before the establishment of the state. New immigrants are required to apply for Israeli citizenship within a defined period, although they are permitted to hold double citizenships if their countries of origin allow this, as the U.S.A. and some European nations do. For men under twenty-eight, military service is required, even if it entails loss of original citizenship. Besides reflecting the basic value system of the kibbutz, these membership requirements seem to eliminate the possibility of anti-Zionistic, anti-Israeli, and anti-socialistic persons joining the kibbutz.

6. Interestingly, the assumption that an insufficient supply of potential mates is the reason for not marrying proves to be false in most cases. Frequently the person marries in the kibbutz after returning from leave.

7. External work is labor done outside the kibbutz and branches; its increase is attributed mainly to industry. In the Ichud Federation, external work fell from 6.2 per cent of workdays in 1970 to 4.5 per cent in 1972. In the same period, the financial contribution of external work fell from 5.7 per cent to 5.6 per cent (Sikumei Haavoda 1973; Sikumin Mishkiim 1973).

8. The "conquest of work" (*kibbush ha'avoda*), a basic tenet of the ideology of the Second Aliyah, is described in the writings of Aharon David Gordon, a prominent thinker of the Second Aliyah and the kibbutz movement. For more details, see Chapter 4.

9. See especially Rosenfeld (1951, 1957, 1958), Schwartz (1957, 1958), and Diamond (1957). The role conflict described by Eva Rosenfeld is characteristic of the group and is a classic case of the detrimental effects of preconceived ideas in scientific research.

10. The possible categories which may give rise to groups are age, seniority (which usually overlaps with age), nation of origin, category of

production or service, movement background (youth movement or, in some cases, kibbutz origin—see Meier-Cronenmeyer 1969).

11. The statutes made by most kibbutzim deal with higher education, vacations abroad, and rights of people who leave the kibbutz.

12. The frequency of convening the General Assembly varies according to size of the kibbutz. In small kibbutzim, the General Assembly is summoned almost every week; the number of Assemblies per year varies from forty to forty-seven. In larger kibbutzim, there are usually not more than twenty to thirty a year.

13. In some kibbutzim, these Assemblies have the special name of Annual Assembly; frequently their decisions cannot be changed by a regular General Assembly. The Annual Assembly may elect a special chairman, rather than be chaired by the outgoing secretary. The Annual Assemblies usually convene around the fall or spring holidays.

14. In Hebrew, Va'adat haverim—literally, "committee of members." Etzioni (1958) proposed a structure with three instead of two main committees. He advised the kibbutz to separate the value function and the integrative function. Although his recommendations were intensively studied, most kibbutzim rejected his Parsonian analytical approach and argued that value considerations are ubiquitous in kibbutz life, and their compartmentalization into a separate committee is incompatible with the kibbutz atmosphere. Nevertheless a very few kibbutzim adopted his scheme, calling the new committee "the social committee" (Va'adat hevrah) rather than control committee (Va'adat bakkarah) as Etzioni suggested.

15. Contrary to the description by Spiro (1958), who suggested that ideas about sex roles develop only at kindergarten age.

16. Such an investigation is now being carried out at the Haifa University by Dr. Ben-Raphael. The collection of data on desertion is very difficult and complicated, especially for the early years of the kibbutzim. Kibbutzim are not interested in people who have left and do not maintain data on them. Moreover, the number of deserters is a delicate detail of the life of every kibbutz, and data are not made easily available.

17. These are relative majorities. There were Marxists among the Second Aliyah immigrants, and non-Marxists among the people of the Third Aliyah. Both workers' parties were founded in the Second Aliyah, but the relative preponderance of the Marxist element in the political life of the workers became obvious after the Third Aliyah.

The dates of the Aliyah phases are commonly agreed to be
Second Aliyah, 1903-17

Third Aliyah, 1918-23
Fourth Aliyah, 1924-32
Fifth Aliyah, 1933-39
Haapalah (Illegal Aliyah) 1940-48

18. This deterioration began with the Slansky Trial in Prague in 1952, continued with the Physicians' Affair in 1953, and ended with the Twentieth Congress of the Communist Party of the U.S.S.R. in 1956, with the revelations of Kruschchev.

19. The population of Israel grew from 872,000 in 1948 to 1,789,100 in 1955, a growth of 105 per cent within seven years—an average annual growth of 15 per cent (Statistical Abstracts of Israel 1973). This enormous increase made the first years of the nation extremely difficult both economically and socially.

20. As far as the present situation is concerned, there are some data about the percentage of all workdays completed by hired nonkibbutz personnel. The source for the data are unpublished demographic and economic reports of the three kibbutz federations; the data on the religious kibbutzim are from the Ichud accounts. These are the available figures; the records do not distinguish between Arab and non-Arab workers, but one estimate is that at the most, 20 per cent of all workdays by hired people were of Arab personnel.

21. See, for example, Ben David (1971).

Chapter 4

1. Nahal is an acronym for *Noar Halutzi Lohem* (Fighting Pioneer Youth), a special unit in the special defense force. After graduation from high school, members of all the various youth movements organized themselves in *garinim* (nuclei). Each nucleus affiliates with a kibbutz that needs additional manpower. After three to six months' training in the kibbutz, they join the army; there, each group remains together as much as the different training for men and women permits. After finishing army service (the boys a year later than the girls), most join the kibbutz where they previously served. New settlements on the nation's borders are first manned by such Nahal groups, which have received both agricultural and military training. An especially strong Nahal group may turn such a temporary settlement into a fully "civil" one and thus found a new kibbutz. However, most Nahal

groups join existing kibbutzim. About a thousand youngsters join the Nahal every year; about 25 per cent ultimately remain in the kibbutz.

Chapter 5

1. Women's Farms and Groups were special institutions established in such places as Kinereth, Nahalat Yehuda, and Nahalel to give girls agricultural training.
2. The numbers are based on the statistical publications of the Jewish Agency.
3. Israeli television has one channel. It telecasts children's shows from 5:30 to 6:30 P.M., an Arabic program from 6:30 to 8:00, and Hebrew programs for adults from 8:00 till 11:00. In most kibbutzim there are only two or three sets, in public places, and members watch together. A few very prosperous kibbutzim have supplied sets to all families. Apart from the very high prices—a black-and-white set costs about 2,200 I£ (about $500), a color set I£9,000 ($2,140)—kibbutzim are reluctant to supply sets to families for fear that TV-watching will atomize the community.
4. Family sociology is not highly developed in Israel (Weller 1974). However, the available research material supports our assumption (Bar Yoseph 1970).

Chapter 6

1. The average is higher than we indicated. When the secretary is on annual vacation, the acting chairman may forget to keep a record of participation; the average number of Assemblies is, in fact, about forty a year.
2. The parents of members have a special status in the kibbutz. They have all rights except political ones (a vote in the General Assembly and eligibility for offices and committees), but no duties. They may work if they want to, but this is not required. They may keep income from external sources without curtailment of their full economic and social maintenance.

3. In local folklore, the two storerooms are considered the centers of kibbutz gossip. The most commonly offered source of a rumor is "I heard it in the storeroom." This is presumably because the workers there usually sit together in a big room, doing manual work that requires little concentration and permits an unobstructed flow of talk. Women in the storerooms angrily reject the accusation that they are the main gossipers and claim that men gossip even more than they. It may be true, but most men do not have comparable circumstances in which to do it. An earlier gossip center, the communal shower, disappeared in the early fifties, with the building of larger apartments.

4. Some kibbutzim have established service committees or consumption committees to diminish this important difference between the production and service branches.

5. We do have two groups that approximate control conditions. The accounting department of the industrial plant is all-female. The head of it, the only licensed accountant, is a salaried clerk from outside the kibbutz. Between him and the four kibbutz women who work in the office lie the distance of professional prestige and the difference between kibbutznik and outsider. These distances work in opposite directions and neutralize one another. The women, as we would have predicted, are reluctant to accept authority, have strained relationships, and maintain no primary relationships with one another after work. A similar, if impure, case is the accounting department of the whole kibbutz. It is a mixed-sex team headed by a woman, a senior accountant; there are two more women, and a man whose special task is cost accounting. A hierarchy does exist, on the pattern we would expect. The second accountant is reluctant to accept the authority of the senior accountant; in fact, the senior accountant is more successful in imposing her authority on men inside and outside the team (for instance, on the treasurer and general manager) than on the women who work under her. The only man on the team, a man of considerable intelligence and skill, serves to a great extent as a mediator not only for his team but for the accounting team of the industrial plant.

Chapter 7

1. One of the founders of Degania, the first kibbutz, and apparently the strongest personality among the founders; he had both an ideological and practical effect on the settlement's development.

2. For a detailed discussion, see *inter alia,* Golan (1958, 1959), Segal (1970, 1971), and Shepher (1974).
3. Nevertheless, more complaints are made about the irrelevance of high-school education to girls' futures. For example, see Porat (1960), Artzi (1960), and Tene (1956).

Chapter 8

1. Six kibbutzim are not a representative sample, but our work had been completed when the war ended, so we had to settle for a strategic, if small, sample of kibbutzim to whose data we had easy access.

Chapter 9

1. The matrix of the correlations and the complete analysis are reproduced in Appendices D and E.

Chapter 10

1. Because it may reflect the situation which these facts describe, and because the author is a woman who is an important columnist for the general newspaper of her kibbutz federation, we quote the following article by "Nira" which appeared in *Igeret Le'Chaverim,* No. 1097, February 11, 1975, page 3 (trans. by J. S.):

. . . In the beginning of the year we began "The International Year of the Woman." Indeed, we have a lot to be reminded of but I regret that it was focused on women's liberation. What liberation? What do women want to be liberated from? From washing dishes? From emptying the garbage can? From cleaning the home? Are these *the problems* of women?

It is *the man who is discriminated against in our society*. He is discriminated against by his very creation. He misses the most miraculous thing in all that only the woman has: the capability to bear a child, to be pregnant, to deliver, to nurse—the supremely complete process of creation that the man makes such a small contribution to. You, the woman, have received the greatest delight when you hold the small creature in your arms for the first time, after having given him life—The greatest experience that, however many times it is repeated, its intensity never fades.

Oh, please! Do not tell me about industrial production lines, about your will to be managers, to be superiors, to be bigger, more equal! We are big enough. And equal? Equal to whom? Nature created man and woman and created different tasks for them. All the Women's Liberation Leagues in the world cannot change and will not change this basic fact.

In the first moment we hear the alarm signal, they go—and we stay and then equality is over. Our task is indeed important and indispensable for them. We symbolize everything they dream of in the hell of fire. We are the light in the window when they come home. But we are *here* and they are *there*. They may leave there a limb or even their soul, they may not return . . . and then, my dear ones, that is the end of equality. Disappeared. Workers, and among them women workers, have something to fight for; you have to focus on essentials: *equal conditions, equal payment for equal work of men and of women and of the minorities*. Yes, gentlemen, there are distortions. They exist in the rabbinical marriage laws, according to which we conduct ourselves and act. These distortions hurt women. We have to fight against them and to try to correct what has to be corrected. But I do not think we have to fight for equality in division of labor and promotion between men and mothers (single women invest a lot anyway in their career and achieve a lot if they give up family life). Employers have the right to prefer a man for a vacancy, even if his absence from work because of reserve service is not less than that of women on maternity leave.

Work *recompensates* a man. That is the place where he can and has to prove himself. For you, women, that is secondary. Nothing will help. Family, motherhood, that is your calling, and it is deeply rooted in your self.

When the man is absent from home for a vacation or for the reserves, he will forget the home *for some days* and will enjoy his new environment, but soon he will yearn for and worry about the home. But if *you* leave for a vacation it comes *within hours* and you "die" to know what is going on at home: Is it equality? Inequality? *It is the truth.*

The kibbutz probably is the best example: sweeping changes that have developed during a relatively short period. When the kibbutz was founded, there was maximal equality between the sexes. Women worked with men everywhere, in all heavy work, they were equal to men and also similar to them. Then the reaction came. A fierce reaction and the daughter of the kibbutz retired to her home, exaggerated her self-nurturance, her homemaking, her care for husband and children—all this with the active support of the men, who enjoyed the change. Her activity and her commitment to the commune consequently diminished.

Today we witness a more balanced situation. Women are again starting to take managerial jobs. In many kibbutzim the secretary is a woman. Women chair important committees, are in charge—almost exclusively—of health and education, manage service branches and have high responsibility and wide authority. Woman remains woman and yet—her value is great in our society.

Bibliography

Abernethy, Virginia D. "Dominance and Sexual Behavior: An Hypothesis," *American Journal of Psychiatry,* vol. 131, no. 7 (July 1974).
————. "Social Network and Response to the Maternal Role," *International Journal of Sociology of the Family,* vol. 3, no. 1 (March 1973).
Altman, A. "The Japan Kibbutz Association," *Asian and African Studies* (Jerusalem), vol. 6 (1970).
Amir, Y. "The Effectiveness of the Kibbutz-Born Soldier in the Israel Defence Forces," *Human Relations,* vol. 22, no. 4 (1969).
Anderson, Barbara G. "The Frenchwoman," in Carolyn J. Matthiasson, ed., *Many Sisters: Women in Cross Cultural Perspectives.* Glencoe: The Free Press, 1973.
Arian, A., ed. *The Election in Israel—1969.* Jerusalem: Jerusalem Academic Press, 1972.
Arian, A. *Ideological Change in Israel.* Cleveland: Case Western Reserve Press, 1968.
————. "Utopia and Politics: The Case of the Israeli Kibbutz," *Journal of Human Relations,* vol. 14, no. 3 (1966).
Artzi, F. "Reflections on the Status of the Kibbutz Girls," *Niv Hakvutza* (in Hebrew), vol. 9, no. 3 (1966).
Bamberger, Joan. "The Myth of Matriarchy: Why Men Rule in Primitive Society," in M. Z. Rosaldo, and L. Lamphere, eds., *Woman, Culture, and Society.* Stanford: Stanford University Press, 1974.
Baratz, J. *A Village by the Jordan.* Tel Aviv Reference Library: Ichud Habonim, 1966.
Bardwick, Judith M. *Psychology of Women: A Study of Biocultural Conflict.* New York: Harper & Row, 1970.
Barkai, H. "The Kibbutz—An Experiment in Microsocialism," in Irving Howe, ed., *Israel and Arabs: View from the Left.* New York: Bantam Books, 1972.
Barrett, C. J., and others. "Implications of Women's Liberation and the

Future of Psychotherapy," *Psychotherapy: Theory, Research and Practice,* vol. 11, no. 1 (Spring 1974).

Bar-Yosef, R. "The Pattern of Early Socialization in the Collective Settlements in Israel," *Human Relations,* vol. 12 (1959).

Barzel, Alexander. *Der Begriff 'Arbeit' in der Philosophie der Gegenwart.* Bern: Herbert Lang, Peter Lang, 1973.

Bein, A. *The Return to the Soil.* Jerusalem: Youth and Hechalutz Dep. of the W.Z.O., 1952.

Bell, Norman Ward, and Vogel, Ezra F. *A Modern Introduction to the Family.* 2d ed. New York: The Free Press, 1968.

Ben David, Y. "Change in the Kibbutz," *Kibbutz A New Society?* Ichud Habonim Publications, 1971.

Bernard, Jessie. *The Sex Game: Communication between the Sexes.* New York: Atheneum, 1972.

Berger, P., Berger, B., and Kellner, H. *The Homeless Mind: Modernization and Consciousness.* New York: Vintage Books, 1974.

Bettelheim, Bruno. *The Children of the Dream.* New York: The Macmillan Co., 1969.

Blumberg, Rae L. "The Women of the Israeli Kibbutz," *The Center Magazine,* vol. 7 (May/June 1974).

Blurton-Jones, Nicholas. "Comparative Aspects of Mother-Child Contact," in N. Blurton-Jones, ed., *Ethological Studies of Child Behaviour.* Cambridge: Cambridge University Press, 1972.

Booth, Alan. "Sex and Social Participation," *American Sociological Review,* vol. 37 (April 1972).

Borochov, Ber. *Nationalism and Class Struggle.* Westport, Conn.: Greenwood Press, 1972.

Bott, Elizabeth. *Family and Social Network.* London: Tavistock Publications, 1957.

Bowlby, John. *Separation.* New York: Basic Books, 1974.

———. *Attachment.* New York: Basic Books, 1969.

Breznitz, S., and Kugelmass, S. "The Perception of Parents by Adolescents: Consideration of Instrumentality-Expressivity Differentiation," *Human Relations,* vol. 18 (1965).

Brown, J. "A Note on the Division of Labor by Sex," *American Anthropologist,* vol. 72 (1970).

Burgess, E. W., and Locke, H. J. *The Family from Institution to Companionship.* 2d ed. New York: American Book Co., 1953.

Callan, Hilary. *Ethology and Society,* Oxford: Clarendon Press, 1971.

Campbell, Bernard, ed. *Sexual Selection and the Descent of Man: 1871-1971.* Chicago: Aldine Publishing Co., 1972.

Chomsky, Noam. *Language and Mind.* New York: Harcourt Brace Jovanovich, 1968.

————. *Aspects of the Theory of Syntax.* Cambridge, Mass.: MIT Press, 1966.

Conway, Jill. "Stereotypes of Femininity in a Theory of Sexual Evolution," *Victorian Studies* (September 1970).

Cook, Joan. *In Defense of Homo Sapiens.* New York: Farrar, Straus and Giroux, 1974.

Count, Earl W. *Being and Becoming Human: Essays on the Biogram.* New York: D. Van Nostrand Co., 1973.

Crowley, Joan E., Levitin, Teresa E., and Quinn, Robert P. "Facts and Fictions About the American Working Woman," Employment Standards Administration, U.S. Department of Labor (January 1973).

Dahrendorf, R. *Homo Sociologicus.* London: Routledge and Kegan Paul, 1973.

Dar, Y. *Sex Differences in Academic Achievements among Kibbutz High School Students* (in Hebrew). Tel Aviv: Ichud Research Institute, 1974. Mimeographed.

Darin-Drabkin, H. *The Other Society.* London: Victor Gollancz, Ltd., 1962.

Davis, Elizabeth Gould. *The First Sex.* New York: G. P. Putnam's Sons, 1971.

Davis, Kingsley. *Human Society.* New York: The Macmillan Co., 1949.

————. "Final Note on a Case of Extreme Isolation," *American Journal of Sociology,* vol. 50 (1947).

————. "Extreme Social Isolation of a Child," *American Journal of Sociology.* vol. 45 (1940).

Dearden, John. "Sex-Linked Differences of Political Behavior: An Investigation of their Possibly Innate Origins," *Social Science Information,* vol. 13 (April 1974).

De Beauvoir, Simone. *The Second Sex.* New York: Alfred A. Knopf, 1953.

Devereux, E. C., and others. "Socialization Practices of Parents, Teachers, and Peers in Israel: The Kibbutz versus the City," *Child Development,* vol. 45 (1974).

Diamond, Stanley. "Kibbutz and Shtetl: The History of an Idea," *Social Problems,* vol. 5, no. 2 (1957).

Dodge, Norton T. *Women in the Soviet Economy.* Baltimore: Johns Hopkins Press, 1966.

Douard, G. *Du Kolkhoze au Kibbutz.* Paris: Plon, 1961.

Duverger, Maurice. *The Political Role of Women*. Paris: UNESCO, 1955.

Eisenberg, John F. "Mammalian Social Systems: Are Primate Social Systems Unique?" *Symposia of the Fourth International Congress of Primatology*, vol. 1 (1973).

———. "The Social Organization of Mammals," *Handbuch der Zoologie*, vol. 10, no. 7 (May 1966).

Epstein, Cynthia. *Woman's Place*. Berkeley: University of California Press, 1970.

Etaugh, Claire. "Effects of Maternal Employment on Children: A Review of Recent Research," *Merrill-Palmer Quarterly of Behavior and Development*, vol. 20, no. 2 (1974).

Etzioni, A., ed. *The Semi-Professions and Their Organization: Teachers, Nurses, Social Workers*. New York: The Free Press, 1969.

Etzioni, Amitai. "The Organizational Structure of the Kibbutz." Unpublished Ph.D. Dissertation, University of California at Berkeley, 1958.

———. "Solidaric Work-Groups in Collective Settlements," *Human Organization*, vol. 16 (1957).

Fenz, Walter D., and Fogle, Barry R. "Differences Between Male and Female Reactions to Psychosocial and Physical Stressors: A Review of the Literature and Some Comments," in L. Levi, ed., *Society, Stress, and Disease*, vol. 3. New York: Oxford University Press, forthcoming.

Figes, Eva. *Patriarchal Attitudes*. Greenwich, Conn.: Fawcett Books, 1971.

Firestone, Shulamith. *The Dialectic of Sex*. New York: William Morrow & Co., 1971.

Fowler, Heather Trexler. "An Investigation in the Relationship Between Testosterone Levels in Human Females and the Dominance They Exhibit in Small Group Situations." M.A. Thesis, University of Missouri, 1973.

Fox, Robin. "Evolution and Race" in *Encounter with Anthropology*. New York: Harcourt Brace Jovanovich, 1973.

———. "Alliance and Constraint: Sexual Selection and the Evolution of Human Kinship Systems," in B. Campbell, ed., *Sexual Selection and the Descent of Man: 1871-1971*. Chicago: Aldine Publishing Co., 1971.

Freeman, Derek. "Social Anthropology and the Scientific Study of Human Behavior," *Man: The Journal of the Royal Anthropological Institute*, vol. 1, no. 2 (1966).

French, J., and Golomb, H. "Introduction to Kibbutz Research," *New Outlook,* vol. 13, no. 1 (1970).

Friedan, Betty. *The Feminine Mystique.* New York: W. W. Norton and Co., 1963.

Friedman, G. "The Kibbutz Adventure and the Challenges of the Century," in G. Friedman, ed., *The End of the Jewish People?* New York: Doubleday and Co., 1967.

———. "L'Aventure Kibboutzique et les Défis du Siècle," *Revue Française de Sociologie,* vol. 5 (1964).

Frommer, Eva A., and O'Shea, Gillian. "The Importance of Childhood Experience in Relation to Problems of Marriage and Family-Building," *The British Journal of Psychiatry,* vol. 123, no. 573 (August 1973).

Galbraith, John Kenneth. *The Affluent Society.* Boston: Houghton Mifflin, 1958.

Garai, J., and Scheinfeld, A. "Sex Differences in Mental and Behavioral Traits," *Genetic Psychology Monographs,* vol. 77, 2d half (May 1968).

Gavron, Hannah. *The Captive Wife.* New York: Penguin Books, 1968.

Geertz, C. "Ideology as a Cultural System," in David Apter, ed., *Ideology and Discontent.* New York: The Free Press, 1964.

Gershon, M. *Education and Family in the Reality of the Kibbutz* (in Hebrew). Tel Aviv: Sifriat Hapalim, 1968.

Ghiselin, Michael. "Darwin and Evolutionary Psychology," *Science,* vol. 179 (1972).

Gilder, George. *Naked Nomads.* New York: Quadrangle Books, 1974.

———. *Sexual Suicide.* New York: Quadrangle Books, 1973.

Gluckman, Max. "A Bandwagon Full of Monkeys," *New York Review of Books* (October 1972).

Golan, Sh. *Collective Education* (in Hebrew). Tel Aviv: Sifriat Hapalim, 1961.

———. "Collective Education in the Kibbutz," *Psychiatry,* vol. 22, no. 2 (1959).

———. "Collective Education in the Kibbutz," *The American Journal of Orthopsychiatry,* vol. 28 (1958).

Goldberg, Steven. *The Inevitability of Patriarchy.* New York: William Morrow & Co., 1974.

Goldenberg, Sheldon, and Wekerle, Gerda R. "From Utopia to Total Institution in a Single Generation: the Kibbutz and the Bruderhof," *International Review of Modern Sociology,* vol. 2 (September 1972).

Goode, W. J. *World Revolution and Family Patterns.* Glencoe: The Free Press, 1963.

Gordon, A. D. *The Nation and the Work* (in Hebrew). Jerusalem: The Zionist Library, 1952.

Gould, Stephen Jay. "The Nonscience of Human Nature," *Natural History* (April 1974).

Grebenik, E. "On Controlling Population Growth," in J. W. S. Pringle, ed., *Biology and the Human Species.* Oxford: Clarendon Press, 1972.

Greer, Germaine. *The Female Eunuch.* New York: McGraw-Hill, 1971.

Hamburg, Beatrix A. "The Biological Bases of Sex Differences," in S. L. Washburn and P. Dolhinow, eds., *Perspectives on Human Evolution,* vol. 3. New York: Holt, Rinehart and Winston, 1975.

Hamburg, David. Report to Second International Experts' Conference on Human Aggressiveness. Paris: UNESCO, 1972.

————. "Recent Research on Hormonal Factors Relevant to Human Aggressiveness," *International Social Science Journal* (UNESCO, Paris), vol. 23, no. 1 (1971).

————. "Emotions in Perspective of Human Evolution" in P. Knapp, ed., *Expression of the Emotions in Man.* New York: International Universities Press, 1963.

Harlow, Harry F., and Lauersdorf, Helen E. "Sex Differences in Passion and Play," *Perspectives in Biology and Medicine,* vol. 17, no. 3 (Spring 1974).

Hashomer Hatsair. *Kehiliatenu.* Hashomer Hatsair, Haifa, Geda Road, 1922.

Hedblom, Jack H. "Dimensions of Lesbian Sexual Experience," *Archives of Sexual Behavior,* vol. 2, no. 4 (1973).

Heyer, Paul. Marx and Darwin: A Related Legacy on Man, Nature, and Society. Ph.D. Dissertation, Rutgers University, 1975.

Hinde, Robert A. *Biological Bases of Human Social Behaviour.* New York: McGraw-Hill, 1974.

Holter, H. *Sex Roles and Social Structure.* Oslo: Universitetsforlaset, 1970.

Horner, Matina. "Toward an Understanding of Achievement-related Conflict in Women," *Journal of Social Issues,* vol. 28, no. 2 (1972).

Howell, Mary C. "Employed Mothers and Their Families (I)," *Pediatrics,* vol. 52, no. 2 (August 1973).

Hutt, Corinne. "Sex Differences in Human Development," *Human Development,* vol. 15 (1972a).

————. *Males and Females*. Harmondsworth, England: Penguin Books, 1972b.

Ichud Habonim. *Kibbutz: A New Society?* Tel Aviv: Ichud Habonim Publications, 1971.

Iglitzin, Lynne B. "The Persistence of Patriarchal Thinking: Women-as-Property," *The Center Magazine* (May/June 1974).

Infield, H. F. *Co-operative Communities at Work*. London: Kegan Paul, French, Trubner and Co., 1947.

Janeway, Elizabeth. *Man's World, Woman's Place*. New York: William Morrow & Co., 1971.

Jarus, A., and others, eds. *Children and Families in Israel. Some Mental Health Perspectives*. New York: Gordon and Breach, 1970.

Johnston, Jill. *Lesbian Nation*. New York: Simon & Schuster, 1973.

Joravsky, David. *The Lysenko Affair*. Cambridge, Mass.: Harvard University Press, 1970.

Kanovsky, E. *The Economy of the Israeli Kibbutz*. Cambridge, Mass.: Harvard University Press, 1966.

Kanter, R. M. *Commitment and Community*. Cambridge, Mass.: Harvard University Press, 1972.

Kaplan, Helen Singer. *The New Sex Therapy*. New York: Brunner-Maazel, 1974.

Kedenburg, Dean, Kedenburg, Annette, and Kling, Arthur. "Plasma Testosterone and Aggressive Behavior in a Patient Population," *Archives of General Psychiatry* (in press).

Klein, Viola. *Working Wives: A Survey of Facts and Opinions Concerning the Gainful Employment of Married Women in Britain, Occasional Papers No. 15*. London and Weston-super-Mare. Lawrence Brothers, Ltd, n.d.

Konopnicki, M. *La Cooperation en Milieu Rural Israelien*. The Hague: Martinus Nijhoff, 1968.

Kruez, L., Rose, R., and Jennings, R. "Suppression of Plasma Testosterone Levels and Psychological Stress," *Archives of General Psychiatry*, vol. 26 (1972).

Kugelmass, S., and Breznitz, S. "Perception of Parents by Kibbutz Adolescents: A Further Test of the Instrumentality-Expressivity Model," *Human Relations*, vol. 19 (1966).

Lancaster, Jane. "In Praise of the Achieving Female Monkey," *Psychology Today* (September 1973).

Langston, T. *Women's Status in the Chinese Political Economy*. Proceedings of Women's Anthropology Workshop, London, 1973. Mimeographed.

318 / *Women in the Kibbutz*

Larsen, Ray R. "On Comparing Man and Ape: An Evaluation of Methods and Problems." Paper presented at 73d Annual Meeting American Anthropological Association, Mexico City, November 19-25, 1974.

Laslett, Barbara. "The Family as a Public and Private Institution: An Historical Perspective," *Journal of Marriage and the Family* (August 1973).

Leacock, Eleanor. Book review, *American Anthropologist*, vol. 76, no. 2 (June 1974).

————. "Introduction," in F. Engels, ed., *The Origin of the Family, Private Property, and the State.* New York: New World Paperbacks, 1972.

Lee, Richard Borshay. "Male-Female Residence Arrangements and Political Power in Human Hunter-Gatherers," *Archives of Sexual Behavior*, vol. 3, no. 2 (1974).

————. "The Contribution of Hunter-Gatherer Research to the Study of Adaptation and Evolution." Lecture to Wenner-Gren Foundation Supper Conference, April 17, 1970.

Leon, Dan. *The Kibbutz: A New Way of Life.* Oxford: Pergamon Press, 1969.

Leshem, E., and Cohen, E. "Public Participation in Collective Settlements in Israel," *International Review of Community Development,* nos. 19-20 (1968).

Levine, Adeline, and Crumrine Janice. "Women and the Fear of Success: A Problem in Replication," *American Journal of Sociology,* vol. 80, no. 4 (January 1975).

Liegle, L. *Familie und Kollektiv im Kibbutz.* Berlin: Baltz Verlag, 1971a.

————. *Kollektive Erziehung im Kibbutz.* Munich: Munchen Piper Verlag, 1971b.

Lifschitz, M. "Gender and Psychological Identification" (in Hebrew), *The Quarterly of Social Research*, vol. 4 (1973).

Lifton, Robert Jay. *Revolutionary Immortality: Mao Tse-tung and the Chinese Cultural Revolution.* New York: Random House, Vintage Books, 1968.

Liska, Allen E. "The Impact of Attitudes on Behavior: Attitude-Social Support Interaction," *Pacific Sociological Review*, vol. 17, no. 1 (January 1974).

Livingstone, Frank. Book review, *American Anthropologist*, vol. 76, no. 2 (June 1974).

Lorenz, Konrad. "Analogy as a Source of Knowledge," *Science,* vol. 185 (1974).

Maccoby, Eleanor E. Book review, *Science,* vol. 182, no. 4111, 1973.

Maccoby, Eleanor E., and Jacklin, Carol Nagy. "Comments on the Etiology of Sex Differences." Paper presented at AAAS meeting, Washington, D.C., December 28, 1972. Mimeographed.

Maccoby, E., ed. *The Development of Sex Differences.* Stanford: Stanford University Press, 1966.

MacLean, Paul D. "New Findings Relevant to the Evolution of Psychosexual Functions of the Brain," *The Journal of Nervous and Mental Disease,* vol. 135, no. 4 (October 1962).

Margalith, E. *Hashomer Hatzair, From Youth Movement to Revolutionary Marxism 1913-1936* (in Hebrew). Tel Aviv: Hakibbutz Hamuchad, 1971.

Marler, Peter, and Griffin, D. R. "The 1973 Nobel Prize for Physiology or Medicine," *Science,* vol. 182 (November 1973).

Marrett, Cora Bagley. "Centralization in Female Organizations: Reassessing the Evidence," *Social Problems,* vol. 19, no. 3 (1972).

Maslow, Abraham. *The Farther Reaches of Human Nature.* Harmondsworth, England: Penguin Books, 1973.

Meier-Cronemeyer, H. *Kibbutzim Geschichte, Geist und Gestalt. Teil 1.* Hanover: Verlag fur Literatur und Zietgeschehen. Geschichte, 1969.

Melman, S. "Managerial vs. Cooperative Decision Making in Israel," *Studies in Comparative International Development,* vol. 6, no. 3 (1970-71).

Meri, Ury. "Changes in Leisure Patterns in the Kibbutz," *The Kibbutz Interdisciplinary Research Review* (in Hebrew). Higher Education and Research Authority of the Federation of Kibbutz Movements, Tel-Aviv, 1973.

Mibifnim. *Periodical, Kibbutz Meuchad Federation* (in Hebrew), 1932.

Mill, John Stuart, and Mill, Harriet Taylor. *Essays on Sex Equality.* Chicago: University of Chicago Press, 1970.

Millett, Kate. *Sexual Politics.* New York: Doubleday & Co., 1970.

Mimoetza Lemoetza. *Report to the Seventh General Council of the Kibbutz Artzi Federation, 1942-47* (in Hebrew), n.d.

Mitchell, Juliet. *Psychoanalysis and Feminism: Freud, Reich, Laing, and Women.* New York: Pantheon Books, 1974.

Money, John, and Ehrhardt, Anke A. *Man & Woman, Boy & Girl: The Differentiation and Dimorphism of Gender Identity from Conception to Maturity.* Baltimore and London: The Johns Hopkins University Press, 1973.

Montagu, Ashley. "Sociogenic Brain Damage," *Man's Most Dangerous*

Myth: The Fallacy of Race." 5th ed. New York: Oxford University Press, 1974.

Moore, Barrington, Jr. *Reflections on the Causes of Human Misery and Upon Certain Proposals to Eliminate Them.* Boston: Beacon Press, 1972.

Morin, Edgar. *Le Paradigme Perdu: La Nature Humaine.* Paris: Editions Seuil, 1973.

Myrdal, Alva, and Klein, Viola. *Women's Two Roles.* London: Routledge and Kegan Paul, 1956.

Natan, Michael, and Schnabel, O. "Attitudes of Second Generation Kibbutz Adults towards Premarital Sex Relations," *Education in the Kibbutz* (in Hebrew), vol. 2 (1972).

Nerlove, Sara B. "Women's Workload and Infant Feeding Practices: A Relationship With Demographic Implications," *Ethology,* vol. 13, no. 2 (April 1974).

Neubauer, P. B., ed. *Children in Collectives: Child Rearing Aims and Practices in the Kibbutz.* Springfield: Charles C. Thomas, 1965.

Nichols, Paul L., and Anderson, V. Elving. "Intellectual Performance, Race, and Socioeconomic Status," *Social Biology,* vol. 20 (December 1973).

Nicholas, Ralph W. "Social and Political Movements," *Annual Review of Anthropology,* vol. 2 (1973).

Niv Hakvutza. *Periodical of the Hever Hakvutzot Federation,* vol. 6, part 3 (1949).

O'Faolain, Julia, and Martines, Lauro. *Not in God's Image: Women in History from the Greeks to the Victorians.* New York: Harper Torchbook, 1973.

Olive, Helen. "A Note on Sex Differences in Adolescents' Divergent Thinking," *The Journal of Psychology,* vol. 82 (1972).

O'Neill, W. L. *Everyone Was Brave: The Rise and Fall of Feminism in America.* Chicago: Quadrangle Books, 1968.

Orbach, Eliezer. *Comparative Organization in Israel: The Kibbutz and the Moshav.* Madison: Center for the Study of Productivity Motivation, University of Wisconsin, 1968.

Ounsted, Christopher, and Taylor, David C. *Gender Differences: Their Ontogeny and Significance.* Edinburgh: Churchill Livingstone, 1972.

Oz, Amos. *Elsewhere, Perhaps.* New York: Harcourt Brace Jovanovich, 1973.

Pallman, Martin. *Der Kibbutz. Zur Strukturwandel eines Konkreten*

Kammunetypus in nichtsozialistischer Umwelt. Basel: Kyklos, 1966.

Piepmeier, K. B., and Adkins, T. S. "The Status of Women and Fertility," *Journal of Biosocial Science,* vol. 5 (1973).

Porat, Shulamit. "The Image of the Kibbutz Girl," *Igereth Lehinuch* (in Hebrew), vol. 2 (1960).

Poznansky, M., and Shkhoury, M., eds., *Haverot in the Kibbutz* (in Hebrew). Ein Harod, 1944.

Rabin, A. I. *Growing Up in the Kibbutz.* New York: Springer, 1965.

Raphael, Dana. *The Tender Gift: Breastfeeding.* Englewood Cliffs: Prentice-Hall, 1973.

Reinisch, June M. "Fetal Hormones, the Brain and Human Sex Differences: A Heuristic, Integrative Review of the Recent Literature," *Archives of Sexual Behavior,* vol. 3, no. 1 (1974).

Rosaldo, M. Z., and Lamphere, L., eds. *Woman, Culture, and Society.* Stanford: Stanford University Press, 1974.

Rosenblatt, Ellen, and Greenland, Cyril. "Female Crimes of Violence," *Canadian Journal of Criminology and Corrections,* vol. 16, no. 2 (1974).

Rosenfeld, Eva. "The American Social Scientist in Israel: A Case Study in Role Conflict," *American Journal of Orthopsychiatry,* vol. 28 (1958).

—————. "Institutional Changes in the Kibbutz," *Social Problems,* vol. 5, no. 2 (1957).

—————. "Social Stratification in a Classless Society," *American Sociological Review,* vol. 16 (1951).

Rosenfeld, H. "Changes, Barriers to Change and Contradictions in the Arab Village Family," *American Anthropologist,* vol. 70 (1968).

Rosner, Menahem. "Changes in the Concept of Woman's Equality in the Kibbutz," *The Kibbutz Interdisciplinary Research Review* (in Hebrew). Higher Education and Research Authority of the Federation of the Kibbutz Movements, Tel Aviv, 1973.

—————. *Worker Participation in Decision Making in Kibbutz Industry.* Israel: Givat Haviva, 1972.

—————. *The Kibbutz as a Way of Live in Modern Society.* Israel: Givat Haviva, 1971.

—————. "Communitarian Experiment, Self-Management Experience and the Kibbutz," *Group Process,* vol. 3 (1970).

—————. "Social Aspects of Industrialization in the Kibbutz" C.I.R.C.O.M. International Symposium on the Role of Group Action in Industrialization in Rural Areas, Tel Aviv, 1969.

————. *Temuroth Bitfisa al Shivyon Haisha Bakibbutz* (Changes in the Perception of the Woman in the Kibbutz). Israel: Givat Haviva, 1969.

————. "Direct Democracy in the Kibbutz," *New Outlook*, vol. 8, no. 6 (1956).

Sanday, Peggy. "Female Status in the Public Domain," in M. Z. Rosaldo and L. Lamphere, eds., *Woman, Culture, and Society*. Stanford: Stanford University Press, 1973.

Schmalenbach, H. "The Communion," in T. Parsons, and others, eds., *Theories of Society*. Glencoe: Free Press, 1961.

Schreiner, Olive. *Woman and Labour*. Toronto: Henry Frowde, 1911.

Schwartz, R. D. "Democracy and Collectivism in the Kibbutz," *Social Problems*, vol. 5, no. 2 (1957).

Segal, M. "Collective Education: the Background," in Ichud, *Kibbutz: A New Society?* Tel Aviv: Ichud Habonim Publications, 1971.

————. "The Child and his Family in the Kibbutz: School Age," in A. Jarus, and others, eds., *Children and Families in Israel: Some Mental Health Perspectives*. New York: Gordon and Breach, 1970.

Seligman, M. E. P., and Hager, J. L. *Biological Boundaries of Learning*. New York: Appleton-Century-Crofts, 1973.

Shapira, A., ed. *The Seventh Day*. New York: Charles Scribner's Sons, 1971.

Shashua, L., and Goldschmidt, Y. *Economic Progress in the Kibbutz Sector During the Sixties*. Tel Aviv: Inter-Kibbutz Economic Advisory Unit, 1972.

Shepher, Joseph. "Service publique au dehors du kibbutz," in *Sociétés Villageoises: Auto-développement et inter-cooperation*. Paris: Mouton, 1974.

———— . "Education in the Kibbutz," in H. Ormian, ed., *Education in Israel* (in Hebrew). Jerusalem: Ministry of Education and Culture, 1973.

————. *Self Imposed Incest Avoidance and Exogamy in Second Generation Kibbutz Adults*. Ann Arbor: Xerox Monograph Series nos. 72-871, 1971.

————. "The Child and the Parent—Child Relationship in Kibbutz Communities in Israel," *Assignment Children*, no. 10 (UNESCO, Paris) (June 1969a).

————. "Familism and Social Structure: the Case of the Kibbutz," *Journal of Marriage and the Family*, vol. 31 (1969b).

————. *The Reflections of the Housing System of the Children in the*

Social Structure of the Kibbutz (in Hebrew). Tel Aviv: Ichud Habonim Publications, 1967.

———. "The Kibbutz in the Eyes of an American Sociologist," *Niv Hakvutza* (in Hebrew), vol. 1, 1952.

Shirom, Arie, and others. "Job Stresses and Risk Factors in Coronary Heart Disease Among Five Occupational Categories in Kibbutzim," *Social Science and Medicine,* vol. 7 (1973).

Shur, Simon. *Kibbutz Bibliography.* Higher Education and Research Authority of the Federation of Kibbutz Movements, Tel Aviv, 1972.

Sidel, Ruth. "The Long March of Chinese Women," *Human Behavior* (November 1973a).

———. "The Human Services in China," *Social Policy* (March/April 1973b).

Siegel, Claire Lynn Fleet. "Sex Differences in the Occupational Choices of Second Graders," *Journal of Vocational Behavior,* vol. 3, no. 1 (January 1973).

Sikumei Ohlosia. Unpublished demographic data of the Ichud Federation, 1973.

Simpson, R., and Simpson, I. H. "Women and Bureaucracy in the Semi-Professions," in A. Etzioni, ed., *The Semi-Professions and Their Organization: Teachers, Nurses, Social Workers.* New York: The Free Press, 1969.

Singer, Irving. *The Goals of Human Sexuality.* New York: W. W. Norton and Co., 1973.

Singer, Irving, and Singer Josephine. "Periodicity of Sexual Desire in Relation to Time of Ovulation in Women," *Journal of Biosocial Science,* vol. 4 (1972).

Smith, Dorothy. "Women's Perspective as a Radical Critique of Sociology," *Sociological Inquiry,* vol. 44, no. 1 (1974).

Sommer, Barbara. "Menstrual Cycles: Changes and Intellectual Performance," *Psychosomatic Medicine,* vol. 34, no. 3 (May/June 1972).

Spiro, M. E. "Is the Family Universal?" (Addendum), in N. W. Bell and E. F. Vogel, eds., *A Modern Introduction to Family.* London: Routledge and Kegan Paul, 1960.

———. *Children of the Kibbutz.* With the assistance of G. Spiro. Cambridge, Mass.: Harvard University Press, 1958.

———. *Kibbutz, Venture in Utopia.* Cambridge, Mass.: Harvard University Press, 1956.

———. "Is the Family Universal?", *American Anthropologist,* vol. 56 (1954).

Statistical Abstract of Israel. Jerusalem, Tel Aviv: Central Bureau of Statistics, 1973.

Steinem, Gloria. "Essay," in Dom Moraes, ed., *Voices for Life.* New York: Frederick Praeger, 1975.

Steinmetz, Suzanne K. "The Sexual Context of Social Research," *The American Sociologist,* vol. 9, no. 3 (August 1974).

Sullerot, Evelyne. *Women, Society and Change.* New York: McGraw-Hill, 1971.

Sutton, Constance R. *American Anthropological Association Annual Report 1973* (April 1974).

Talmon-Garber, Yonina G. *Family and Community in the Kibbutz.* Cambridge, Mass.: Harvard University Press, 1972.

―――. "Sex Role Differentiation in an Egalitarian Society," in T. E. Laswell, J. H. Burma, and S. H. Aronson, eds., *Life in Society.* Chicago: Scott, Foresman and Co., 1965.

―――. "Mate Selection in Collective Settlements," *American Sociological Review,* vol. 29 (1964).

―――. "The Family and the Housing System of the Children," *Niv Hakvutza* (in Hebrew), 1958.

―――. "Differentiation in Collective Settlements," *Scripta Hierosolymitana* (Hebrew University, Jerusalem), vol. 3 (1956a).

―――. "Division of Labor According to Sex" (in Hebrew). Jerusalem: University of Jerusalem, 1956b. Mimeographed.

Tavris, Carol. "Field Report: Women in China, The Speak-Bitterness Revolution," *Psychology Today* (May 1974).

Tene, Shoshana. "On the Formation of the Image of the Kibbutz Girl," *Igereth Lehaverim,* vol. 166 (1956).

TIAA-CREF. *The Participant* (July 1973).

Tiger, Lionel. "Interview," in Dom Moraes, ed., *Voices for Life.* New York: Frederick Praeger, 1975a.

―――. "Sex-Specific Friendship," in Elliott Leyton, ed., *The Compact.* Toronto: University of Toronto Press, 1975b.

―――. "Biology, Rhetoric, Reform; The Allure of Low-Born High Ideals," *Social Science Information,* vol. 12, no. 5 (1973).

―――. *Men in Groups.* New York: Random House, 1969.

Tiger, L., and Fox, R. *The Imperial Animal.* New York: Holt, Rinehart and Winston, 1971.

―――. "The Zoological Perspective in Social Science," *Man: Journal of the Royal Anthropological Institute,* vol. 1, no. 1, (1966).

Tinbergen, Nikolaas. "Ethology and Stress Diseases," *Science,* vol. 185 (July 5, 1974).

————. *The Animal in Its World.* Cambridge, Mass.: Harvard University Press, 1973.

————. "On Aims and Methods of Ethology," *Zeitschrift fur Tierpsychologie,* vol. 20 (1963).

Trigger, Bruce. "Engels on the Part Played by Labour in the Transition from Ape to Man: An Anticipation of Contemporary Anthropological Theory," *The Canadian Review of Sociology and Anthropology,* vol. 4, no. 3 (August 1967).

Urbanowicz, Charles. "Mother Nature, Father Culture." Anthropology Section, Oregon Academy of Science, 1970. Mimeographed.

van den Berghe, Pierre. *Age and Sex in Human Societies: A Biosocial Perspective.* Belmont, Ca.: Wadsworth, 1973.

Viteles, H. *A History of the Co-Operative Movement in Israel, A Sourcebook,* vols. 2 and 3. London: Valentine Michell, 1966.

Wade, Nicholas. "Bottle-Feeding: Adverse Effects of a Western Technology," *Science,* vol. 184 (1974).

Washburn, Sherwood L., and Lancaster, Chet S. "The Evolution of Hunting," in R. B. Lee and I. DeVore, eds., *Man the Hunter.* Chicago: Aldine Publishing Co., 1968.

Wershow, Harold J. "Aging in the Israeli Kibbutz: Some Further Investigation," *International Journal of Aging and Human Development,* vol. 4, no. 3 (1973).

Whiting, Beatrice, and Edwards, Carolyn Pope. "A Cross-Cultural Analysis of Sex Differences in the Behavior of Children Aged Three Through Eleven," *Journal of Social Psychology* (December 1973).

Wilensky, H. L. "Women's Work: Economic Growth, Ideology, Structure," *Industrial Relation,* vol. 7, no. 3 (May 1968).

Wilmore, Jack H. "Strength, Endurance and Body Composition of the Female Athlete." Paper presented at the American Medical Association's 15th National Conference on Medical Aspects of Sports, Anaheim, California, December 1, 1973.

Wurm, Shalom. *The Bussel Book* (in Hebrew). Tel Aviv: Tarbut ve-Hinuch, 1960.

Wolf, Arthur P. "Childhood Association and Sexual Attraction: A Further Test of the Westermarck Hypothesis," *American Anthropologist,* vol. 72, pp. 503-15 (1970).

————. "Adopt a Daughter-in-Law, Marry a Sister: A Chinese Solution to the Problem of Incest Taboo," *American Anthropologist,* vol. 70, pp. 864-874 (1968).

————, "Childhood Associations, Sexual Attraction and the Incest Taboo: A Chinese Case," *American Anthropologist,* vol. 68, pp. 883-898 (1966).

Yaari, M. "Bederech Leshivayon" (On the way to Equality), in *Bederech Arucha* (On a Long Way). Merhavya Sifriat Poalim, 1947.

Young, M., and Willmott, P. *Family and Kinship in East London.* London: Routledge and Kegan Paul, 1957.

Zborowski, Mark, and Herzog, Elizabeth. *Life Is With People: The Culture of the Shtetl.* New York: Shocken, 1969.

Index

Abernethy, Virginia D., 241, 275
Abortion, 12
Achdut Ha'avoda (The Unity of Labor) party, 61, 62
adult-store manager (*machsanait chaverim*), 150–51
agriculture: creating, 76; labor polarization, 112; *moshavot*, 82–83; sex typing of labor, 82-83, 92, 93, 99
Amir, Y., 58
Anderson, Barbara, 28
Annual General Assembly, 41
antifemaleness, historical, 4
Antonovski, M., 254
Arabs: guerrilla wars (1930's), 184; hostility and terrorism, 183, 203, 204; intransigence of, 64
Arian, A., 62
attitudes, kibbutz members, 242–58; on authority in decisions, 257; toward division of domestic tasks, 256–57; female/male work, 247–48; on impact of familism, 245, 254, 258; interviewees (from 1973), 246–59; of political activities, 251–54; present work, 248–49; satisfaction with kibbutz life, 246; sexual division of labor, 243–51
authority, division of work and, 229–33, 257

Bamberger, Joan, 20
Baratz, Joseph, 161–62
Bardwick, Judith, 21
Barkai, H., 43, 54
bar mitzvah ceremony, 160, 161
Bar Yosef, 166
Barzel, Alexander, 75

Basic Training Camp of Chen, 74
bat mitzvah ceremony, 161
Bein, A., 59
Beit Trumpeldor, 72, 81
Bernard, Jessie, 11, 14, 122
Bettelheim, Bruno, 34, 68, 160, 227–28, 329
Bill of National Security (1949), 186
biogrammar, at birth, 265, 271–72, 274, 278
Biosocial Bases of Sex Difference, The (Hamburg), 21–22
birth rate, 41, 84, 219–20
Blumberg, Rae L., 117, 125
Blurton-Jones, Nicholas, 272, 274, 276
Borochov, Ber, 59
Bott, Elizabeth, 233
Bowlby, John, 274
branch managers (*merakezei anaf*), 41–42
Breznitz, S., 166
Brown, J., 24
Buber, Martin, 60, 67
Burgess, E. W., 233
Bussell, Joseph, 207

Callan, Hilary, 272
Campbell, Bernard, 22
Center for Social Research, 200
Chaverot Bakibbutz, 82
chaverot (female comrades), 77–78, 79, 124
Cheil Nashim, *see* Women's Army
childbirth, 37, 40
child care, 162
children: age groups (*kitah*), 151; IQ scores, 20; placement of, 50; of